The
Pleasure
Areas

The Pleasure Areas

A New Theory of Behavior

H. J. CAMPBELL

DELACORTE PRESS / NEW YORK

Text first published in book form in Great Britain by Eyre
Methuen, Ltd., London.
Copyright © 1973 by H. J. Campbell
Illustrations Copyright © 1973 by Robert Osborn
Manufactured in the United States of America
First printing

Library of Congress Cataloging in Publication Data

Campbell, Herbert James.
The pleasure areas.

Bibliography: p.
1. Pleasure. 2. Psychology. I. Title.
BF515.C35   152.4   73-4666

TO

Stephen

WHO ALSO BELIEVED

IN THE WRONG PEOPLE

Diagrams

Preface

A book such as this takes many a year in the making as the author's mind gropes and grapples with the problem of applying laboratory science to general issues. During that time there are untold discussions and correspondences with colleagues and other interested persons who make their views known, introduce new vistas and generally help to shape the author's approach to his subject. To all the many who have, often unwittingly, contributed to this book I testify my gratitude. I know they would not wish to be part of a list of printed names.

My grateful thanks are also due in no uncertain measure to the Population Council, Inc., New York, and to the Mental Health Trust and Research Fund, London, for the past and present financial support of the experimental work on which this book is based. Those who believe in the usefulness of such research might bear in mind that these agencies cannot support science unless they receive monetary support from the public.

Finally, the book would be far less readable if I had not received unstinted expert assistance from my publishers and literary agents. To them, too, I offer my thanks.

Prelude

If the reader is not a plant, he is a pleasure-seeker, for that is what all animals are. One of my intentions in writing this book is to examine the evidence for this assertion from both the neurophysiological and the behavioral points of view, and in doing so it is necessary, on the one hand, to refer to experimental work on the brain done by myself and other workers, and on the other, to ignore vast amounts of similar research in order to keep the size of this book manageable. The fact that the book can be written at all implies many thousand hours spent by hundreds of scientists over many decades, gradually accumulating knowledge about the brain and what it does for us. Most of these scientists remain unsung in this book. But it is on their work that this story of *human* mental evolution is based. *Human* because most people are predominantly subhuman. For example, many people draw upon the advantages of the human scene much in the manner of parasites: wearing clothes, talking after a fashion, using a knife and fork; yet they contribute nothing from the great power of their brains, and exhibit behavior that is only superficially different from that of monkeys.

My aim is to demonstrate facts—such as what crocodiles do if you offer them an electrical kiss; and to derive reasonable interpretations of observed facts—such as that sportsmen tend to be neuter in mental gender. Interpretations such as these have led to the new theory of behavior that is expounded in this book. These interpretations may turn out to be false and will certainly have to be modified in the light of new knowledge. I give them because many people have already shown much interest in them. They have been promulgated at about thirty lectures to scientific audiences and have been incorporated into university courses for psychiatrists. They have also been "covered" in short form by about a hundred journals and newspapers throughout the world, and they have been broadcast several times in several countries on radio and television. Whether I think so or not, there can be no question that the ideas evoke acute interest.

Another reason I wrote the book is that I and others believe that the ideas discussed in it can be of use to people. It should provide a better understanding of what goes on in the brain, showing what the fundamental mechanisms of behavior are, so that no one can believe any longer that they have something as simple as a telephone exchange inside their cranium. At the same time, in among all the complexity of actual operations of brain processes, there is the simple principle of pleasure-seeking to serve as a focal point. Recognition of that principle alone should be enough to engender at least a few changes in many people's self-assessment.

The way in which pleasure-seeking is carried out has profound implications about who and what we are. Pleasure-seeking in certain ways completely strips us of humanness and even of that prized, but often imaginary possession, individuality. Other forms of pleasure-seeking testify to our elevated level in the animal hierarchy but still leave us, most of us in fact, as robots or automata —walking computers with other people's programs. And yet, with full understanding of certain observed facts about behavior and brain function, the way is clear for every person to be both human and individual, happy yet accomplished.

The way may be clear but it is not simple or effortless. Searching for pleasure is something no one can avoid. Contrary to popular self-pitying belief, we need make little effort to obtain it, which is what keeps so many people on the level of the lizard. I hope that the early chapters show undeniably how our bodies have come to be constructed with a mass of sense organs whose basic function is to produce pleasure. All we have to do to cause pleasure in the proper scientific sense of the term is to look, listen, touch, taste, or move. Few of us have much trouble in doing these things and it is easy to convince ourselves, especially with social approval, that such activities have human value, when in fact we are simply doing what comes as naturally to us as to a fish. Every day in my laboratory, fish in their simple, honest fashion do with their eyes, ears, skin, taste buds, and muscles what millions of people do complexly and hypocritically. It is in this sense that I shall use the term *subhuman*—seeking pleasure by the use of neural mechanisms that form the only means of pleasure-seeking in lower animals. One of the strongest reasons why man's social development is retarded is this very ease of obtaining pleasure. This is what keeps wild animals in their allotted place.

Men do not have only the limited brain mechanisms for producing pleasure that exist in the lower animals. No one except the blatantly abnormal need suffer the epithet subhuman. Indeed, the unique ways in which some people can and do behave like human beings are the essential reason why the human scene is so different from that of the lower animals. There is little hope of quickly righting the wrongs of our societies unless every individual takes a deep and truthful look at his motives, his way of life, his contributions to society. Self-examination, if done honestly, is one of the most potent means of producing *dis*pleasure. Until it becomes a means of making changes in lifestyle, which in itself brings pleasure, no one can consider himself mature, either mentally, socially, or neurophysiologically—for it is all in the brain, all part of neurophysiology.

I hope to show that human thinking and behaving, human personality and human systems of value are in no way causally related to planetary positions, tea leaves, gods, or spirits. I reiterate the message of neurophysiologists, psychiatrists, psychologists, and sociologists, that every single aspect of human conduct and aspiration is firmly rooted in material events in the brain. All the manifold evidence of the recent decades of brain research leads to this conclusion. Unless we come to reject all ideas about the nonmateriality of the psyche, unless we accept that our personalities, our hopes and fears, our likes and dislikes, are but external representations of patterns of electrical activity in our brains, we are unlikely to attain freedom. We remain in the neural slavery of indoctrination, objects of exploitational brainwashing, seeking pleasures as dictated by others, while all the time arrogantly considering ourselves to be free. The great advantage of accepting the *fact* of the materiality of mind is that only then does the individual realize that any personality, any hope and fear, any like and dislike *can be changed.* And changed, what is more, in a practical and relatively easy, though time-consuming way by utilizing techniques for altering brain patterns that are employed daily by those who spend their lives in straightening crooked minds.

We shall see that brain function, with special reference to the pleasure areas, is all that needs to be invoked to understand why some men are homosexual, why horoscopes are in vogue, why football is unproductive and art serene. In the accessible recesses of the brain we shall find what really *is* the mind and why it desires pornography, why people sing in the bath and dream in bed, why they go to the movies or write about heaven. Among the nerve cells we shall look upon the forces that drive young people into rebellion and violence, drugs and pacifism. We shall see, too, the material basis of compassion, love, and sex—even when the latter is just another name for adrenalin—and we shall become aware of exactly how important it is to breast-feed, to marry, and to raise a family.

Here and there we shall be surprised to find areas that are crying out for the attention of the women's liberation movement and yet which have been ignored in favor of trivial matters such as brassieres. In the overall view we will survey and ponder deeply the long, slow climb of each individual from his apelike birth to some sort of human maturity, with so many people not quite making it. Much will be deplorable, a lot of it sad, some of it enraging, but at the end of it all there is the neural blueprint for the new genesis—the *psycho*genesis that will lead to a psychocivilized society, or, to express it another way, to a society made up of human beings.

The Science of Pleasure

Part One

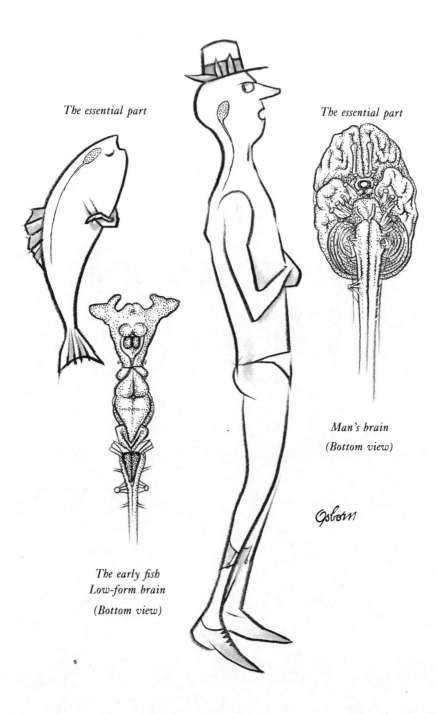

The essential part

The essential part

The early fish
Low-form brain

(Bottom view)

Man's brain
(Bottom view)

Osborn

Chapter 1

The Brain and Behavior

The brain is the most complex entity known, housing about a million times the computational prowess of the Houston Space Center. Twenty years of studying it have allowed me only to scratch the surface of what is known and to glimpse the great unknown area ahead.

The brain in the human skull can be considered to consist of two main parts, as long as it is understood that these are not separated anatomically or functionally, any more than the two parts of the arm. One part of the brain is very much the same as in the oldest vertebrates, judging by current simple backboned animals. This part, comprising the brain stem and parts of the "limbic system," first appeared about 500 million years ago, in the

Ordovician period, filling the skulls of jawless fishes, the ostracoderms. Although it has been pulled around somewhat, this archaic brain tissue is still part of our heritage from lower creatures—one of the myriad pieces of evidence that humans are part of the succession of animal life. Two of the brain regions, the pons and cerebellum, which are concerned mainly with the muscular system, evolved with the reptiles about 300 million years ago; they are of little importance in psychic matters. The rest of our brain, the "highest" regions comprising the great mass of convoluted cerebral cortex and its associated regions, first occurred in the earliest mammals some 100 million years ago, although it was not as great or as convoluted; nor is it as complex in lower mammals now. So there was a period of about 400 million years during which animals existed well enough with just their limbic brains to ensure that humans would eventually appear. The human cerebral cortex has existed for at the most a million and a half years.

Many features have changed in recent mammals compared with those jawless fishes. Limbs have appeared, gills have gone, kidneys have occurred, fingers are formed, and we have eyelids and ears and voices. If we strip away from a man everything not present in the ostracoderms we are left with precious little but a spine, gut, sex organs, which are all greatly modified, and a limbic brain which is practically identical. The very persistence of the limbic system throughout that almost unimaginable amount of time, through all those radical changes in body form and way of life, should suggest at once that there is something of great fundamental value in it, something which has been absolutely essential to the continuance of animal life whereas fins and gills could be dispensed with. What the basic feature of the limbic system is, what there is about it that not only sustained our countless ancestors but that serves to keep us alive and much more—for the limbic system is in fact the "brain" of sport and pop and sex—I hope to be able to demonstrate.

But, first, how do our present, full-grown brains work? The "brick" that builds the brain is the nerve cell, and there are several hundred millions of them. Every nerve cell or neurone is made up of two components, a cell "body" and two kinds of fibers or "processes." The cell body looks very much like other cells, for example those in the liver; it is roughly spherical and contains a nucleus. From certain regions on the surface of the cell body quite short fibers grow out; these are called "dendrites" and are in contact with nearby neurones, bringing information *from* them to the cell body. At one point on the surface of the cell body, one relatively long fiber grows out; this is the "axon" and it may end near another nerve cell in the brain, near another nerve cell in the spinal cord, or in an organ such as a muscle somewhere in the body at large. Information passes *away* from the neurone to other cells along the axon.

If we look at any small region of the brain, of about a cubic centimeter, we may find that it has a very light appearance, whereas another region nearby is darker. The dark regions (gray matter) contain mostly cell bodies; the light regions (white matter) are masses of axons en route to other regions. The collections of cell bodies are called "nuclei" and are grouped together because they all have to do with the same function. For example, electrical stimulation of one particular brain region (lateral nucleus of the hypothalamus) causes angry behavior. The electricity excites several thousand nerve cells all of which are involved in the "rage reaction." Some axons from this hypothalamic nucleus will be concerned with insuring that the pupil dilates, some will cause extra saliva to be formed, others will evoke raising of the hair, others still will be concerned with vocalizations. We cannot say with any certainty what any single nerve cell does; all we can do is point to clusters of neurones and give a word or phrase (such as "anger") to what is in fact a complex set of bodily reactions. Nor can we point to any one cluster—such as this particular hypothalamic nucleus—and say that this is *the* brain region that generates anger, for many other parts of the brain are required for the full response. Nevertheless, if the lateral nucleus of the hypothalamus is destroyed, it is practically impossible to make an animal angry. If certain other parts of the brain are destroyed instead, we obtain a "partial response" when we upset the creature; it is clearly annoyed but does not show *all* the signs of rage.

In much the same way all other brain functions require several brain regions for the full normal range of components in any labeled piece of behavior; nevertheless they are heavily dependent upon one or a few critical brain regions. Thus there are no "centers" for functions; only areas and regions and the networks of fibers that interconnect them. Nor does any region or area have only one function. For example the nerve cells in the lateral hypothalamus that look after the diameter of the pupil will do this sometimes even if the animal is not angry—as when it looks toward a dark scene. There are cells in the lateral hypothalamus that send instructions to the pupil if they are "told" by the eye that it is getting dark or by the ear that an enemy is about. All nerve cells receive information from several different sources and then proceed to cause a particular response. Nearby are other neurones that are sensitive to only some of these sources of information, for example from the eye and skin but not from the ear; these will cause another related response such as making the retinal receptors more receptive.

The reason the brain can be studied so well by stimulating it electrically is that the generation of electricity is part of normal brain function. Electrical charges are generated by underlying chemical changes—movement of ions—rather like the way a dry battery works. We could stimulate the brain with ions, and some brave research workers do, but it is infinitely more difficult than

Osborn

with electric current. Our experiments duplicate crudely and grossly what happens in the brain when we are not experimenting with it. If, for example, the skin is touched, chemical changes are caused in a tactile receptor and similar changes are propagated along the nerve fiber that connects the receptor to the brain. This is the nerve impulse and it can be detected by looking at its electrical features. In fact, touching a tactile receptor will cause dozens of nerve impulses to stream into the brain; the total number and rate depend upon how hard and how long the receptor is touched. Much the same applies to all other kinds of receptors in the body.

When the nerve impulses reach the other end of the nerve fiber in the brain they cause different chemical changes. Substances that are normally stored in the nerve terminals diffuse through the walls of the fiber and across the minute space to the cell body or dendrites of a nearby neurone. If enough of this "transmitter substance" crosses the gap, then the other nerve cell begins to generate its own impulses, which pass down its axon to some distant region. If insufficient transmitter substance reaches the other nerve cell then it only "gets ready" to generate impulses and the level of its state of readiness—its sensitivity—depends upon the amount of transmitter substance present. These quanta of transmitter substance are in fact the "information" referred to earlier. They "tell" the other nerve cell to "get ready" or to "go, go, go."

Every nerve cell receives information from several sources. If a given neurone receives five quanta of transmitter substance from a touch fiber (telling it to stand by, it is *likely* to be needed) and then another three quanta from a visual receptor (telling it to stand by, it *may* be needed), the neurone will receive a total of eight quanta, which may well be enough to make it generate impulses, whereas either one of these pieces of information would have been insufficient. In this way neurones sum up a total situation and make a decision based on impulses from both skin and eye. In reality there would be many more than two inputs. What is more, some of the transmitter substances are inhibitory, that is they tell the neurone *not* to discharge impulses or to be *less* ready to discharge. The receiving neurone might, for example, receive ten quanta of excitatory substance from a skin receptor fiber and ordinarily this would be enough to make it send impulses to a muscle to withdraw from the stimulus. But if at the same time it receives five inhibitory quanta from a visual receptor the algebraic sum is only five excitatory quanta, so the neurone does not discharge—and the man does not brush the ladybug off his arm. All this, of course, is tremendously oversimplified but the gist of it applies.

The neurone receives information from several sources, some of it conflicting, works out a sum using chemicals instead of numbers, and then does or does not send its own information along its axon, that is, the nerve cell "integrates," takes several inputs but gives out only one. The neurone at the other end of that axon receives information that has already been analyzed or "processed" by the previous neurone. This process is going on all the time everywhere in the brain, sometimes concentrating on some places, sometimes on others. Always, every neurone is in a state of sensitivity to incoming quanta of information, the level of the state depending upon what has just been happening to it in the way of transmitter substances. Whether it discharges impulses depends upon what happens to it in the near future, or what new quanta arrive.

And this is where a matter of great importance arises, because what happens to it in the near future depends overwhelmingly upon what has been happening all through life and not just upon what is happening in the world outside. Neural information goes from place to place in the brain, sometimes spreading out in several directions at once—the information follows pathways. On the face of it there seems no reason why information follows *particular* pathways—why information from the skin should go to a neurone that can move that bit of skin away from the stimulus. In fact, at an early stage of intrauterine development nerve impulses do *not* follow particular pathways. At birth a few such pathways have come into existence but still only a tiny fraction of what will be present in the adult. But as the baby repetitively comes in contact with stimuli in the environment, and as some of its responses to these contacts cause pleasure and displeasure, the responses whose pathways are associated with pleasure become "preferred." Changes occur in the brain that, so to speak, decrease the resistance between certain nerve cells, so that information passes more readily between them than between other nearby neurones. Every appropriate response in an adult is the result of a preferred pathway for neural information. The process of "learning" to play the violin or even to write with a pen is simply the gradual setting up or "establishing" of preferred neuromuscular pathways.

Appropriate responses are easy enough to see when they involve relatively simple things like muscular movements; they are rather more obscure when patterns of thinking are concerned. Whenever we think, we are using preferred pathways in our brains. As we develop, not only are our simple muscular movements in response to stimuli rewarded or punished, that is cause pleasure or displeasure, but our complex activities and attitudes, too, become dependent upon preferred pathways. These become established between different thinking regions of the cerebral cortex and between the cortex and the older, deeper structures. If we knew exactly what the pattern of preferred pathways was in any individual we could predict exactly what he would do and think under any given set of circumstances. Conversely, if we *construct* particular preferred pathways in ourselves or in others, we and they behave according to the constructions.

There is, in neurophysiological fact, no such thing as free will at any instant in time. (Our mental reaction to that statement is a consequence of our present preferred pathways!) The only sensible meaning we can attach to the concept of free will is that by exposing ourselves to particular environmental changes and by deliberately thinking along certain lines, we may establish new preferred pathways. For many people, of course, this may be long overdue, but much needs to be said before we can return to this point. It all begins in the laboratory.

Chapter 2

Pleasure and Displeasure

SELF-STIMULATION OF THE BRAIN

The scientific study of pleasure took an enormous leap forward in 1954 because of an accidental discovery. James Olds, a psychologist, was interested in the alerting reaction, which is the behavioral change seen in an animal when it shifts from the drowsy to the alert state or from sleeping to waking. It had been known for some years that the alerting reaction is due to electrical excitation of a region of the brain called the reticular activating system. Olds inserted electrodes in what he thought was the region of the reticular activating system in rats in order to study certain special aspects of the alerting reaction. However, when he sent a small amount of electricity into the animal's brain from time to time with a hand-operated switch, there was no sign of alerting whatever. Some scientists would have rejected the animal and tried another, but James Olds watched the creature attentively and made a discovery that created profound interest among neurophysiologists throughout the world.

Olds noticed that the rat was not wandering about the cage in a more or less random fashion, but was repeatedly returning to the corner where it had first received stimulation of its brain. He now made a point of closing the switch only when the rat was in that corner of the cage and soon the animal never left it, but stayed there evidently awaiting the next pulse of electricity. There was no doubt—the rat *wanted* the stimulus.

This was a completely new and unparalleled discovery. Never before had an animal shown the slightest interest in having its brain stimulated. Experimenters could to some extent control an animal with electrical pulses, make it move or eat or drink or attack another animal, but always in a mindless way, the animal acting like a radio-controlled toy. But here was a rat actually seeking electrical stimulation of its brain. By staying in the right corner of the cage, or by going back when it strayed too far, the animal insured, as far as it could, that it would obtain more electricity.

When Olds later checked the position of his electrodes, it was found that they were not in the reticular activating system at all. The electrodes were in the limbic system of the brain, the functions of which were highly obscure although it was known to be involved in many activities. Olds therefore reduced his work on the alerting reaction and concentrated on this new and fascinating pleasure-seeking behavior, establishing the technique that has come to be called intracranial self-stimulation.

The general pattern of experiments on intracranial

self-stimulation initially involves a little simple and safe surgery, during which extremely thin wires are inserted into the animal's brain in a predetermined place and a small electrical socket is fixed to the upper ends of the wires. Implanting the electrodes takes about twenty minutes and within an hour or two the animal is back to normal and gives no indication that it is in any way aware of the wires or the socket. Patients have stated after this same operation that they have no consciousness of anything in their brains. When the animals have fully recovered, the test sessions begin. For these, a miniature plug is placed in the socket to connect the electrode wires with external electrical apparatus. This equipment varies in detail with different workers but in essence it supplies a pulse of very weak electricity every time the animal presses a switch. The strength of the electric current may be as low as ten microamps and would have to be made ten thousand times greater to make a light bulb glow. The time during which the current flows is determined automatically by settings on the apparatus and ranges from a few milliseconds to about half a second. In order to receive more electricity the animal must press the switch again and the equipment automatically counts the number of times this happens, so that a quantitative assessment of pleasure-seeking is obtained. By altering various controls it is possible to establish the strength and duration of stimulus which any particular animal prefers; this so-called preferred stimulus is then the one used throughout a given experiment. Most often, the switch is made into a lever on which the animal can step, although I use a special form that rabbits can press with their chins.

It was soon found that rats would press the lever at different rates, depending upon where the electrodes were in the brain. When they were placed in regions which make up about 60 percent of the brain substance, the animal pressed the lever no more when the current was supplied than when it was not. These are the neutral regions and include the entire cerebral cortex, the highest and latest region of the brain. When the electrodes were in various other parts of the brain within the limbic system, making up about 5 percent of brain volume, the animals pressed the lever fewer times when the stimulus was supplied than when it was not; clearly the creature disapproved of having these particular areas activated and kept away from the lever. When the electrodes were in other places, still in the limbic system, comprising some 35 percent of brain substance, the animals would press the lever almost continuously, reaching rates of around five thousand times an hour. There could be absolutely no doubt that the animals were experiencing pleasure and so those regions of 35 percent of the brain have come to be called the pleasure areas. Those regions where the animal avoids pressing the lever are consequently called displeasure areas.

When a naïve animal with electrodes in one of the pleasure areas is connected to the stimulator and placed in a cage where the lever switch is available, it does not at first know what is happening. It wanders around the cage, touching, smelling, and licking anything it happens to find. Quite by accident it presses the lever and obtains the first artificial activation of one of its pleasure areas. I have watched this happen many times and the animal always does what might be called a double take. It becomes instantly more attentive to its surroundings, moves about quickly in various directions, sniffs, licks, and touches everything again, as though searching for something. After a while it will inevitably press the lever again, and will go in search of the source of pleasure again. This is repeated a number of times because the animal takes a while to establish the connection between the "feeling" of intense pleasure and the uninspiring bit of metal jutting through the wall of its cage. Similarly, humans would take some time to establish the chain of cause and effect if we had an orgasm every time we passed a telephone booth.

In my own experiments with rabbits I leave the animals in their home cages all the time and bring the lever to them. Most rabbits learn within three days that the lever supplies pleasure and routinely come forward as soon as they see the apparatus. They bend their heads forward to have the plug inserted into the sockets. Over the next two to four days their pressing rate rises quite rapidly, while the animal discovers how to press the lever with the greatest economy of movement. After those initial days the animals are on what is called the plateau of response—from now on they press the lever at about the same rate day after day with only minor fluctuations. When animals have reached this plateau, experiments are carried out to determine the various factors involved in pleasure-seeking.

With this technique it was possible to study pleasure in a locatable, measurable way for the first time, in physiological terms as opposed to the necessarily vague and largely introspective terms of psychology. It was demonstrably obvious that pleasure is not just a feeling. It is as much a material fact as the contraction of a muscle or a beat of the heart. Pleasure is simply the name we give to the subjective feeling we experience when our limbic areas are electrically active. It is easy now to show fairly precisely which parts of the brain are concerned with pleasure and also to measure quantitatively the effect of a wide series of factors on the production of pleasure and on the drive to seek or avoid pleasure.

Experiments with intracranial self-stimulation soon

made it apparent that what was being studied was not merely pleasure in any parochial sense but what is clearly the ultimate pleasure, the font of all behavior. Among the earliest experiments were ones designed to measure the relative strengths of the desire for stimulation of the limbic areas compared with the wish for some more usual reward. It was found that animals that were deprived of food for a few days and knew that a certain lever would provide a pellet when pressed did not press that lever if another lever was available that they knew would give brain stimulation. Further experiments showed that animals preferred the electrical pleasure when influenced by a number of other desires, including the drive to drink in thirsty animals and the drive to mate in sexually deprived animals. In every case, the wish for activation of the pleasure areas wholly overwhelmed the attractiveness of natural pleasures.

Even more impressive, perhaps, were the experiments designed to measure the drive for intracranial self-stimulation in absolute terms. In this type of experiment the animal has to overcome a difficulty or undergo an unpleasant experience in order to obtain its goal. It is well known that hungry rats will cross a cage in which the floor is an electrified grid in order to press a lever for food, and the strength of their hunger can be evaluated in terms of the voltage that can be applied to the grid. Animals will cross a grid of much higher voltage for limbic stimulation than for food or any other normal reward.

When the lever supplying stimulation to the pleasure areas is made continuously available, the most remarkable and unusual behavior is seen. The animal does nothing but press the lever. It falls to the floor exhausted, sleeps, awakens, and immediately begins to press the lever again. So it goes on, cycle after cycle, so acutely and persistently that the investigator removes the lever in order to save the animal's life. I emphasize again that with the electrodes squarely in a pleasure area and a lever to activate them, the animal wishes to do nothing but press the lever and has no desire to engage in any other behavior whatever.

However, even though the animal working a self-stimulation lever appears to be oblivious of its environment, the electricity or its effect in the brain is not somehow hypnotizing the creature or preventing any other

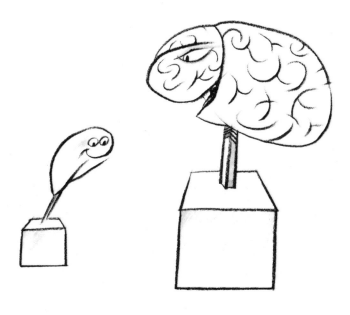

Early brains   *Later brains*
                          (*still* pleasure *seeking*)

activity. Experiments have shown that if made to do so, animals can perform quite complicated parallel tasks, such as auditory discriminations, even when pressing the lever at maximum rate. The animal on intracranial self-stimulation is fully aware of its environment but utterly uninterested in it.

Although the vast majority of these experiments have been performed with rats, the same phenomenon has been demonstrated in a wide range of species—fish, mice, guinea pigs, hamsters, rabbits, cats, dogs, dolphins, monkeys, and even humans. It is a constant feature of the vertebrate nervous system. The limbic system, of course, is one of the oldest parts of the brain; indeed sections of it represent the very first swelling of the spinal cord to form a head, some 450 million years ago. Having endured right up to the human species, it is therefore not surprising that it should be concerned with some very vital and widespread functions.

In many ways the most interesting species studied in this field is the human. The material, of course, is limited severely in numbers and the range of manipulations is narrow, for no one would implant electrodes into human brains solely for experimental purposes. Studies were made with mental patients in Sweden and in the United States to try to alleviate mental abnormality by generating pleasure. As might be expected, the responses of people were more flexible than those of lower animals. With some electrode sites the patients wished for the prolonged stimulation characteristic of the rat; with other parts of the limbic system the desire was frequently to start and stop stimulation. Again it was found that displeasure areas are always close to pleasure areas, though some of the former generated vague, mild anxiety rather than distinctly unpleasant feelings. Regions causing mild anxiety closely abutted areas that gave rise

to feelings of mild comfort and relaxation. Such mild-
ness of effect is not apparent in self-stimulating lower
animals.

An enormous advantage with human subjects is that
they can be asked why they keep closing the switch and
what they feel when doing so, although all reports at the
moment originate from mentally ill people and are
therefore somewhat suspect. Even so, these reports of
patients about their subjective feelings contain nothing
bizarre or surprising, so it is likely that much the same
experiences would be found in normal people. It is of
great interest that different kinds of pleasure are experienced with electrodes in different sites within the
limbic system. Stimulation of one site was described as
"about to produce a memory"; another as causing sexual
thoughts and the feeling of imminent orgasm; yet another limbic region gave a "drunk" feeling and the elimi-
nation of bad thoughts; while another simply made the
patient "feel good" as compared with the "feel great"
effect of another site.

These patients stimulated their brains at rates of up to
1100 times an hour and were quite happy to continue
doing nothing but this for up to six hours, the maximum
period allowed. As with the lower animals, there were
no serious signs of anger or frustration when the switch
was taken away, but obvious pleasurable anticipation
when it was brought back again next day. A remarkable
finding and one not easy to interpret, pending studies on
normal volunteers, was that some patients went on closing the switch repeatedly long after the current was
turned off. They were not aware that the doctor had cut
off the electricity and seemed still to be experiencing
pleasure. It is possible that this feature is a peculiarity of
the mentally abnormal person, but there is also the
chance that the limbic system may contain reverberating

circuits (well known in other parts of the brain) in which activation continues after the cessation of an input, due to nerve impulses traveling around closed loops of nerve fibers. Further research may show that in the human brain some forms of pleasure are self-sustaining for short periods. Self-stimulation was certainly of great benefit in the short-term view and was also possibly of some long-term help.*

In the human and in all other animals tested, there is found to be an optimum strength of stimulus which produces the highest number of lever presses. As the strength is reduced below optimum, the response rate diminishes and finally stops; obviously the level of pleasure is correlated with the degree of activation of the pleasure areas. When the strength of stimulus is raised above optimum, the rate of lever-pressing again decreases, eventually reaching zero, but this time the animal clearly shows aversive behavior in the way it avoids the lever. The most likely explanation is that the electricity at higher levels spreads to nearby displeasure areas. Moving the electrode a couple of millimeters in animals or a centimeter in the human can shift them from highly rewarding sites to undeniably displeasurable regions. But when the electrodes are located roughly at a junction between these two types of limbic areas, animals show an ambivalent attitude to the lever. They press it and run away, return and press it again, over and over again, running up quite high scores, though not as high as when the electrodes are in the center of a pleasure area. Some time is spent eyeing the lever as though deciding whether to come back for more. This type of behavior is not entirely unknown in the human and frequently accompanies the introduction of some young

*The psychiatric aspects of this work will be dealt with in chapter five.

people to such behaviors as smoking and drinking alcohol. In a radio broadcast I called it the "stop it, I like it" reaction; the radio critic of *The Times** preferred to describe it as the "go on, you are hurting me" response, revealing two very different attitudes to ambivalent phenomena. But whatever expression we use, it seems that it is the simultaneous excitation of pleasure and displeasure areas that has given rise to the concept of "pleasure that is almost pain." This neural mechanism may well be involved in sadism and masochism.†

The behavior of an animal pressing a lever for limbic stimulation may appear decidedly unusual, but we should be wrong to believe that the *events in the brain* during intracranial self-stimulation are especially remarkable. There are several reasons for this. The current required must be at about the level that would occur in the brain under normal conditions. Animals that are given a lever that produces a gradually increasing strength of current very soon learn to press another lever that maintains the present strength. In this way each animal is able to determine for itself the stimulus intensity it wishes to experience, first of all pressing the "increase" lever and then, when the stimulus reaches the preferred level, alternating its presses of the "increase" and the "maintain" lever. The level of stimulus strength chosen by each animal proves to be constant over long periods of time and is always in what is called the physiological range, that is the same sort of electrical strength that occurs naturally in the brain. Again, when animals were allowed to press a lever that supplied a continuous stimulus, the situation was found to be aversive and they quickly learned to work another device that switched off

---

* *The Times*, London, February 20, 1971.
†See p. 203.

the current. They would then alternate between the two switches, reproducing in their brain the same kind of interrupted electrical activity that occurs when bursts of nerve impulses reach the limbic system.

Further evidence for the relative normality of the neural events that occur during intracranial self-stimulation is that the various agencies or factors that affect other forms of behavior also affect self-stimulation responses. In view of the close association of drug-taking with pleasure-seeking in the human, it is not surprising that drugs were studied very early on in relation to the pleasure areas. In humans one cannot predict precisely the short-term effect of a given drug because this is the result of many interacting factors such as the dose, route of administration, state of health of the subject, whether the subject already has some other drug (such as alcohol or nicotine) in its system, and many other imponderable factors. Nevertheless, drugs can be divided roughly into three groups according to their main effects. These are the depressants, the stimulants, and the hallucinogens. All three types have been given to animals receiving intracranial self-stimulation, with results that closely parallel what would be expected.

In all experiments involving reasonably small doses of drugs and reasonably large numbers of animals opposing effects are always found, and this is not limited to experiments on intracranial self-stimulation. Even so, it is invariably found that the majority of animals exhibit a given effect, although some animals do not respond at all and a few show the opposite effect. Thus when a depressant such as chlorpromazine (often prescribed as a tranquillizer) is given to animals engaged in self-stimulation, a small percentage behave as if they had not received the drug, another low percentage show a slightly increased rate of lever-pressing, but the overwhelming majority exhibit a marked decrease in this form of pleasure-seeking. The effect of chlorpromazine, and all the other depressant drugs tested, seems to be the same therefore on self-stimulation as on behavior in general, namely an overall reduction in emotional involvement.

Conversely, a sharp rise in pressing rate is found in animals treated with stimulants such as amphetamine, so here again the drugs produce the same kind of effects as when more ordinary forms of behavior are being studied. But there is the important difference that stimulants given under ordinary conditions evoke behavior in which the animal shows heightened awareness of the environment and seeks every kind of pleasure, behaving in a restless, agitated manner, whereas when stimulants are given to animals engaged in intracranial self-stimulation they simply increase their attempts to acquire the electric current. This again indicates that activation of the limbic areas supplies the ultimate pleasure.

Hallucinogenic drugs given to volunteers under ordinary conditions generate behavior that objectively is not easily distinguishable from tranquillization, inasmuch as the individual tends simply to relax into immobility and shows little active interest in his surroundings. Many subjective accounts, however, are available to testify to the strange and terrifying hallucinatory experiences that usually accompany administration of drugs such as LSD, indicating that the internal neural events are quite different from those produced by depressants. The subjective nature of the effects of hallucinogens renders studies on lower animals rather less profitable than with the other classes of drugs. It is not easy to determine whether animals are experiencing hallucinations. These drugs, when given to animals engaged in self-stimulation, cause complete and rapid cessation of lever-pressing, and future research is required to discover why this is.

Experiments with LSD have hinted at how complex is the anatomy and chemistry of the pleasure areas and have provided long-term work for researchers. Serotonin, a substance that occurs in the brain, is concerned with the transmission of information from one nerve cell to another. When it was given to animals which had already been treated with LSD the expected reduction in lever-pressing did not occur when the electrodes were in some pleasure areas but occurred as usual when the electrodes were in others. Clearly the detailed pattern of pleasure mechanisms is fully as complicated as other brain functions. We should always bear in mind that the term "pleasure areas" does not apply to a homogeneous set of nerve cells all doing the same thing, but refers to a neuronal system of great intricacy.

The importance of chemical factors in the experience of pleasure is also shown by experiments with hormones. These are compounds that are manufactured in various glands in the body and which are secreted into the bloodstream and carried to distant sites to exert their actions. The full picture of the effects of these chemical messengers on pleasure-seeking has yet to be painted, but several interesting results have already been obtained. A number of investigators have carried out experiments on animals such as rats. A complication enters here with the females because, as in the human, they undergo cyclic release of eggs from the ovary associated with periodic fluctuations in hormone levels. My own experiments were carried out with rabbits, which do not have this disadvantage, both sexes having stable, noncyclic hormonal patterns.

When the male sex hormone, testosterone, is administered to male or female animals, the pressing-rate for intracranial self-stimulation is raised quite rapidly by several hundred percent. Conversely, when oestradiol, the female sex hormone, is injected, both male and female animals exhibit a dramatic fall in pleasure-seeking. Similar results have been obtained in other species and indicate that among mammals, at least, it is the male sex hormone that maintains the normal level of pleasure-seeking. In untreated animals there is no difference between the pressing rates of males and females and it can be assumed that the female's pleasure-seeking drive is maintained by the small amount of male hormone known to be manufactured by the outer part of the adrenal gland.

I tested this assumption in two ways. By the simple operation of castration the major sources of sex hormones can be removed. When this was done in males we found that the animals showed a rapid and profound reduction in pleasure-seeking to extremely low levels that persisted for weeks, until testosterone was administered, upon which their pressing rates rose to normal. On the other hand, when the ovaries were removed from female rabbits, the rabbits continued to press the lever at their normal rates. Obviously, the female sex gland has little to do with the normal level of pleasure-seeking.

The second line of attack involved the use of antiandrogens. These chemical compounds do not prevent the manufacture of testosterone, nor its release into the bloodstream, but they inhibit the action of testosterone upon its target tissues. When rabbits were treated with the antiandrogen cyproterone acetate, both sexes showed the same kind of sharp reduction in pleasure-seeking that the male shows after castration. In the male, then, cyproterone acetate had the effect of chemical castration, and in the female of suppression of adrenal gland function, so pleasure-seeking in both species is apparently kept at a normal level by the male sex hormone, and fluctuations in blood level of this hormone may well be related to fluctuations in pleasure-seeking. For many years sexual frigidity in women has been treated success-fully by the administration of derivatives of testosterone. However, this does not mean that female hormones have no part at all to play in pleasure-seeking.

When an egg has been released from the ovary, this

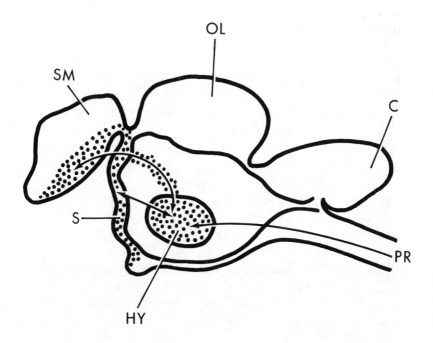

DIAGRAM 1

Simplified section through fish brain.
C, cerebellum; HY, hypothalamus; OL, optic lobe; PR, pathway from peripheral receptors; S, septum pellucidum; SM, smell brain.
The pleasure areas are dotted.

gland ceases to manufacture oestradiol and makes a hormone called progesterone instead. If the animal becomes pregnant the ovary continues to make progesterone in large quantities during the whole course of gestation. At parturition the production of progesterone stops and oestradiol is manufactured once again. I examined the effect of progesterone on my rabbits and found that daily injections of this hormone produced a slow and gradual decline in pleasure-seeking, extending over weeks rather than the sharp drop found with antiandrogen and oestradiol. When the pressing-rates were plotted on a graph, the curves obtained were indistinguishable from those obtained with pregnant rabbits, for when a rabbit which has been pressing at about three hundred times in fifteen minutes becomes pregnant, her responses drop to about fifty in fifteen minutes over three weeks. The day after she has her litter her pressing-rate is back in the region of three hundred. The obvious interpretation is that high levels of progesterone in the bloodstream, whether from injection or from pregnancy, in some way reduce the drive for pleasure-seeking. This ties in with the many reports of feelings of content and satisfaction that women experience during pregnancy; they frequently show less desire to engage in their previous pleasure-giving activities.

Much work remains to be done on the effect of other hormones on the limbic pleasure mechanisms, upon the effects of different dosages and especially upon whether different effects are produced with electrodes in different regions.

The age-old anatomical terms for the brain regions that are now called pleasure areas are parts of the hypothalamus and thalamus, the preoptic and septal areas and the amygdaloid nucleus. Those are the regions delineated by Olds and other early workers in this field. Since then other parts of the brain have been shown to have rewarding properties when stimulated, but most of them are probably way stations leading to the pleasure areas proper.

It can be seen from Diagram 1 that the pleasure areas form an interlocking system of nerve fibers and nerve cells starting from the front of the brain sweeping backward deep inside the brain in two branches that curve around to the sides of the brain. Thus the limbic system occupies a relatively large space, although only parts of it are indisputably pleasure and displeasure areas. As with any other important function—and pleasure-seeking is *vital*—the neural equipment subserving the search for pleasure is not lodged in any small or localized region but is spread out, so that damage to any part will not destroy the overall function.

When workers have studied pleasure-seeking by destroying parts of the limbic system in no case was the response abolished, though results differ much in detail with regard to the exact effect of the destructions of neural tissues. The limbic system is a very old part of the brain and it is a neurological truism that the older a part of the nervous system, the more important it is for survival. The sum total of pleasure cannot be deliberately destroyed without killing the animal. Thus, even if it were desirable, an animal cannnot be alive without being able to experience pleasure.

This is because the brain regions involved have functions other than the pursuit of pleasure. Inextricably interwoven among the nerve fibers and nerve cells subserving pleasure-seeking are those which control the beating of the heart, the filling and emptying of the lungs, the expansion and contraction of blood vessels so necessary in the control of blood pressure, and a number of other unconscious and basic physiological phenomena. By placing stimulating electrodes in the correct places in the limbic system, animals can be made to eat or drink or make love or fly into a rage, none of them at the animal's own volition, of course. All these acts of behavior already play a vital part in the animal's normal life even though they are not lodged in the pleasure areas. Nevertheless their remarkable proximity and their similar antiquity strongly suggest that they are controlled by neural messages from the pleasure areas. Future research may enable us to distinguish between various parts of the pleasure system in terms of the kind of behavior they produce when they are relatively inactive, because it is likely that while the pleasure areas are active—that is, when pleasure is being experienced—they bombard the other behavioral regions with impulses which reduce electrical activity. Only when the pleasure ceases and the limbic areas become inactive do these inhibitory impulses stop flowing out of the pleasure areas, releasing the kind of behavior controlled by these other areas of the limbic system.*

Thus all the fundamental behavioral reactions that are concerned with survival of the individual and of the species are grouped together in this ancient region which also contains the pleasure areas.

Perhaps the pursuit of pleasure is likewise an ancient and vital form of behavior. Indeed, there is much to be said for the concept that the pursuit of pleasure is the *only* form of behavior.

*See chapter five.

Chapter 3

The Pursuit of Pleasure

PERIPHERAL SELF-STIMULATION

Other scientists have done more detailed work than I on intracranial self-stimulation, and their results have illuminated much that was obscure about higher brain functions. I have no reservations therefore about studies with intracranial self-stimulation being of great importance for the advance of neurophysiology. But its unnaturalness worried me greatly.

The sight of animals with limbic electrodes endlessly pressing levers and not wanting to do anything else is unnerving to the physiologist whose concern is with the normal functions of the body, with special reference to the brain and behavior; but there is nothing normal about my lever-pressing rats and rabbits. I do not question the ethics of this valuable work, but I question its relation to normal function and everyday life.

A number of highly competent and imaginative workers have attempted to erect theories of motivation, drive, emotion, and the mechanisms of reward by direct reference to results obtained with intracranial self-stimulation. I was more interested in finding the natural counterpart of this fascinating phenomenon and going on to theorize from *that*.

It was obvious that animals experience pleasure without first having a scientist implant electrodes into their brains. They play, enjoy their food, and clearly find sex rewarding. Equally without question humans, too, experience pleasure without direct electrical stimulation of the brain. In the vast majority of animals, then, the limbic pleasure areas are somehow activated in normal life. Somehow our pleasure areas must at times show much the same kind of electrical activity that they would show if we were provided with electrodes and a lever to press. I wanted to find out what in normal life activates the pleasure areas. Being predominantly a scientist and only occasionally a philosopher, I did not ask what pleasure is; that one came later when I was in a more solid position to answer it. At first I simply thought about the ways in which the limbic areas could be activated by events in everyday life. The very idea of pleasure being produced by *events* led me to see that the simplest way for this to happen was through the senses, because it is by means of the senses that we detect events in the first place. There is abundant evidence of anatomical connections from well-known sensory pathways to the newly known pleasure areas. These neural connections were observed and recorded by the early anatomists but their significance, understandably, had not been recognized.

I formed the view that in normal animals, including

man, the pleasure areas deep inside the brain are activated when the sense organs on the periphery of the body are stimulated. When light enters the eye or sound vibrates the eardrum or touch stimulates the skin, nerve impulses pass from the peripheral sensory receptors along nerve fibers to the limbic areas, causing the animal to experience pleasure. This does not imply that every kind of peripheral stimulus gives rise to pleasure. All intense stimuli and quite a few mild ones are well-known to be unpleasant. According to my view this kind of stimulus activates the displeasure areas, but since most normal volitional behavior is concerned with pleasure my emphasis lies in this direction.

This then was my hypothetical answer to the problem of the normal counterpart of intracranial self-stimulation. I felt sure that it would be possible to test these ideas in the laboratory. If I were right, I should be able to arrange for animals to perform some task, entirely at their volition, the reward for which would be more stimulation of one of their senses. There would be no electrodes in the brain and no conventional rewards such as food or sex, but simply the stimulation of the sensory receptors in the eye, ear, skin, or other part of the body in a perfectly intact and normal animal. The correctness of my ideas would be indicated if I could demonstrate *peripheral* self-stimulation. I set out to do just that.

When a totally new piece of scientific research is about to begin, the investigator's feeling of intellectual excitement and hopes of establishing the truth of a new concept must give way to serious consideration of matters such as money, laboratory space, apparatus, and time to devise new equipment. Though free to pursue his chosen line of research, the scientist has an obligation to his employer to use his time effectively, and a duty to his financial supporter to spend the money wisely. It is not easy to be impersonal about such considerations, whereas it is simple to convince oneself that the new ideas are worthwhile. In this case I was particularly fortunate; I had eight aquariums of tropical fish at home, so I could do pilot experiments with these without infringing professional time or money.

I made a plastic frame in the shape of a pair of goal posts, on each of which was mounted a platinum wire electrode. These were connected to a source of electricity, the "stimulator." A pencil of light could be shone across the electrodes onto a photocell, so that if the light beam was obscured the stimulator sent a pulse of electricity across the electrodes, through the water between the electrodes and into whatever was between the electrodes, cutting off the light. If a fish were there, its skin receptors would be stimulated. In my study one evening I set up the equipment in association with a fully furnished, three-foot aquarium, putting the electrodes down at one end of the tank where the fish need not go if they did not wish to. I expected a long wait, but within minutes fish which had been serenely gliding back and forth throughout the aquarium began to dart backward and forward through the light beam while the stimulator kept clicking and the electricity kept pulsing across the gap between the electrodes. One fish after another would join the throng until in the end every fish in the tank was jostling for the tingle in its skin that the electricity produced. These tropical fish left me in no doubt that peripheral self-stimulation was a fact.

More rigorous experiments were now justified, so I moved the work into the laboratory and devised more sophisticated equipment that would automatically record the performance of single fish, so that I could express the results in numerical form. Using several fully furnished aquariums, I found that when the stimulator was disconnected each fish swam through the light beam an average of twenty-one times during ten-minute test sessions. But this control figure rose to sixty-six on average in over two hundred tests on twenty-two fish when the stimulator was in circuit. There seemed no reason to think that the fish were engaging in this behavior in order to swim through the light beam, but were doing it to obtain electrical stimulation of their skin receptors. Even so, I tested this by putting a small amount of local anesthetic in the water. The fish swam about in an ordinary manner, according to impartial observers, but their traverses of the light beam fell to the control value of about twenty-one. The local anesthetic had numbed their skin receptors so that they could no longer feel the electricity, could no longer obtain pleasure from traversing the electrode assembly. In 1880 a great psychologist, B. von Anrep, showed that cocaine anesthetized the tactile receptors in fishes but left the chemosensory (taste) cells still sensitive. So almost certainly my self-stimulating fish were having their touch receptors activated by the electricity and were experiencing pleasure from a kind of tickling or fondling sensation—just as fish will zoom up against objects in the aquarium from time to time, presumably enjoying the tactile sensation produced; and the marine clown fish will spend much of its time weaving about among the tentacles of sea anemones. Who among us does not like to have his back scratched?

Some fish demonstrated how intelligence can be brought to bear on pleasure-seeking even at this low level of animal organization, by devising a technique for minimizing their muscular effort. During the test sessions they hovered just below the light beam and waved their large dorsal fins from side to side through it, obtaining an electrical caress with every wave.

For reasons that will appear later, it is important to note that the factor of deprivation does not enter into these experiments. In practically all other behavioral experiments on animals in which they are expected to perform some task thought up by the investigator, such as pressing a lever or treading on a pad, it is either impossible or extremely difficult to induce the animal to cooperate unless it is first deprived in some way. For example, it is starved and then given a food pellet as a reward for performance. In my experiments with fish, and in all of my other work on peripheral self-stimulation, the animals were all properly fed and watered, kept under conditions with a full range of normal environmental stimuli and tested in their usual home environments. Thus, the animals were not filling a prearranged gap in

their lives by seeking sensory pleasure, but were adding
something new and positive to it.

Much the same apparatus as I have described has now
been used to test the peripheral self-stimulation responses of amphibians and reptiles, and similar results
have been obtained. Japanese fire-bellied newts and red-
eared terrapins showed the same kind of "approach
behavior" toward electrodes that stimulated their skin
receptors. But the real value of these lower groups, intermediate between fish and mammals, to my mind, is the
most impressive demonstration of the power of peripheral self-stimulation shown by the crocodile. The
creature I work with is in fact a caiman, but we need not
split nomenclatural hairs; to all ordinary eyes it is a
crocodile. Like most of its kind, its life is predominantly
sedentary. I have frequently thought it dead when
finding it in exactly the same position in the morning as
it was in the night before. It shows purposeful activity
on two occasions only. The first is when my assistant
proffers its thrice-weekly feed of lean steak, and the other
is when there is a chance of obtaining an electrical fon-
dle.

There are two to three inches of water in its tank and
from time to time a set of goal post electrodes is placed
in this water at one end of the tank. When this is done,
the crocodile lumbers off the stone slab on which it
spends many hours basking in the warmth of a lamp. It
trundles slowly through the gap between the electrodes,
ponderously turns and sets off back again. On good days
it will do this some fifty times in fifteen minutes, which
is tremendous physical activity for a crocodile, comparable only to the energetic activity of capturing prey. On
bad days it will drag itself through the light beam only
about half a dozen times but, rather like the hovering
fish, will obtain plenty of "fondling" by slowly wagging

The crocodile and the electrode

his tail through the beam or by sitting with its throat just above it, so that its respiratory movements set the stimulator going several hundred times during the test sessions. The epithets "good" and "bad" days refer to me, not to the crocodile, for its application of low cunning on bad days thoroughly confuses my numerical records. I have now outwitted it by using a beam of infrared light, which it cannot see, so it *has* to engage in whole-body effort if it wants to be kissed.

The crocodile's many hours of immobility make it unnecessary to carry out an experiment with local anesthetic. While it basks on its slab, microscopic, single-celled plants attach themselves to its scales and multiply, so that after a few weeks it is visibly coated with an insulating layer of this green alga. Under these conditions it shows no interest in the apparatus, but once scrubbed down it will immediately renew its interest in the device, avidly lumbering back and forth.

In the view of several biologists the comparatively strenuous effort exerted by the crocodile to obtain stimulation of its skin receptors is among the strongest evidence for the reality of peripheral self-stimulation as a source of pleasure and for its comparability—though by no means its *identity*—with intracranial self-stimulation. Even so, most of us gain more confidence in the general applicability of a phenomenon if it can be demonstrated in animals rather higher than fish, newts, terrapins, and crocodiles. The occurrence of peripheral self-stimulation in these lower forms, however, has a very special significance.

The first mammal I tried was the rabbit, on which I have done so much work with intracranial self-stimulation. For this I developed a new technique. I used a device called a capacitance probe which is sensitive to being touched. It can be connected to any piece of apparatus to act as a switch so that when the probe is merely touched the apparatus is turned on. The probe looks and feels like a metal rod; it gives no special stimulus to the hand. Nothing has to be moved with this device so very little muscular effort is required and the probe does not wear out in the way conventional levers do when pressed thousands of times daily. To go with the capacitance probe I designed a new stimulator which is in effect a highly complex switching machine that can turn on one or more of several kinds of stimuli for selected periods of time at predetermined strengths, at the same time making a permanent record of everything that is going on. When the probe is touched, the stimulus comes on for, perhaps, five seconds and then ceases. For a repetition the probe must be released and touched again.

In deciding on the first stimulus to try on mammals I had to determine what receptors I was going to allow the animals to stimulate and precisely how to stimulate them. The stimulus should be a "pure" one, that is, without meaning to the animals. Other research workers have described how monkeys will show themselves certain slides on a projector in preference to others, landscapes instead of lamp posts, for example. But for my theory I wanted a stimulus that could not be thought to evoke any kind of psychological reaction, that would not conjure up visions of freedom in the forests, but would simply make some peripheral receptors active in what would ordinarily be called a meaningless way and yet would activate the pleasure areas.

So I chose white light. The capacitance probe and stimulator were connected to a high wattage bulb placed a few inches in front of the animals' cages. Once more the tests were carried out without any kind of deprivation of food or drink or sensation. The animal stayed in its usual cage under the ordinary animal house conditions and the apparatus was set before it from time to time. When this was done the rabbits came forward and pressed the probe with their noses or chins many times above the chance level which resulted in the lamp lighting. The response rate was not nearly as high as that for intracranial self-stimulation in these creatures, so even though the flash of light was rewarding, it was not as pleasurable as direct stimulation of the brain. We shall see later why this is to be expected and how it explains a lot of what we do and why we do so much.

This positive result with plain white light pleased me greatly, for although the skin tingle in fish is readily understandable, the pleasure from mere light is not readily analogous to common experience. In order to explain it we *must* agree with the postulate that was in my mind when I designed the experiment—stimulation of peripheral receptors results in electrical activation of the pleasure areas irrespective of whether the stimulus is one that has come to be commonly associated with pleasure. Many stimuli are used by people in this "unknowing" way.

The next step was to demonstrate peripheral self-stimulation in a primate. Monkeys are social creatures and I did not want to keep them under the semi-isolated conditions that are usual in animal houses. I preferred to have them in the laboratory where they could enjoy the long-term company of other primates (my assistants and myself) and plenty of generalized stimulation—people coming and going, talking and shifting things about. These requirements limited the choice of monkey. In the end I decided to use squirrel monkeys from Peru. They are diminutive creatures, friendly and reasonably quiet. They exhibit none of the frenzied, irritating and utterly unnecessary screaming and aggressive posturing that persists in rhesus monkeys, which are so often used in behavioral research. Our squirrel monkeys live on the laboratory bench in cages large enough for them to swing about on tree branches; they whistle and chirrup all day, try to play with us whenever they can, and have never attempted to bite or even to adopt aggressive postures. They keep *us* company nicely and are always an added pleasure for visitors.

When the capacitance probe is first pushed through the bars the squirrel monkeys come running up to investigate it. They handle it spontaneously in the way monkeys manipulate any new object they come across. Unless it proves edible or can be made love to, the new object is soon tired of and ignored. But our squirrel monkeys did not tire quickly of the capacitance probe. During the first test session they touched it about thirty times, sporadically and rather absentmindedly after the initial decision that it was neither meat nor mate. Their limbs happened to come in contact with the probe as they moved about the cage and stared at the five-hundred watt lamp that went on and off a few inches in front of them without their understanding why. When tested for fifteen minutes daily, the squirrel monkey took about three days to be quite sure that the probe controlled the light and to learn that it must keep touching it and releasing it to obtain more than five seconds of stimulation. On about the fourth day the monkeys touched the probe some two hundred times in fifteen minutes, and within a week they reached out and grabbed the probe before it could be pushed through the bars. After that they touched the probe at a fairly steady rate of about three hundred to five hundred times during a test session, with the light actually on for a total of about thirteen minutes. This means that they learned to release the probe and touch it again in an average of two-tenths of a second. Such results have been identical for statistical purposes in eight squirrel monkeys of both sexes.

In some ways these results are as impressive as those with the crocodile, quite apart from the fact that they were obtained with primates. Monkeys are a direct contrast to the crocodile in that, provided they are warm and healthy, they are usually on the move. Our squirrel monkeys are incessantly jumping and swinging around their cages, picking up bits of food, chewing them, dropping them, running about again, peering in every direction, taking note of every sound and movement in the environment. When the probe was within reach they settled down on the nearest perch, curled their tails around their necks and worked away at touching and releasing the probe while they stared at the lamp. From time to time they would reach down and pick up a nut and eat it without interrupting their manipulation of the probe. Sometimes they would pop over to the water bottle for a drink and then return immediately to the probe. When the bright light stimulus was available, the squirrel monkey severely curtailed its usual cavortings and settled down to the serious business of obtaining sensory pleasure. Comparable singleness of purpose is seen only when the monkeys are given a fresh supply of food or become engaged in coupling. Peripheral self-stimulation has, in fact, been demonstrated in the primate group.

Over the next few years much work will be done on peripheral self-stimulation and a great deal more found out about its detailed properties and characteristics, but even now it is possible to sketch in some of the main features of this widespread phenomenon. One is that the response rate is reduced as the wattage of the lamp is lowered; clearly, the intensity of the stimulus determines the effort generated to obtain it. This is comparable with the increasing lever-pressing rates obtained with intracranial self-stimulation as the current is raised from low levels toward optimum strength.* When the intensity is reduced to zero, that is, when everything is as before but the light does not come on, the monkeys touched the probe thirty to thirty-five times during a test session. Some of these touches presumably are random manipulations; others are hopeful attempts to light the lamp; the probe itself is clearly of little interest.

A five-hundred-watt lamp emits a noticeable amount of heat, even when alight intermittently, and it might be thought that the monkeys were not so much interested in the meaningless light but touched the probe to obtain

*See p. 29.

the physically important stimulus of warmth, and this could explain why they respond so poorly to a low-wattage lamp (45 touches for 40 watts; 105 for 100 watts). But when I placed a sheet of quarter-inch plate glass between the lamp and the monkeys, which made the heat of the bulb imperceptible to a thermometer or to the back of my hand when placed behind the glass, there was no difference in the response rates. Under some conditions monkeys would almost certainly carry out a task to obtain heat; experiments have been done on hairless mice and even on pigs, who will tread on a switch to turn on infrared lamps hanging above them. But in these other experiments the animals were cold; they were not seeking *mere* pleasure, mere sensory stimuli, but were performing a task in order to bring back a normal ambient temperature. When pigs were placed in a warm environment they ignored the switch. This behavior is what would be expected, for the pig, in these experiments, is homeostatically oriented while my monkey is not—because the laboratory is kept properly warm.

Another indication that the monkey's search for sensory stimulation has little to do with the surrounding environment is indicated by tests carried out with different degrees of lighting in the laboratory during the experiments. The animals have been tested at night with all other lamps extinguished, at different times of the day in winter from dull, overcast weather to bright, sunny conditions, and even in the powerful glare of the lights set up by a television film crew. In all circumstances the monkeys responded at their usual levels for the bright light they could control by their own efforts. It has been known for a long time that monkeys in a light-tight box will press a lever to open a panel in the wall or to switch on a lamp in the box. This is obviously very different from my squirrel monkeys who, as with the heat, were not trying to produce a return to ordinary conditions from a situation of deprivation, but were thoroughly enjoying the extra stimulus of the lamp.

Rather similarly, the squirrel monkeys have been tested both before and after their morning feed, again with no consistent change in response rate. Nor did the rate alter when they were tested again after a rest period of weeks or months; as soon as they were given the probe again they touched it at their usual rate. Thus, the response obviously has a strong identity in its own right and does not arise out of a special set of environmental conditions, in contrast to so many behavioral experiments with monkeys. But the response rate is by no means independent of all other factors; it can be readily altered by hormones, for example.

If my belief that peripheral stimulation is the natural counterpart of intracranial self-stimulation is correct, it might be expected that the peripheral responses would be affected by hormones in much the same way as the intracranial responses. This type of investigation is being actively pursued at the moment and the results so far obtained are not as numerous as those obtained with rabbits. Nevertheless treatment with male sex hormones appears to cause a remarkable increase in response rate in fish and monkeys; and a severe reduction in response rate occurs when they are treated with female sex hormone or antiandrogen. These effects upon pleasure-seeking are the same as those obtained when these hormones were used with intracranial self-stimulation, so they support the view that peripheral self-stimulation is the way in which animals obtain electrical activation of the limbic pleasure areas.

The success of experiments with white light suggested that it would be interesting to try the monkeys with colored light. Although it is not yet certain, most investigators agree that squirrel monkeys are fairly accurate at discriminating most colors but a little deficient with reds. I tested mine with yellow, green, blue and red lamps. Using forty-watt colored lamps, the responses were the same as for a white light of the same intensity; the monkeys were poorly interested and made no apparent distinction among the colors. Again, when I used colored lamps of an intensity equivalent to 250 watts, the animals responded for each color just as eagerly as they did for white light of that brightness. If this suggests that to the squirrel monkey it is all the same whether the stimulus is white or any other color because all the fun is in the brightness, further experiments showed that this is not the case.

They indicated also that peripheral self-stimulation comes close to everyday living in another respect. In some sessions the probe and a bright light, either white or colored, were made available continuously instead of for only fifteen minutes. Under these conditions there was a rapid fall in responding, right down to unstimulated levels within two hours, whatever color was supplied during the session. This "satiation effect" is another aspect of great importance. On the face of it, the experiments so far described give no evidence that monkeys are aware of the different colors supplied to them. But when the probe was made continuously available and the color of the lamp was changed every fifteen minutes, all the monkeys went on pressing at high rates for up to four hours. Although they soon become tired of any one form of stimulus, even changing the color was enough to sustain interest in bright light. When colored telephones were first shown in the United States there was an immediate demand for large quantities of *black* telephones. Manufacturers know what they are doing when they bring out "the same product in an exciting new package."

I moved on to the use of sound in peripheral self-stimulation and found, as I had expected, that producing intense pleasure in this sensory modality is more difficult than with light. White light is made up of many wavelengths and is more or less permanently and pervasively present in our lives. The intense white light that monkeys love to shine at themselves is nothing more than an especially interesting form of what is always with us. On the other hand, white sound, made up of many frequencies occurring simultaneously, has to be made by constructing elaborate electronic circuits and it is a most disconcerting noise. It did not seem to me to be profitable to start the monkeys off with sound that is so unpleasant. Nor, as with my choice of visual stimulus, did I wish to use a meaningful sound. It would not help my thesis if monkeys touched the capacitance probe to obtain monkey noises. To be reasonably sure that the stimulus sounds were psychologically meaningless meant using completely artificial ones and then the problems of auditory discrimination and acuity arise. Mammalian eyes are similar in terms of sensitivity to white light, but hearing ability differs very much, and practically nothing is known about aural function in the squirrel monkey. I was sure that they are sensitive to a fair range of frequencies because they utter high-pitched, "I'm lonely" squeals and some of their "let's be buddies" chirrups are quite low-pitched. With regard to intensity, not only different species but different members of the same species vary in terms of acceptable loudness, as any parent of an adolescent will testify. With all these factors operating, I had to find out by trial and error.

At first I tried the monkeys with a series of pure tones

from a signal generator that was switched on by the capacitance probe. Using closed circuit television so that my presence was no distraction, I watched the animals touch the probe while I varied the frequency and intensity of the sound stimulus which came from a twelve-inch loudspeaker just in front of the cage. One fact was immediately obvious. While the monkeys were by no means indifferent to the sounds, they did not find them as attractive as the light. With some very low frequencies around the 40–400 Hz region they seemed distinctly displeased, though neither angry nor frightened. Similar reactions were noted with shrill sounds when the frequency was above about 2 KHz. It seemed that neither very high nor very low (to my ear) volumes were pleasing to the monkeys. I use the word "seem" often because at this stage one could only observe the animals' behavior and make intelligent assessments about what they were doing. Short of spending several years trying out one frequency after another with full quantitative analysis, this was the best I could do. I settled on a medium-pitched sound at an intensity just high enough to make my assistants and myself pleased when the test sessions ended. The signal was impressed on magnetic tape to give uniformity to the daily test sessions.

I found that the monkeys touched the probe for the sound stimulus at about one-third of the rate they did for light, which is still, of course, far above control values. Although I have not chosen the quintessential sound stimulus for squirrel monkeys, should one exist, these experiments demonstrate that peripheral self-stimulation for activation of the ear as well as the eye occurs in primates.

My next set of experiments was based upon the supposition that monkeys might like music. I was wrong; only some monkeys like music. When the stimulus takes the form of bright light or a pure tone, there is no significant difference between the response rates of different monkeys. The simple light or simple sound causes about the same amount of pleasure in all the monkeys. But when the capacitance probe switches on a tape recording of Beethoven's *Pastoral Symphony*, only one of two monkeys so tested will touch the rod for it. The other monkey touches the probe once or twice, hears a few bars and then leaves the probe untouched for the rest of the session. The monkey with the musical ear is not as enthusiastic about Beethoven as he is for the light, but at least the symphony seems to give him pleasure. These results show experimentally what we know from ordinary life: there are some pleasures that are near universally enjoyed, while with others there is a difference of opinion. Experiments with peripheral self-stimulation using animals with different known backgrounds and experience might well produce evidence for why some of us like brandy while others prefer gin; why Van Gogh appeals to some and Gainsborough to others; or even why certain individuals demand democracy while others clamor for Communism.

There are some features which are common to both peripheral and intracranial self-stimulation and although it is the *differences* that are really important, the similarities should not be ignored. One such common feature is the effect of hormones. Another is that the task —lever-pressing, probe-touching—is carried out willingly. Another is that under experimental conditions both the peripheral and intracranial forms of self-stimulation are nonhomeostatic, that is, what the experimental animal seeks, whether it is electricity, light, or sound, can in no way be said to have survival value or to be essential to its day-to-day life. Under natural conditions when an animal obtains stimulation of the peripheral receptors—the taste buds—by eating it does *incidentally* acquire nourishment; the reward is in fact homeostatic. But the animal (unless it is human) does not know that. As far as the animal's volition and pleasure are concerned it is the same whether the ear, the eye, or the taste buds are being stimulated, because either one of them will activate the pleasure areas of the limbic system. With indwelling electrodes there is simply a by-passing of the sensory pathways and the pleasure cells of the brain are stimulated directly. What is often called the animal's normal "homeostatic behavior" is merely a semantic distinction; the creature seeks sensory stimulation and some of this happens, happily, to be homeostatic. We shall see that these features have profound implications with regard to the processes of evolution, extinction, and survival.

Another feature of both peripheral and intracranial self-stimulation indicates the essential similarity of the brain processes. This is called rapid extinction of response. With most tasks that animals learn, for example lever-pressing to obtain a morsel of food, the animal will eventually not press the lever if the reward is no longer supplied. The learned response is said to have been extinguished due to lack of reinforcement by the reward. But the animal will go on pressing the lever during a significant number of trials before it gives up hope. An observer who is not told that in a series of ten trials the reward will be withheld after the fifth, cannot tell from the animal's behavior that there is any difference between the trials.

With self-stimulation behavior the situation is different. If the stimulus is cut off there is an immediate drop to zero in the animal's response; it may press the lever once or twice, but then goes right away from it and only comes back at rare intervals for a single press. An uninformed observer can determine within seconds when the stimulus is withdrawn. A reasonable explanation is that with experiments involving conventional rewards the animal has been made hungry or thirsty and is impelled by this deprivation to pursue a vain course of action in the hope of obtaining a pellet. With my self-stimulation experiments there is no such internal pressure; the animals can take it or leave it, and they give up as soon as the pleasure stimulus ceases.

These similarities between the two forms of self-stimulation strongly support the belief that the two forms of behavior cause activation of the pleasure areas of the brain. However, the impetus that initiated my research was the impossibility of accepting intracranial self-stimulation as normal and the wish to establish peripheral self-stimulation as a physiological mechanism. I felt sure that there must be observable differences between the two forms that would emphasize the normality of peripheral self-stimulation. The most obvious difference is that in peripheral self-stimulation the neural elements that are being brought into a state of activity are all well-founded in classical neurophysiology. These elements are the receptors, sensory pathways, sensory centers in the brain. There is nothing odd or peculiar about an animal doing something that results in peripheral receptors being stimulated, thereby giving rise to impulses that pass to various parts of the brain. Indeed, oddity would arise if an animal did *not* do this. On the other hand, as happens in intracranial self-stimulation, it is unique for a part of an animal's brain to become active without some other part being made active first by contact with the environment.

But the really important difference, one that forms the cornerstone of the new theory of behavior, is that *satiation* is not characteristic of intracranial self-stimulation but is a constant feature of peripheral self-stimulation. Whether one considers the fish or the crocodile cutting their light beams or the rabbits and monkeys touching their probe, all of them reach a point quite rapidly when they do not want any more of that particular stimulus. They voluntarily go away from the source of stimulation and busy themselves with some other activity. After a while they return and seek the stimulus anew, only to reach satiation again within a short time. All of us are aware that whatever is giving us pleasure *now* does not do so later on. However exciting a barrel full of strawberries may be to the eye, it becomes a source of indifference to the palate after a number have been consumed. The number varies within limits from person to person and from time to time, but we should seriously question the normality of a person who ate a whole barrel of strawberries at one sitting. Similarly, we enter a concert hall full of anticipation of the pleasure to come and we thoroughly enjoy the music, but most of us would be distressed if after two-and-a-half hours we had to bear another two hours of encores. And it is no accident that

Osborn

the exquisite pleasure of orgasm is so short-lived. Experimental sensory pleasure-seeking shows the same kind of end-point mechanism that we find in the pleasure-seeking of ordinary living.

Peripheral self-stimulation has been convincingly demonstrated in fish, amphibians, reptiles, and primates. It also happens in humans, in such clearly recognizable forms as television, the arts, eating, and mating, as well as in many other, more subtle activities. The limbic regions have great phylogenetic antiquity; we can now see that its behavioral mechanisms are also ancient because the neurological processes of sensory pleasure-seeking are present in fish, which have the simplest vertebrate brain. Since the same neurological equipment and the same behavioral patterns are present in humans, we cannot reasonably doubt that the fundamental mechanism of sensory pleasure-seeking is the same in humans as in fish.

Chapter 4

A New Theory of Behavior
"ACTIVATE THE PLEASURE AREAS!"

My intention is to establish that behavior, at least in vertebrates, is directed by the brain, completely rejecting any dualism involving a nonmaterial "mind" or "soul" as unnecessary, unprofitable, and probably untrue. The present viewpoint negates all supernatural intervention, direction, or control over animal behavior, including humans; the responsibility for what people do rests entirely upon their shoulders, literally, inside their skulls. The thoughts and feelings that appear to guide their actions are generated solely by electrical activity in neurones.

Pleasure is the end point of all animal behavior, and pleasure is not merely a feeling but is a fact of neurology.

Pleasure can now be demonstrated with oscilloscopes, meters, counters, and pen recorders, or it can still be detected by the "feeling" we have when experiencing it. Pleasure can now be measured, its degrees established, and the factors that affect it examined. Pleasure, and therefore all behavior, has been brought within the precise, quantitative domain of scientific instrumentation, in just the way that blood pressure has, or the constituents of blood, or the constituents of urine, or the volume of air in the lungs. To the long-known physiological measurements of bodily phenomena can now be added what were once psychological guesses. But some people rebel against the idea that an instrumental yardstick can be applied to their "feelings" although they do not object to a sphygmomanometer or to a cardiograph. They seem to regard their feelings as particularly private and personal, not to be meddled with by the impersonal methods of science. This attitude arises, on the one hand, from conceit about the particularity of the "self," and on the other, from a hankering after spiritual attributes. Many people do not wish to believe that their opinions, thoughts, and actions are as much down-to-earth biological matters as what goes on in their kidneys. They consider it some kind of attack upon their identity as an individual.

However, just as the cardiograph in no way alters heart function and the sphygmomanometer has no effect on blood pressure, so a more realistic, scientific, and materialistic understanding of it need not alter anyone's attitude to pleasure. It is unnecessary to feel less pleasure in a given activity simply because one knows that the feeling arises from electrical activity in a given part of the brain. Everyone is aware that certain pleasures are intimately connected with taste buds or the tactile receptors in the erotic zones, without considering the value of gastronomy and sex lessened thereby. Indeed, greater knowledge of the physiological factors and principles involved in eating and mating, rather than attributing deficiencies to "I'm made like that," has enabled many people to increase their enjoyment from these activities. In a similar way it is likely that a better understanding of the fundamental brain mechanisms involved in behavior, especially with regard to the distinction between subhuman behavior and the uniquely human form, may well lead to a change in orientation toward pleasure-seeking that gives greater rewards. It is still entirely a matter for the individual to decide. Surely it is no reduction in mental life to switch from the behavior of an elaborate monkey, entirely sensorially oriented, to that of even a simple man. And for those who do not wish to believe, consciously or unconsciously, for those who wish to remain elaborate monkeys, the knowledge that they are subhuman does not compel them to evolve any more than merely measuring their blood pressure forces them to stop running up stairs.

In the previous chapters I have shown how various localized and interconnected regions of the brain give rise to a subjective experience of pleasure when electrically active, and there is convincing evidence that under ordinary conditions the pleasure areas are electrically activated by stimulation of the peripheral receptors. Thus the evidence indicates that the normal counterpart of intracranial self-stimulation is peripheral self-stimulation. Animals normally generate pleasure by bringing about situations in which their sense organs are stimulated. It is no coincidence that we speak of "feeling" pleasure.

With intracranial self-stimulation both lower forms and people behave in a compulsive and exclusive fashion. They wish to do nothing other than the minimum requirement to obtain limbic stimulation, pressing the lever repetitively with no thought for food or drink or any other necessity of life. This compulsiveness, this exclusiveness, suggested to me that everything the animal does in its normal life, its entire behavior is directed at evoking electrical activity in the pleasure areas of the brain. The only reason animals do anything at all is to produce what could be obtained so easily by pressing the lever. Whatever else they do simply accomplishes in poor degree what the lever supplies sublimely and exquisitely. So I have suggested the principle which is an axiom of my theory of behavior, namely that the pleasure areas *must* be activated if life is to continue; it is a built-in property of nervous systems, at least of the complexity of vertebrates, to generate behavior that insures that the limbic brain regions are maintained in a state of electrical activation. Putting it operationally, all that we need postulate to explain animal behavior is that a single "command" was given to the ancestral brain-computer: "Activate the pleasure areas!"

If we recognize that the limbic system evolved from earlier neural mechanisms and also remember that even the simplest animals, the single-celled protozoa, move toward pleasant things and away from unpleasant ones, we can see that our discussion is not really limited to vertebrates. We shall be predominantly concerned with them, partly because it is in them that the experimental evidence resides but more importantly because *we* are vertebrates. Nevertheless, it would be unreasonable to assume that pleasure-seeking arose suddenly in concert with a spine. There is every reason to believe that the driving force in the whole of the animal kingdom is the pursuit of pleasure, with other structures than the limbic system serving as a focal point in the more primitive groups. Unfortunately, the transition from the invertebrate to the vertebrate nervous system is abrupt and there are no available links to show us how the limbic system came into existence. The fact that it is the "highest" part of the brain in the earliest vertebrates suggests that the limbic system evolved as a more efficient organizer of pleasure-seeking than our closest invertebrate ancestors possessed. But nevertheless, in their simple groping way, the spineless animals also search for neural joy.

It is this very feature that separates animals from plants. It is why animals do things and plants do not. All the other differences, such as the manner of obtaining food, sensitivity, movement, and so on, are derivative characteristics, not primary differences. To be an animal is to be a pleasure-seeker. Not to be a pleasure-seeker is to be a plant or an inanimate thing.

Derivative functions are rife even within the animal kingdom, too. Each organ does not contribute its own particular function for the good of the whole body. The function of each organ is incidental to the main purpose, which is to keep the pleasure mechanisms active. We can see now that the whole of animal evolution has been a gradual process of developing better ways of obtaining pleasure, by the natural selection of more efficient muscular abilities and the survival of the fittest sense organs for exploring the environment for pleasure. For an animal to continue living, various organs must function properly; these are the vital organs such as the heart, lungs, liver and adrenal cortex (which provides hormones essential to resistance). But merely being alive, though suitable for plants, is insufficient for animals. In animals other, nonvital organs must also function efficiently; these are muscles, skeleton, alimentary canal, various glands. But the point of an animal's existence is not for its bodily organs to function but that events shall occur in the brain. For these events to occur, other organs have their jobs to do. Thus we can see these other organs as derivative, secondary structures whose existence is justified only by the effect they can have on maintaining brain function.

This is very much a reversal of what has long been the popular view, namely that the whole point of living is to use such organs as the muscles, with the brain being subservient to that end—activity for the activity's sake. But the focal point for all bodily activity, internal or external, is to aid the maintenance of electrical activity in the limbic system in vertebrates.

Just as all other parts of the body are subservient to the brain, so all other parts of the brain are subservient to the limbic system. Not naturally, in the sense that they are controlled or dominated by the limbic system, but in the sense that other parts of the brain exist and carry out their tasks solely to contribute to the proper activation of the limbic system. This applies with equal force to the higher as to the lower brain regions. The cerebral cortex survived and evolved because its intricate neuronal organization is superlatively efficient at keeping the limbic system active. Thus every part of an animal's body, high or low, exists to aid in the generation of pleasure.

It would be a mistake, though, to think that the word pleasure is here being used in its everyday sense. It is used in its strictly modern scientific sense of being identical with activation of the limbic areas of the brain. To the average person the concept of pleasure has a highly positive connotation, a situation which is *extraordinarily* acceptable or desirable, and of course this is understandable. Given that the pleasure areas must be activated, then when they are stimulated in high degree it is reasonable that we should apply a special word to what we feel. It happens that the word is "pleasure." In some

ways it is unfortunate that the same term was introduced
into the scientific work described earlier, but there is no
way now of replacing it without adding confusion. From
the point of view of this theory and the scientific research on which it is based, it must be clear that the term
is used in a much broader sense than usual. In essence
there are only two states. If a situation is not pleasurable,
it is displeasurable; if a situation is not displeasurable, it
is pleasurable. Quite often a situation has elements of
both but only under abnormal conditions does a zero
state exist in which neither pleasure nor displeasure is
produced. Thus in the present scientific connotation
there is nothing extraordinary about pleasure, only certain forms of it.

For normal people the sets of circumstances that they
would describe as neutral or having no pleasure or displeasure in them are those that have very little of either,
those in which the limbic areas are not much activated.
Such activity as walking to work along a city street may
not possess much in the way of pleasure or displeasure
—mainly because the available stimuli are familiar. The
same motor behavior along a seashore or in some rural
scene, with new stimuli to charm the eye and ear, will
be considered pleasurable because the feeling is more
intense.

We spend much time in eating and drinking, but few
of us can choose for every meal exactly what we would
like to consume. When we can choose, our eating and
drinking causes fairly intense activity in the pleasure
areas and those are occasions when we might say that we
had a pleasurable meal. At other, usually more numerous, times, when we have eaten more ordinary food, we
are quite likely not even to comment upon it. Nevertheless, the mundane meal was not displeasurable so it must
have given some pleasure or we would not have eaten it

because we were probably not really hungry. Thus we can get more pleasure, in the scientific sense, from some things than from others, but we usually restrict the term to outstanding examples. In this book I am not restricting it. By pleasure I mean activation of the limbic areas and I leave the reader to decide on each occasion what value he will attach to the precise form under discussion.

So, limiting the discussion for the moment to subhuman animals, let us return to the statement that all animal behavior is directed at pleasure-seeking. This statement resolves into the claim that everything animals do is aimed at stimulation of the peripheral sensory receptors in order to produce electrical activation of the pleasure areas. Only the reason is new. Common sense shows that everything an animal does stimulates the sense organs of one kind or another, and numerous experimental psychologists have put this view into scientific terminology and called it stimulus-seeking, sensation-seeking, search for stimulus change, desire for novelty, exploratory instinct, and other terms. But animals not only do these things, they *must* do them. Yet they do no particular thing for very long.

With intracranial self-stimulation animals will continue to press the lever indefinitely if allowed to do so. But a sharp distinction is found with peripheral self-stimulation in which, whatever the stimulus, the search for it diminishes and disappears when it is continuously available. This is a most important feature of my theory of behavior. The limbic pleasure areas must be maintained in a state of electrical activation. If this requirement were met by direct activation through electrodes in the limbic system, the animal would die, if only because it would neither eat nor drink. Fortunately, under the natural conditions whereby the limbic areas are activated by stimulation of peripheral receptors, no act of behavior can maintain this state for very long. This is due to a three-fold neural mechanism that characterizes the sensory system. To begin with, a phenomenon known as "adaptation" occurs at the peripheral receptors. This means that although a sense organ will respond to the initiation of a stimulus by generating a barrage of nerve impulses which pass into the brain, the receptor gradually slows down and eventually ceases to discharge impulses even though the stimulus continues. Although it is normally demonstrated by rather complex electrophysiological apparatus, there is a simple example of this. If the eye is directed at a small object and not allowed to move away from it, then in a short time the point disappears, even though light is still being reflected from the object into the eye. This is difficult to demonstrate to oneself because however much one tries to fixate the eye on a small object, say a printed letter in this book, one cannot do it voluntarily because a complex neural mechanism maintains our eyes in constant motion, movements so small that we are unaware of them yet large enough to make the light reflected from an object fall on different retinal receptors every few seconds. If a contact lens is placed on the eyeball and from this a rod extends outward with a small object on the end, then the eye and the object move together, so that the image of the object remains on the same retinal receptors. Under those conditions the object suddenly disappears from view and is replaced by featureless grayness, because the retinal receptors have adapted.

Incidentally, one of the reasons my crocodile and all other lower animals spend so much time motionless is that they do not have these so-called saccidic eye movements. Shortly after such a creature comes to rest, the environment becomes uniformly gray because of visual adaptation. When something in the environment moves, its image passes to another set of receptors and the animal can see it again; usually it is prey so the animal lunges forward to catch it.

Adaptation has been shown to be a feature of all receptors, whatever the mode of sensation, and we are all subject to it. When we first sit down in a chair we are consciously aware of the points of contact between the chair and our bodies, but in a short time, unless our conscious attention is drawn to it, we are quite unaware that certain tactile and pressure receptors are being stimulated by our weight in the chair. Even so, adaptation of receptors is probably not the most important mechanism of satiation in mammals. A much more likely candidate is "habituation," which happens in higher regions of the brain on the way to the pleasure areas.

Habituation occurs at places in the brain where incoming sensory impulses arrive at a junction between several nerve cells. The impulses, turning up in a single nerve fiber, can be sent on into several nerve fibers going to different places. Precisely which secondary nerve cells the impulses enter depends upon various electrochemical processes which occur at the junction. One of these processes results in habituation—the nerve impulses do *not* pass on. Although the external stimulus continues and although the peripheral receptors are still generating impulses, the information does not get past certain regions deep inside the brain. This neurological process is not the same as the habituation used in popular psychology for becoming "used to" violence, for example. There are similarities but not identity. There is also an important distinction between habituation and adaptation.

The process of adaptation of peripheral receptors is automatic and will happen at any time, with any receptor, with any animal. This is not the case with habituation, for in this the role of learning and experience is of great importance. When we cease to hear the engines of a ship after a while it is because our auditory system has become habituated to the sound. What has happened is that the brain has decided not to pay attention to the sound of the engines any more, because it has continued for some time without untoward event, and we have learned long since that under those conditions there is nothing to worry about. When the engines stop, there might be cause for concern, so we start hearing them again. This is not to suggest that with some stimuli habituation does not occur, for it will eventually occur with any sensory input. The distinction is that although we are all equally subject to adaptation, the exact point at which habituation will occur with any given stimulus will depend upon what has happened to us up to that point in time. This is one of the ways in which behavior is so profoundly influenced by past experience.

The third mechanism by which sensory pleasure-seeking can be controlled and brought to an end is called "centrifugal control of receptors." The nerve fibers that pass from the brain and travel out to end near sensory receptors carry impulses in that direction. These outgoing impulses have the effect of varying the sensitivity of the receptors to applied stimuli. Thus brain regions can control to some extent the number of impulses generated by any receptor and the period over which they are generated, independently of the stimulus that is activating the receptor. This mechanism has actually been shown to control behavior with regard to food intake. For example, many animals are fond of sweet fluids and even if they are not thirsty will consume them. When an animal is not hungry or thirsty it will reject a weak sugar solution and accept a strong one; if the same animal is hungry it will accept the weaker solution. Electrophysiological methods have shown that in the hungry animals the taste receptors generate a large number of impulses when a weak sugar solution is applied to them, whereas the same solution evokes only a small number of impulses from the taste receptors of the well-fed animal. The process of becoming nearly or fully satiated with food includes the production of changes in brain regions controlling the receptors, so that the receptors do not respond to gustatory stimuli as they would do under nonsatiated conditions.

These results were obtained some years ago, but they fit well into the present theory. Part of the mechanism of satiation, of bringing a given piece of sensory pleasure-seeking to an end, is that brain regions send inhibitory impulses out to the peripheral sensory receptors, thereby reducing the number of impulses arriving in the pleasure areas. In this way, although a given stimulus is still applied to the same organ, its sensitivity has been so altered that it is no longer capable of maintaining the proper activation of the pleasure areas required by the ancient command.

Thus during any given behavioral activity that initially results in sufficient activation of the pleasure areas, three factors are inevitably at work. Adaptation, habituation, and the centrifugal control of receptors all insure that in time those particular receptors send less and less impulses into the pleasure areas and a point is reached where so little activation occurs that the behavior ceases to be rewarding and the animal changes its behavior in order to stimulate some other receptors. And all this is absolutely vital.

Names are given to various kinds of behavior that are easily recognizable, such as mating, eating, exploration, aggression, and each of these behaviors, like any other, is engaged in because it gives pleasure. But however innocuous or even advantageous any one of these behaviors may be when indulged in over short periods, every one of these would prove fatal if engaged in continuously to the exclusion of all others. However pleasant, however "homeostatic" the form of behavior, it cannot maintain an animal's existence. If any animal could find in the environment a form of behavior that were able to provide the ultimate pleasure supplied by the limbic electrodes, it would as surely succumb from that behavior as from lever-pressing, if only from starvation. But in fact whatever form of behavior is under way at any given moment, its pleasure-giving properties *must* decrease with time, so the animal halts that behavior because it only began it in the first place for the pleasure to be obtained.

When a particular form of behavior is brought to an end in this way, it is not the end of behavior but the beginning of a new form. Under natural conditions, with the lower animals who have so little control of their environment, this is usually exploratory behavior. This produces a low level of pleasure from the eyes, ears, and skin and serves the purpose of scanning the environment to detect another sensory situation that will bring greater pleasure. When such is found another "labeled" form of behavior begins.

Probably the simplest and clearest example of this type of satiation process is seen with eating in the lower animals. Exploratory behavior involving touching, smelling, licking, and tasting objects in the environment brings the animal upon an object that stimulates the taste buds and thereby causes the generation of sensory impulses in profusion, which evoke heightened activity in the pleasure areas. The animal therefore continues with the behavior that is producing this effect, namely taking material into the mouth, chewing it, and swallowing it, because it is more pleasurable than the exploratory behavior. But the animal does not eat indefinitely even when there is a plethora of food, however flavorsome; although the intake on any occasion varies, it does so within narrow limits. We say it has "had enough," not realizing that we have not said anything meaningful. A meaningful description is that the neuronal processes of satiation have stopped enough nerve impulses arriving in the pleasure areas, so that the animal has no wish to continue. Under normal circumstances, satiation occurs when a sufficient amount of nutriment has been taken in to tide the animal over the next few hours, without at the same time bursting its stomach or even just loading it down too much to escape an enemy; this is one of the reasons why certain animals have survived. But they know nothing of this. They stop eating because there is no fun in it any more. But this normal mechanism can become unhinged.

Thus an essential feature of this new theory of behavior is not simply that because the pleasure areas must be activated animals engage in peripheral self-stimulation. Because an animal must do that and because of the inevitable intervention of satiational mechanisms, the animal is forced to engage in sequential behaviors of different types, thereby bringing it into contact with the sensory phenomena that are essential for its well-being and indeed for its life.

Diagram 1 (p. 34) explains the continuing, cyclical activity of animal organisms. The pleasure areas are the focal point upon which nerve impulses from the peripheral receptors impinge and from which, when activation decreases, nerve impulses are sent to the motor centers that control the muscles involved in exploratory behavior, until the animal finds a new source of sensory stimulation and a new source of temporary pleasure. This scheme is to be regarded as the most fundamental and basic neural mechanism of behavior, and one which can be acted upon by a multiplicity of factors ranging from heredity through hormones to bacterial toxins, thereby allowing the great range of behavior actually observed, especially in higher forms. This neural scheme is the only one operative in lower animals right up to the apes, and there can be no doubt that it is also at work in much of the behavior of people, who engage in a great deal of subhuman behavior not only in the primitive forms of mating or eating, but also in the tremendous plurality of sensory self-stimulation associated with technological civilization.

But some people obtain pleasure without the use of the sense organs at all, or by means in which the sense organs play only an ancillary role. People, unlike lower animals, derive pleasure from mathematics, logic, philosophy, linguistics, law, religion, hope, anticipation, reverie, and introspection, sources of joy that need not involve any sensory receptors. Sense organs play only an auxiliary part, for example, in the pleasure generated by classical music, painting, sculpture, architecture, writing, reading, and all other activities in which the eyes and ears are simply means to an end. Clearly, the behavioral mechanism just described does not embrace the totality of behavior seen in people, even though it may cover a vast amount of it.

It is in this respect, and this respect only, that we may draw an unequivocal dividing line between lower animals and humans. Criteria such as the making of tools or the power of reason do not sufficiently include all people and exclude all lower animals. The argument that only humans possess a soul cannot be pursued intelligently if the term is used to mean some kind of immaterial aura. "Soul" can be used to mean merely the total personality, but then those who work closely with animals are under no illusion about people's exclusive prerogative in this respect. The only clear and observationally undeniable difference between man and the lower animals lies in the

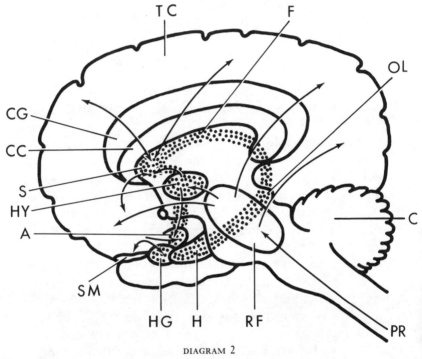

DIAGRAM 2

Simplified section through human brain, across midline.

A, amygdala; *C*, cerebellum; *CC*, corpus callosum; *CG*, cingulate gyrus; *F*, bundle of nerve fibers ("fornix") connecting septum with hippocampus; *H*, hippocampus (archicortex, id); *HG*, hippocampal gyrus (palaeocortex, ego); *HY*, hypothalamus; *OL*, optic lobe; *PR*, pathway from peripheral receptors; *RF*, reticular formation; *S*, septum pellucidum; *SM*, smell brain; *TC*, tertiary areas (neocortex, superego).

Pleasure areas are dotted.

organization and use of the brain with respect to activation of the pleasure areas. It is from this that the differences in behavior, such as they are, arise.

Many careful experiments in neuroanatomy and
neurophysiology have demonstrated that nerve impulses
pass from the very highest regions of the brain, the cerebral cortex, down to the lower, older areas including the
limbic system. A common example of this downflow is
seen in psychogenic insomnia, in which nerve impulses
generated by anxiety or excitement in the thinking regions of the brain bombard the reticular activating system* and so maintain a state of wakefulness, even though
there is a conscious desire to sleep. There is every reason
to believe that the same downward flow of nerve impulses from the higher regions to the limbic system is the
source of human pleasure. That is, the clearest distinction we can make between the subhuman and human is
that the human is able to evoke electrical activity in the
limbic pleasure areas by processes occurring in the
thinking regions of the brain. This form of pleasure-
seeking seems to be totally absent from the lower animals. It is almost totally absent from some people, too.

Diagram 2 represents the whole of animal behavior,
including that which is uniquely human. It shows that
in the human there is still the original, fundamental
neural mechanism of behavior indicated in Diagram 1
but now there is two-way traffic between the limbic pleasure areas and the higher regions (neocortex, palaeocortex, archicortex) and higher processes (attention, recognition, association, memory). When human behavior
occurs, it is mediated by the use of these added pathways;
all else that people do is subhuman.

This diagram will be referred to in order to clarify the

*See p. 19.

neural interrelations involved in specific behaviors mentioned later, but at the moment we can see, broadly, that people can be divided into three main classes, between which there will inevitably be some overlap and in which we are dealing with their *predominant* mode of pleasure-seeking. However, we should recognize that we all possess some features of all three classes. In one class there are people who might be called the feeling-doers. They are those people whose high evaluation of pleasure, throughout the major part of their lives, lies in what can be obtained by the sensory input and only in a small amount from any form of thinking or intellectual activity. Second, there are the thinking-doing people who derive their pleasure predominantly from processes of thought which are then converted into material form. Third, there is the very small group of thinking people who derive most of their pleasure from the operation of higher mental processes alone and whose "doing" is largely communicative by writing and speaking.

I will return to the characteristic features and behavior patterns of these different kinds of people, but these are the salient features. The feeling-doing people are those who do not take advantage of the advanced evolution of their own brains and while apparently engaging in human behavior in fact are utilizing mainly the sub-human neural mechanisms shown in Diagram 1. Among them are the gluttons, sportsmen, mountain climbers, spelunkers, dancers, pop-disciples, satyrs, and nymphomaniacs. In none of these activities are the capabilities of the human cerebral cortex fully realized; the higher regions play about as much part in their lives as in a reasonably sophisticated orangutang, acting as coordinating and discriminating structures bereft of human creativity. In the second category the sensory mechanisms of Diagram 1 have been brought under the creative dominance of the higher regions, and the essentially human faculties of the cerebral cortex are expressed in sensory form. Among these are the classical musicians, painters, sculptors, architects, film directors, television producers, and several sorts of scientists. In them, the sensory components of activities are subservient to the operation of the thinking abilities. It is necessary for them to utilize a sensory modality in stimulating form in order to communicate their ideas, but it is the ideas that form the font of their endeavors. The small group of people who are "pure" thinkers have relegated the neural mechanisms of Diagram 1 to the basic survival functions of eating, mating and staying warm. For pleasure, they utilize almost totally the added mechanisms of Diagram 2, and their motor behavior is not concerned with producing stimulating sensations but with informational ones. They include the philosophers, mathematicians, lawyers, logicians, theologians, theoretical physicists, sociologists, and politicians.

This ascending series of activation of the pleasure areas by cortical regions is also, biologically, an ascending series of humanness. The thinkers are obviously farthest along the line of human evolution and have clearly contributed most to make the human scene different from that of the lower animals. On the other hand the feeling-doers have come but a little way from the jungle and have contributed nothing enduring to the pattern of human life; indeed, they are as much parasitic upon the efforts of the other types as any dog, horse, or flea, inasmuch as they enjoy the fruits of civilization that are due to the brain work of others. They should not necessarily be blamed or despised for this. Those in-between comprise those who have varying proportions of highly evolved features and primitive characteristics, contributing and receiving in a wide range of degrees.

I have described the characteristics as *predominant* because it is likely that every person falls into all three of these categories at different times in his life. However junglelike the sensorially oriented person may be, from time to time he or she is likely to obtain pleasure from mere thought; unfortunately, if it is not thought about imaginary sensory inputs it may well be the kind of thought described as ridicule, superiority, arrogance, or greed. However much the mathematician or philosopher is involved in his mental operations, he will also eat, drink, and make love, thus temporarily joining the subhuman group. If we draw a scale, rather like that of a thermometer, with zero percent at the bottom and 100 percent at the top and call it a scale of ascending humanness, we can see that each individual jumps about up and down the scale from time to time. He is at the bottom when eating or making love, very near the bottom when engaged in sport or dancing, rather near the top when sculpting or designing, and right at the top when composing or solving equations. Nevertheless, there is a region on the scale which represents the "hover point" of the individual's lifestream. By and large, adults are relatively stable in terms of their main kind of pleasure-seeking so each person has his or her hover point on the scale, representing the essential "self" as a reflection of the neural mechanisms predominantly utilized in pleasure-seeking.

If we were able to place dots on the scale to represent people, the vast majority of dots would be toward the lower end. This is by no means totally due to the vast populations in underdeveloped countries, who may be ill-educated. It is a truism that sensory pleasure plays the largest part in the lives of most people. Therefore the dots on the scale become more and more sparse toward the top. The distinction between human and subhuman behavior resides in the utilization of the evolutionary advances found in the human brain. One of the consequences of this great difference is that the people whose dots lie in the higher regions of the scale have produced the social system called civilization that, even though in its infancy, is far too advanced for the majority of people, whose background training and experience lead them to behave only very partially as members of human society. There is nothing automatic about the use of the higher brain regions. The possibility to use them is there, but the extent to which they are brought into use depends enormously upon the interaction of the individual with his environment. Whether it is called teaching or indoctrination or brainwashing, the procedures for inculcating ideas and values are probably the greatest determinants of human behavior, and unfortunately it is a fact that children tend to adopt the pleasure-seeking behavior patterns of their parents. Luckily, this is slowly changing so that sensorially oriented parents may not give rise to so many sensorially oriented offspring. Gradually, as the generations go by, the dots will move toward the top.

This scale of humanness serves another purpose, which is to evaluate the degree of actual, as opposed to chronological, maturity of people. The scale can be said to represent the possible transition from birth to real adulthood. Dots for all newborn babies must be placed at the bottom of the scale because they are entirely sensorially oriented. In this respect the human infant does not differ from the newborn chimpanzee. However, with appropriate observational techniques it can be shown that within a few days of birth the human can differ most fundamentally from monkeys. The human baby can obtain pleasure from problem-solving. But the problem must involve sensory stimuli. The baby exhibits all the signs of pleasure when learning to make simple motor movements to switch on a lamp above its head. Obviously the sensory role of the lamp is important; its brightness as opposed to the dullness of the surrounding environment gives pleasure. But over and above the mere sensory joy, the baby derives activation of its pleasure areas by finding out how to switch the light on himself. The baby can demonstrate *human* behavior.

Unfortunately, so many children never have the opportunity to develop this facility to the full or anywhere near full extent of which they are capable because it does not occur to most parents to present their babies with intellectual problems. Conversely, most parents seem to feel that their job is to keep problems out of the baby's life. At a later age, when the children's motor abilities are such that they can set up problem-solving situations for themselves, they are frequently discouraged because the parents are virtually bereft of the highest human desires. By example and precept they are more likely to be led into the intellectually simple activities of kicking a ball or swimming rather than the strenuous attempt to solve an abstract problem. So the child grows up to be a dot near the bottom of the scale, whereas he possesses all the human potential to be placed somewhere near the top.

In the lives of all people, their dots move gradually up the scale from zero at birth to some higher hover point in chronological adulthood. Thus the final position of the dot is not only a measure of the individual's distance from the jungle but also of his progress from the cradle. Observation of friends and acquaintances, as well as frank introspection, reveals that many people who have the appearance and surface trappings of adults have a personality structure that is essentially a child's. Closer examination of their behavior from the point of view of the pleasure-seeking theory may well show that the cause of this immature personality is the continuing search for sensory pleasure. The adults show all the signs of irritation, frustration, boredom, and tiredness characteristic of a child when confronted with a situation that demands the protracted use of their thinking capacities. Their happiest times, like the child's, are when they are indulging in some form of peripheral self-stimulation.

It is important to recognize, though, that the position of a person's dot on the scale of humanness, or the scale of maturity, is determined by many factors. For the majority it is likely that the genetic pattern is the least important of these. It will be many years before the precise role of genes in the mental development of normal people is established. Until that time, the most profitable attitude is to concentrate on the growing evidence that points to the tremendously important role that experience plays in the developing mind, and to recognize that although early experience is particularly effective, experiences can be effective at any age. The transition of a baby's dot from the bottom of the scale to some higher point can be increased in both rate and extent by appropriate environmental stimuli, including verbal ones. The deepest effects are produced by the earliest experiences, but it would be both unrealistic and pessimistic to believe that these effects cannot be reversed in later life. The factors required to reverse them simply have to be stronger. Any pattern of thinking in terms of the preferred mode of pleasure-seeking laid down in childhood can be rearranged later. No one can take refuge in what has happened to him to justify unacceptable behavior; everyone has the capacity to change under new conditions.

Since pleasure-seeking is the root of behavior it is clearly within the parents' power either to move the child in the direction of the chimpanzee by supporting

and encouraging the search for physical, sensory pleasure, or to direct the child along the pathway that human
beings have followed, by teaching and demonstrating
that pleasure can be obtained by the use of human brain
mechanisms. That is for the future. For the present, all
young people should place under the closest scrutiny the
pleasure-seeking behavior of their parents, to determine
for themselves whether they are being led upward or
downward, and if downward, to take the appropriate
steps to reverse the trend of their lives. There would be
no harm in older people doing this, too.

The ethologist Konrad Lorenz knew that he was exag-
gerating when he stated that the missing link between
the great ape and *Homo sapiens* is man. But the statement
is clearly true for the majority of the world's population.
Lorenz was saying that the majority of people are still at
a very early stage of evolution. The majority do not fit
the description connoted by the term *Homo sapiens;*
rather they should be called *Homo sensoriens.* But it does
not have to be like that, and indeed will not be like that,
as I show later. The rapidity of the change from *Homo
sensoriens* to the real *Homo sapiens* can be accelerated if
people recognize the neural basis of their behavior and
choose to behave as human beings rather than as clever
animals.

The essential features of this new theory of behavior
are:

1. It is a requirement in all vertebrates (at least) that
   the pleasure areas of the brain shall be maintained
   in a state of electrical activity.
2. In subhuman animals the state of activity of the
   pleasure areas is maintained by nerve impulses
   originating from stimulation of peripheral sensory
   receptors.

3. In human animals, uniquely, there is a second manner of activating the pleasure areas, namely by nerve impulses originating from the thinking areas of the brain.

4. All vertebrate behavior, and probably all animal behavior, is directed at pleasure-seeking and must be changed from time to time because satiational processes prevent activation of pleasure areas from continuing with any specific input.

5. In all humans behavior is directed at one of three means of obtaining pleasure: (a) using subhuman mechanisms of sensory stimulation, (b) using a combination of activity in the thinking regions and a sensory modality to represent this activity, and (c) using the thinking regions as the sole source of pleasure.

6. Since the neural mechanisms involved in the activation of the pleasure areas form the fundamental machinery for all behavior, then all behavior, normal and abnormal, may be interpreted in terms of varying detailed function of the neural mechanisms.

7. The neural mechanisms of behavior can be influenced by many factors including heredity, childhood experiences, hormones, drugs, toxins, and alterations in neuronal interconnections, brought about by experiences in childhood and adult life, and by the normal physiological processes of development, maturation, and senescence.

Men have worked on the brain and on behavior for many decades. If my theory is true, much of the knowledge gained in the fields of neuroanatomy, neurophysiology, psychology, and psychiatry should support it.

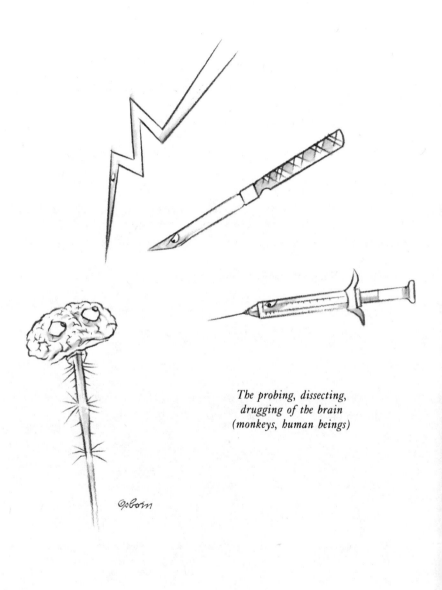

The probing, dissecting,
drugging of the brain
(monkeys, human beings)

Chapter 5

Matter Is Mind

ANATOMY, PHYSIOLOGY
AND PLEASURE

The difference between a hypothesis and a theory is that the hypothesis is an idea about what might be the case. There is very little evidence to support it. When some suitable evidence has accumulated, but not enough to prove the idea beyond doubt, the new idea is called a theory. This traditional approach to the terms hypothesis and theory has rather fallen into disuse lately and a *new* "explanation" tends to be called a theory. In this book, the term "theory" is being used advisedly because there is a wealth of evidence to support it. The evidence is derived from the experiments of other workers in several fields of research, some carried out many years ago with no reference to the present postulations.

What is meant by saying that human behavior can be unique because the human brain is unique? Apart from trivial matters such as weight, shape, and proportional dimensions, the human brain shows no purely anatomical difference from the brain of a lower primate. The uniqueness of the human brain is not due to the existence of any new brain structures. Putting it crudely, nothing can be cut out of a human brain that cannot be cut out of a monkey's brain. The uniqueness does not lie in structure but in function.

Without doubt there is a very close relation between structure and function but it is not a one-to-one relation; one function can be subserved by several structures and one structure can subserve several functions. With regard to the brain, the functional differences that can be demonstrated electrophysiologically and behaviorally between the human brain and the brain of apes lie almost totally in the cerebral cortex. This may be because the functional examination of deeper parts of the brain is not appropriate to routine investigation in the human and so less direct evidence is available. Nevertheless, the few observations made on deep brain regions in the human only show differences from monkeys when the patients are mentally abnormal. Most neurologists would probably agree that they do not expect future research to reveal significant differences in the subcortical regions. This in itself supports my theory. I have claimed that the essential difference between humans and the lower animals is that humans are capable of activating their pleasure areas by means of higher regions, and in terms of basic biology the one place where the human brain differs from that of subhumans is precisely in the higher centers.

In all animals possessing a cerebral cortex there are "primary" areas. For example, one such area is concerned with the visual sense, another with hearing, another with skin senses. Another most important area is concerned with voluntary movement. In some species practically the whole of the cerebral cortex is made up of primary areas. In the rat 90 percent of the cerebral cortex consists of this type of neural tissue; in the rabbit 75 percent; in the monkey 35 percent; in humans 15 percent. Thus the human cerebral cortex has 85 percent of its area available for doing things other than the simple things done by 90 percent of the rat cortex.

This 85 percent of nonprimary cortex is divided, functionally, into secondary and tertiary areas. The secondary areas are concerned with association within a sense modality. For example, the visual association area, lying close against the primary visual area, is involved in the process of learning what objects look like, not merely in order to recognize shape and form but also to know what the object means in the life of the animal. In a dog, for example, the primary visual area simply sees a cat but when this information is transferred to the secondary visual area it recognizes an object that will run away and give the fun of the chase, provided the dog has already experienced that situation.

There is a secondary area for each of the senses and for the system of voluntary muscles, but even when all the primary and secondary areas are accounted for, the major part of the human cerebral cortex remains. It also remains mysterious, especially the vast area of the frontal lobes, for very little detailed knowledge is available about the function of the tertiary areas. Nevertheless, excellent and exacting work by neurophysiologists can be used for a few general statements. The tertiary areas are especially concerned with complex, higher neural functions such as memory, learning, speech, language, conceptualization, and the association of the information supplied by several senses simultaneously. They enable us to "picture" an orange when we smell one and to resurrect whatever emotional attachment for oranges that our past experience has given us. They enable us to look at a printed word instead of an orange and yet carry out the same kind of cognitive processing, hearing its sound and knowing its meaning and being aware of what we can do with it. And here lies the crux of the situation.

The use of the primary and secondary areas alone produces the kind of creature that is an ape or a monkey. The tertiary areas contribute the tremendously valuable power of abstraction, which has enabled humans to produce a system of symbols and so pass on the accumulated wisdom of generations, and to synthesize this information into the valuative scheme of personal philosophy that is often called personality. It is these tertiary areas, which under the microscope look much like any other part of the cortex, that are responsible for the enormous difference between the pattern of life of humans and that of the lower animals. This is because they are free from having to perform elementary tasks (such as simple sensing and simple moving) and are in neural contact with vast areas of the nervous system. My contention is that the survival value of the tertiary areas in the human lies in their ability to activate the limbic pleasure areas. This is what I mean, anatomically and functionally, when I describe humans as using their higher regions to obtain pleasure. I do not suggest that the cerebral cortex plays no part in obtaining pleasure in lower animals; I assert that in the lower animals and in the subhuman behavior of people the only role of the cerebral cortex in obtaining pleasure is that the primary and secondary areas guide the rest of the brain in handling the body in such a way that maximum efficiency is exerted in the acquisition of sensory pleasure.

My theory would have to be totally abandoned if it could be shown that there were no connections between the sensory pathways and the limbic pleasure areas. One cannot claim that the basic neurology of behavior involves sensory impulses from the peripheral receptors activating the pleasure areas unless the vast amount of anatomical study of the brain has produced evidence of neural links that would enable this to happen. One method is to cut thin sections of the brain, stain them with various dyes and examine them under the microscope, and trace the interconnections of the nerve cells laboriously by eye, which is extremely arduous and requires meticulous attention to detail and tremendous patience. I have done a little of this research and so am aware of the great debt which scientists like myself owe to those workers who acquired this fundamental information upon which we may now draw. This method has given way to a nonvisual technique, which though quicker and more accurate still requires superlative technique and dedication. Recording electrodes are placed in the region in which the investigator is interested and other more distant parts of the nervous system are electrically stimulated, and peripheral receptors are activated. If there is a functional neural connection between the two places, then impulses will pass from the region stimulated along unknown pathways to arrive at the recording electrodes. There they will cause electrical phenomena which can be picked up, amplified, and displayed on an oscilloscope or drawn on moving paper. With this semifunctional approach to neuroanatomy it is possible to carry out many determinations in a short time, especially when dealing with the senses. It is possible, for example, to place recording electrodes in a given region of the brain and then to shine a light into the eye, followed by a sound to the ear and then a touch to some part of the skin. By "watching" what comes out at the recording electrodes one can determine whether information from all or some or none of these peripheral receptors reaches the region of the brain where the recording electrodes are lodged.

In looking into the results obtained by these and other techniques, the technical terms for the various brain regions have to be used. But the term "amygdaloid nucleus" is no more frightening than "coconut"; it is simply less familiar and merely refers to an object in the universe.

The main regions that make up the stippled parts in the diagrams are the amygdaloid nucleus (usually called the amygdala), the septum pellucidum (usually called the septum), and the hypothalamus.* There are other parts but to deal with them separately would not contribute to a better understanding.

The amygdala is a closely-packed mass of nerve cells situated deep within the temporal lobe of the brain. Impulses from all the sensory channels can arrive in this part of the pleasure areas via connections directly from the nose for olfactory sensation and indirectly from the other senses via the reticular formation and also from the thalamus. Electrical studies have shown that nerve impulses in several sense modalities can all arrive at a single cell in the amygdala. In other words, at least some cells in the amygdala are not *specifically* sensitive to peripheral stimulation in any particular sensory mode, which fits with my claim that generalized sensation can produce

*See pp. 34 and 78.

pleasure. The cells of the amygdala are, however, differentially sensitive in terms of intensity; the lowest effective stimulus strength is found with touch, then comes the olfactory sense followed by auditory, and last of all visual modes. Thus there is no doubt that any peripheral receptor is able to transfer information to that part of the pleasure areas called the amygdala, which then deals with the information in a clearly nonrandom way that is not yet understood.

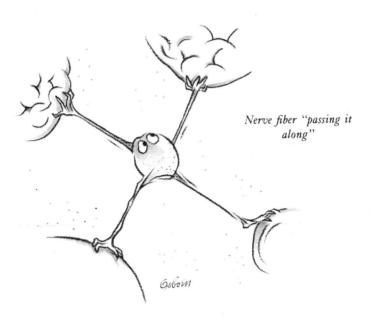

Nerve fiber "passing it along"

Similar results have been obtained by studying the septum, which is the most forward pleasure area and is indeed the front of the brain in the lowest vertebrates. Nerve impulses from all sensory modalities reach the septum from the reticular formation and from the thalamus. The septum also has two-way connections with the amygdala and the hypothalamus and so can receive pleasure-giving impulses from either of these sources, too.

The hypothalamus is a most vital area at the base of the brain that subserves many functions in addition to containing pleasure areas. It receives nerve impulses from the amygdala as well as from the septum and reticular formation, which can and does route information to the hypothalamus from any sensory input. For many years it was thought that the hypothalamus received sensory information only from the internal organs involved in fear, rage, and similar primitive reactions. But it is known now that impulses traveling in the more refined sensory pathways also reach the hypothalamus. Recently, for example, it was shown that stimulation with sound led to the occurrence of electrical activity in the hypothalamus. Also, stimulation of the eye with light and stimulation of the skin receptors causes electrical activation of nearby brain regions with strong hypothalamic connections.

The first conclusion, therefore, is that the pleasure areas undoubtedly receive nerve impulses that originate from any kind of peripheral receptor, the second that the pleasure areas are fully interconnected with each other and therefore can form the basis for the reverberating circuits which serve to extend in time the pleasurable effects of short-term stimuli. Although rather superficially, I have covered that part of the diagram that runs from "peripheral receptors" up to the "limbic areas." Although absolutely necessary, it is still not sufficient to support this theory of pleasure-seeking. The motor system is inextricably involved in behavior so the known connections between the limbic systems and the motor mechanisms and then to behavior must be examined too.

The limbic pleasure areas, like most other parts of the brain, send impulses to many places. There are the impulses that eventually reach muscles and cause movements. Both the amygdaloid and the septum have been shown to have direct connections with the hypothalamus and it has long been known that the hypothalamus is intimately concerned with mediating the muscular contractions associated with emotional behavior. I have mentioned its role with regard to rage, eating, and sex as external forms of behavior, and to heart rate, respiration rate, and blood vessel diameter with regard to internal behavior. In both forms of behavior, therefore, all three pleasure areas are able to exert a direct effect upon the musculature, by sending instructions to the hypothalamus. In the light of its own "knowledge," these will modify the information and relay it to the nerve cells in the brain and spinal cord that cause contraction of both voluntary and involuntary muscle for either external or internal behavior.

Part of the pleasure-seeking theory claims that it is possible for the pleasure areas to be activated by the higher regions of the brain shown in the top part of Diagram 2. What is the evidence supporting the actual existence of neural connections, represented in the diagram by the arrows running to and from the higher regions to the limbic areas? The methods described earlier were applied to this question. It was found that the amygdala has two-way connections with the hippocampus, which in the diagram is also called the archicortex because it is very old, and also with the temporal and frontal lobes. The frontal lobes are especially interesting since it is in their great size that modern man differs so much from early man, let alone from lower animals. It is the frontal lobes, too, that are responsible for man's ability to direct sustained attention to demanding mental tasks.

Connections have also been shown to exist in both directions between the septum and the archicortex and between the septum and the frontal cortex. Similarly, the hypothalamus has been proved to have two-way connections with several parts of the cerebral cortex, including the frontal lobe.

Experiments with recording electrodes have proved that the use of nerve cells in the higher cortical regions, during the process of learning, for example, induces electrical activation in the places now known to be pleasure areas. Conversely, when electrical activity appears in the limbic regions it is soon transmitted to the higher cortical areas. Thus there are very desirable "feedback loops" not only between the various limbic pleasure areas themselves but also between these and the higher regions. One of the great advances in modern neurology is the realization that normal behavior requires the proper interchange of information between several parts of the brain; there is no specific locus for this or that piece of behavior, only preferred pathways between certain brain regions. So past research into the anatomy and physiology of the brain has supplied abundant evidence to support the theory of pleasure-seeking. A suitable neural "wiring diagram" has been thoroughly established.

The responses of the whole animals have also been studied with respect to brain function. This comes a little nearer to what goes on in ordinary life. One of the most interesting and fertile reports on the role of the limbic system in behavior was given in 1939 by two eminent American research workers, Kluver and Bucy, when they described the syndrome that is now known by their names. In their experiments the temporal lobes of a monkey's brain were removed on both sides. This operation, of course, takes away some of the temporal cortex and also the two important pleasure areas, amygdala and archicortex. Subsequent work has shown that the behavioral changes described by Kluver and Bucy are almost entirely due to the absence of these limbic regions, which is not to say that this would be the case in the human, since our temporal lobes are more highly developed.

In the Kluver-Bucy syndrome several facets of behavior are changed and each of them can be interpreted in terms of pleasure-seeking. A most striking change has been called psychic blindness—the animals exhibit a complete loss of the appreciation of the significance of objects. They will pick up and manipulate objects which before the operation gave them pleasure, but they will also include objects that used to cause them grave displeasure. For example, these monkeys, like most others when normal, showed considerable fear of snakes, both live ones and models, whereas after the operation they would handle snakes with complete indifference.

Monkeys put most things in their mouths, but usually each object is subjected to this edibility test only once. After the operation the monkeys showed an excessive tendency to place objects in their mouths and went on doing so even when it was quite clear that the objects could not be eaten. Monkeys investigate every new object in the environment and they normally determine the value of each object very quickly and stop examining it if it is not rewarding. But when the archicortical and amygdalar pleasure areas are removed the animals reexamine all objects within reach incessantly, picking them up, licking and feeling them, throwing them down, only to pick them up again very shortly and repeat the whole procedure on the same object hundreds of times a day. This suggests that as usual the animal is searching for sensory pleasure in the environment but not finding it, because major pleasure areas have been taken away and so cannot be activated even by usually rewarding objects. This fits well with the extension of the pleasure-seeking theory, which claims that meaning will not be attached to any stimulus that does not activate the pleasure areas.

The Kluver-Bucy monkeys also showed greatly exaggerated sexual behavior of many kinds. They repeatedly

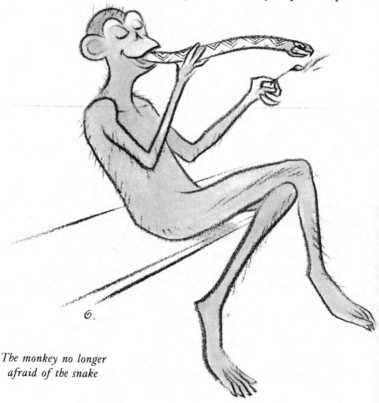

*The monkey no longer
afraid of the snake*

tried to mate with unreceptive females and with many other inappropriate objects such as monkeys of the same sex or anything reasonably large, soft, and furry. The neurology of sexuality is highly complicated and these observations simply illustrate one aspect of it, namely that damage to the pleasure areas causes severe dislocation of a form of behavior which in monkeys is usually precise and efficient.

The type of monkey used in these experiments is normally very aggressive, and aggression may be looked upon as a particular way of activating the pleasure areas. The Kluver-Bucy monkeys were as easy to handle as a dog, whereas before the operation they had to be netted.

These interpretations of the Kluver-Bucy syndrome support my theory, but the position is not as simple as they might imply, mainly because of the loss of cortex overlying the pleasure areas. For example, when the same operation was carried out on a human to try to cure epilepsy, another symptom occurred which was probably present in the monkeys but not so easily detected. This was loss of recent memory. Patients without temporal lobes are unable to remember anything for more than a few seconds or possibly a couple of minutes. They have not lost their memories but have lost the capacity to memorize. If someone he has never seen before comes into the room for half an hour or so, goes out for five minutes and then returns, the patient thinks that two different people are involved. Obviously this will affect many aspects of behavior and it is not possible at this stage to determine if the symptoms described in monkeys are in part attributable to an inability to remember things. Even this explanation is in accord with the pleasure-seeking theory because another extension of it is that no incoming stimulus will be memorized unless it effectively activates the pleasure areas.

Another complication is that in some cases only the temporal neocortex is removed, leaving the subcortical limbic structures intact, and yet this operation produces monkeys resembling those with the Kluver-Bucy syndrome. This is not too surprising because of the extensive two-way connections between the temporal cortex and the limbic regions. Later research workers, in fact, have stated that there are two types of Kluver-Bucy syndrome. One is a mild, temporary, and very variable form caused by removal of the cortex alone. The other follows extirpation of the limbic structures in addition to the cortex and causes behavioral changes that are permanent and much more apparent. It is reasonable to suppose that nearby areas substitute for the functions that have been removed, for this kind of substitution is a well-known property of cortical regions. But there is no redundancy in the pleasure areas, so that when they are removed so are their function and the effect is permanent.

Again, the hypersexuality of the Kluver-Bucy syndrome is not entirely a neurological phenomenon since it can be abolished by the removal of sex hormones and returns if sex hormones are injected. But pleasure-seeking can be shown experimentally to be at least in part dependent upon a proper balance of sex hormones, which in the Kluver-Bucy monkeys probably act upon the remaining pleasure area in the hypothalamus. Sex hormones from the bloodstream are in fact stored in much higher concentration by the limbic areas than by the surrounding neural tissue.

Some kind of intuition may have been at work in the researchers who conducted these experiments in 1957 for they suggest themselves that the hypersexuality resulted from a disorder of perceptual mechanisms. Some workers concerned with other aspects of the Kluver-Bucy syndrome have, independently, attributed the defects in

behavior to dysfunction of perceptual processes, especially with regard to whatever mechanisms are concerned in the selection of behavior appropriate to a given
set of sensory stimuli.

The observations on aggression, too, are puzzling because while the tameness produced by temporal lobec-
tomy in monkeys has been duplicated by destruction of
the amygdala in some species, the reverse occurs in other
species. The normally very savage wild rat becomes
quite equable when the amygdala is removed on both
sides, whereas the same operation in the domestic cat
produces one of the most savage animals it could be
possible to meet. The issue is complicated, and all that
can be justifiably said is that the pleasure areas are involved in aggression in a way that future research may
reveal.

The temporally lobectomized human has been described as showing "an interest that is limited to immediate needs and there is poverty of expression and loss of
all emotion and aggressive behavior." This apathetic approach to life is what one would expect if the individual's
higher centers are unable to activate his pleasure areas
sufficiently because so much of them has been removed.
Fortunately for the individuals who might have been
concerned but unfortunately for the present exposition
there are no cases in man in which the amygdala and
archicortex have been removed and the overlying neocortex left intact. However, the subcortical pleasure
areas have sometimes been found to be affected by disease.

Another means of studying the role of a brain region
experimentally is to place electrodes in it and apply a
reasonably strong current. With this technique some interesting observations of the amygdalar pleasure areas
have been made. Application of current produces a series

of involuntary movements that are not just isolated muscular contractions but are part of an integrated behavioral mechanism. Immediately when the current comes on the animal widens its eyes, dilates its pupils, raises the ears and head, and presents a posture of expectancy and alertness. This process of "collecting itself" is quickly followed by orienting movements of the head, eyes, neck, trunk, and forelimbs. There could hardly be clearer evidence that this subcortical pleasure area is intimately involved with exploratory behavior.

This description is oversimplified because the amygdala is not homogeneous but consists of several distinct regions. Various research workers have shown that different but related behavioral reactions occur when different parts of the amygdala are stimulated. For example, it is possible to produce only a fear response or it is possible to cause an aggressive response; by injecting certain drugs into particular parts of the amygdala it is possible to induce the animal either to eat or to drink. Thus, the amygdalar pleasure areas, like the others, must not be looked upon as a simple arrangement of similar nerve cells all subserving the same function with regard to pleasure.

Another implication of my theory of behavior is that environmental stimuli must activate the pleasure areas so that the learning processes can occur. At first glance this claim seems remarkable since most laymen, and until recently many physiologists, had the impression that learning was pre-eminently a function of the higher brain regions. However, since 1958 many workers have reported findings relating either to stimulation or destruction of the amygdala with respect to learning ability in animals. As yet there is no full agreement about the precise role of the amygdala in learning, except that it is a matter of great complexity. A number of experiments

conducted in the 1960s and since confirmed have shown
unequivocally that the amygdala is vitally concerned in
recognizing the presence or absence of rewarding
stimuli and actually in discriminating between the rewarding value of various stimuli.

A simple example occurs in monkeys. When they are
trained to press a lever for food reward, a normal monkey presses much more quickly for a large amount of
food than for a small amount. But this discrimination is
completely lost in monkeys in which the amygdala has
been destroyed. One worker, Dr. J. R. Smythies, has
written that: "The amygdala may not only be necessary
for determining the reinforcing value of single stimuli,
but also for the most subtle function of inter-relating
different reinforcing stimuli, that is, it enables an animal
to respond to one set of events in relation to another."
In terms of the present theory I would say that in the
normal animal the amygdala is able to control behavior
in relation to the pleasure-giving qualities of the incoming stimuli.

Although I have spoken of the "amygdalar pleasure
area," there is in fact a displeasure area in this region too.
Stimulation can give rise to aggressive behavior ranging
from petulance through mild annoyance to the most intense rage. Sometimes the effect can be very similar to
what is sometimes seen in people. For example, when a
particular part of the amygdala in a cat is stimulated for
ten seconds, the animal behaves perfectly normally except that it refuses to eat for several days. This can occur
in people, too.

Until very recently electrical stimulation of the amygdala has been restricted to animals, but now neurosur-
geons use it on humans from time to time in order to
understand their epileptic condition better. When this
was done, the patients reported a series of sensations

such as pins and needles, heat or chill, or just "a funny feeling." There was no precise analysis of sensation and this is understandable because the stimulation used was far from normal. Nevertheless, these reports show that this subcortical pleasure area does have an extensive inflow of sensory information. Problems in the amygdala can lead to unfortunate behavior in the human, which can be made normal by destruction of the affected amygdalar nerve cells.

There is much more evidence like this, for example the experimental evidence for the mechanisms of satiation. One would expect that by interfering with the pleasure-seeking mechanisms one might be able to remove the process of satiation from an animal, and in fact this can be done easily. Stimulation of certain pleasure areas was shown to cause the animal to continue to direct visual attention at any moving object in the environment, in the response called forced attention or sensory fixation reaction. Under these conditions the normal and rapid process of satiation with visual sensory input does not occur and as early as 1960 the researcher concluded that one of the functions of the archicortex was to prevent an individual from diverting his attention.

Utilizing another sensory mode it has been shown that by destroying certain parts of the hypothalamus an animal loses the capacity to become satiated by gustatory sensations and continues to eat to the point of extreme obesity. Conversely, the appearance of satiation can be simulated by electrical stimulation of the region of the amygdala called the basolateral division. Under these conditions the animal stops whatever it was doing before the stimulus was applied and begins to examine the environment. Such a condition is easily distinguishable from true satiation because an animal which has had enough to eat, for example, does not immediately begin this highly alert exploration but tends to look around rather indifferently. When the current to the amygdala is switched off, the animal goes back to whatever it was doing before. Thus by interfering with the normal electrical events in the pleasure areas, sensation-seeking can be brought to a premature end and the animal made to seek new pleasures from another sensory mode.

When recording electrodes are placed in the amygdala, a characteristic rhythm of electrical activity occurs in the form of periodic waves at forty to forty-five cycles per second. This rhythm declines as satiation of hunger is reached and appears suddenly when a meaningful stimulus occurs. The appearance of this rhythm may be partly responsible for the "feeling" of pleasure that comes in anticipation of a sensory input. It is then maintained by the sensory messages until the mechanisms of satiation come into operation, when it ceases. It is reasonable, too, to suppose that the cessation of this rhythmic activity in the amygdala infringes the ancestral command and thereby excites activity of the motor system so that searching for new stimuli begins.

I have concentrated on the amygdala because it is the region on which much work has been done and it is becoming important in human psychosurgery. But there is also plenty of evidence relating the hypothalamic pleasure areas to sensation-seeking. It has been known for many years that when certain parts of the hypothalamus are destroyed by electrolysis, the animals lose all desire to eat. More recently, work at the University of Pennsylvania has shown that this same destruction causes the animals to show no interest in visual, olfactory, or tactile stimuli. It is interesting that under these conditions of severely reduced sensation-seeking, the animals lost their desire to attack and kill other animals.

Chapter 6

Mind Is Matter

PSYCHOLOGY, PSYCHIATRY
AND PLEASURE

What is the concept of "mind"? The orientation of this present theory of behavior and of the whole book rejects the dualism of mind and matter and considers all behavior and all thinking to be entirely materialistic. I believe that the concept of mind, as distinct from matter, may well have arisen as a function of personal pride, although this does not necessarily make it untrue. Even the most unsophisticated individuals are aware that their bodies are composed of matter, and the more sophisticated they are the more they are aware that the matter in their own bodies is essentially the same as the matter in all other animals. Several experts have pointed out that an astonishing feature of the vast range of living organisms (animals and plants) is the very small number of available kinds of matter of which they are constructed—only about sixteen out of ninety-two elements and only about twenty amino acids out of an almost infinite possible number. So we have no excuse for considering man to be essentially different from any other living creature in terms of what he is made of. We cannot hold the comforting thought that "I" am materially different from other people or from pumpkins.

A way in which we can nurture the concept of having some special, personal evaluation of ourselves and our species is to postulate some kind of non-material entity —spirit, soul, mind. Whether or not this pride, this preoccupation with the value of the self, is an important or useful part of a person's equipment is beside the present point. The theory of behavior expounded here enables everyone, if they wish, to retain as much personal pride as they need to keep them going, and yet at the same time reject completely any non-material basis for these qualities.

Let me make a tremendously oversimplified statement: the present theory implies that we attribute phenomena to matter when the pleasure areas are activated by impulses reaching them along the sensory channels, and we apply the term "mind" to phenomena that are produced when the pleasure areas are activated by impulses reaching them from the higher centers.

The age-old and tedious arguments about dualism are manifold and they involve many aspects of living, but a central feature has been the puzzlement of thoughtful people as to the relationship between two kinds of experience. Many feel that there must be a fundamentally different mechanism at work when we report on something in the environment to ourselves or to others; for example, when we say "I see an apple," we may feel that is different from when we say "I feel sad," because that represents something internal. The first statement seems straightforward because we can all look at, touch, and, as final proof, eat the apple. The fruit has an external reality and so we accept that it has to do with material things like light hitting the retina and nerve impulses traveling around the brain. Agreement breaks down and confusion begins when no object is referred to. The belief has grown up that there is an essential difference between brain processes that are induced by material events in the environment and brain processes that are concerned with what would normally be called internal events, such as thoughts and feelings, concepts and ideas. The point that has been missed, surely, is that when an individual reports on the apple he is in fact reporting upon what is going on in his brain, the various kinds of electrical activity that are occurring. The fact that he is not really reporting on the apple is readily apparent in the various kinds of sensory illusions that seem merely amusing but which in fact throw considerable light on brain function. The individual is conscious of and reports events in the brain and these may or may not be perfectly related to what is actually in the environment.

In a similar way, when the individual reports or reflects upon what are called mental phenomena, he is dealing with electrical events in the brain. What he is conscious of is activation of his pleasure areas and whatever other brain events that leads to. During our development we do not start to pay attention to internal brain events, thoughts and feelings, until we have already spent quite a time entirely preoccupied with external events, and so an unnecessary line of demarcation is drawn between the route of input of nerve impulses to the pleasure areas, ascribing downward impulses to spirit or soul or mind, and upcoming impulses to matter.

Certain patterns of electrical activity in the brain have been given names like sadness, excitement, love, pleasure, or beauty, because we do not yet have a suitable language to describe the physical phenomena themselves. This is a matter only of time and more research. We have seen how simple it is to determine whether that aspect of mind called pleasure is being experienced, we can study the factors that control it and will eventually be able to define in precise neuroelectrical terms what is going on in the brain during it. Perhaps those who do not need the protection of a belief in immaterial mind but simply wish to know the truth will be satisfied when all other "internal" brain phenomena can be similarly described. Much progress has already been made with such primitive mental states as rage, timidity, hunger, thirst, and sexual responsiveness. These states of mind are easily produced in the lower animals; now that safe, harmless experiments can also be carried out with humans it is likely that the more refined, higher "emotions" will soon be related to specific brain mechanisms.

Findings in patients with surgically split brains have already shown that the "mind" is easily studied by the methods of material science. In these patients a set of nerve fibers, which are collectively called the corpus callosum, were severed for medical reasons. These fibers run from one side of the brain to the other and are distributed all the way from front to back. They keep the two hemispheres of the brain in touch with each other. Crudely, they enable the left hand to know what the right hand is doing. When the brain is split it is possible to send sensory information to only one side. If, for example, an object is picked up by the right hand the sensory impulses generated in the peripheral receptors only reach the left hemisphere.

Many fascinating observations have been made with

the ready and valuable cooperation of these patients. For example, if a patient is blindfolded and allowed to handle a common object, such as a spoon, with only one hand, when it is placed in the other hand he cannot say whether it is the same object; only one side of his brain has felt and recorded the spoon. When the patient is normally right-handed and an object is placed in his left hand, he cannot name it although he knows what it is and can use it properly. The problems are not merely sensory; it is here that the observations on patients with surgically split brains are relevant. A female patient would blush when shown a "dirty picture" through one eye but not when she saw it with the other. One man kept pushing his wife away with one hand while the other hand was trying to enlist her aid in some activity. As that great researcher, Professor J. Z. Young, has written: "We are forced by these cases to conclude that many of the actions of people that we classify as characteristics of the mind can be divided by the surgeon's knife." In his book, *An Introduction to the Study of Man*, Professor Young goes on to say: "It may be that this does no more than emphasize that "mind" depends on brain, but even fully to establish this is an advance. Probably those without preconceived ideas would agree that these cases emphasize that our language for discussing cerebral activities needs revision."

Given that the term "mind" may be applied to neural interactions between the pleasure areas and the higher regions of the brain, we may examine an old psychological controversy in a new way. Broadly speaking, psychologists are of two kinds, even though there are many "schools" of psychology. There are those who believe in psychoanalytic doctrines and those who do not. Psychoanalytic concepts were first systematized and enormously developed by Sigmund Freud, who frequently

mentioned that he believed all his principles had a neurophysiological basis that would eventually be demonstrated by brain workers. Unfortunately, in some respects, the great majority of his disciples have kept
strictly away from the brain and from material explanations of mental phenomena. Other psychologists have
equally firmly insisted that all our mental life can be
expressed in terms of biological laws, though some are
far removed from the laboratory. With so much sincere
good work being done by both groups, it is likely that
they are both nearly right. The pleasure-seeking theory
shows how the two viewpoints can be reconciled and
how a neurophysiological basis can be proposed for what
has rather spitefully been referred to as the id-ego-
superego mythology.

Freud and his followers believe that for some time
from birth onward our minds are largely made up of
unconsciously acquired knowledge and valuations,
brought about by direct feed-in from the environment
interacting with the genetic receptivity of the individual. The knowledge and values are stored without criticism in the id; this part of the mind, then, is childish,
selfish, sensual, and unconscious. Gradually we acquire
an awareness of our self, recognizing our existence as
independent of other people and of objects, and this
mental image of our total makeup is the ego. With the
passage of time we begin to experience the concepts of
higher, moral, selfless living and also the symbolic abstractions of human life. Such of these concepts as we
agree with are stored, for reference purposes, in the
third compartment of the mind, the superego. Life as an
adult (or even older child) is executed by the ego, which
stands like a punchball, as it were, between the animalis-
tic, antisocial, sensual "advice" of the id and the godlike,
lady-be-good homilies of the superego. For those of us

who are mentally normal, our lives represent at each instant the ego's operational compromise between the conflicting influences of id and superego, and from time to time one or other triumphs—god or the devil—with no great harm done, except perhaps to our reputations. Should either the id or the ego take over complete command or even exert a too powerful influence for too long, we exhibit one or other form of mental abnormality. Such then, briefly and oversimplified, is psychoanalytic theory.

In Diagram 2 we can see that nerve impulses journey to and from the archicortex. This has the complex neuronal organization characteristic of the newer cerebral cortex but it is very old and even occurs in reptiles. In mammals it has become hidden under the great mass of younger cortex and is therefore classified as "archicortex." We now know that the archicortex is a pleasure area and it is not unreasonable to believe that this was the first "overseer" to take charge of and correlate the sensation-seeking behavior of animals so that sources of pleasure in the environment were more efficiently found and used. There is also clear experimental proof that the archicortex is intimately concerned not only in the process of memorizing but also with *causing memories to stay beyond recall,* that is what physiologists call "active forgetting" and psychologists call "repression." Therefore the archicortex seems an ideal candidate for the position of keeper of the id.

The archicortex also plays a vital role in all learning processes. We can see how the young baby, predominantly concerned with sensory pleasures, gradually constructs his unconscious mind from the positive and negative rewards that come his way. We can see, too, how "deeply" these early experiences will be lodged in his brain, giving physiological substance to the Freudian doctrine that early childhood experiences may come to dominate adult activity. (Many non-Freudian workers have already demonstrated this truth in a variety of down-to-earth ways.) In the newborn child, too, the higher cerebral cortex is very poorly developed, with practically no interconnections between neurones, whereas the archicortex and other lower structures are fully functional.

The higher regions of the cortex gradually increase in anatomical complexity and become properly functional and the child slowly becomes capable of understanding nonsensory components in the environment such as whether his mother is annoyed. This may be expressed as the slow development of the ego or as the slow building up of informational pathways between the lower pleasure areas and the higher cortex, and between the archicortex and the higher cortex. In phylogeny, after the archicortex comes the hippocampal gyrus, which lies on the outside of the brain and has massive connections to the archicortex and to lower pleasure areas. This region, the palaeocortex, seems well-suited to house the early ego mechanisms. Capable of acting in its own right, not dependent upon direct sensory input, it could well restrain and modify the low-level behavior generated by the archicortical id. Overall behavior would still be recognizably subhuman. Animals at this stage of evolution would be expected to exhibit such traits as parental care, a degree of social interaction, and possibly a certain amount of responsibility. This is the type of behavior that is rather typical of chimpanzees and domestic dogs.

But for morality, ethics, concepts of honesty, and selection of nonsensory pleasure, even more complex neural organization is required. These functions of the superego are most logically located in the intricate neuronal mechanisms of the latest, highest regions—the neocortex. The full anatomical development of the neo-cortex is not completed until long after birth, and this explains the psychoanalytic precept that signs of the su-perego's influence are long delayed. Also, if the neocorti-cal superego is to function properly it must have ade-quate connections with the lower pleasure areas and with the archicortex and hippocampal gyrus; and for this there must be repetitive experiences of a nonsensory kind in order that preferred pathways can be established. This is why it is important to have parents who are *human* rather than predominantly sensory. This is why there is little evidence of superego influences in many adults.

The three "mental compartments" have been dealt with separately but in normal development they mature together, though at different rates, through later child-hood and into adult life. Neither the theory of pleasure-seeking nor psychoanalytic doctrine draws sharp demar-cation lines between the id, ego, and superego. They are inextricably interwoven, which is why most of us are such a mixture of human and subhuman, even though one or other may typify us. I intend no exact or limited location of these functions in the brain; no brain region has any significance in isolation, and the archicortex, hippocampal gyrus, and higher neocortex must interact with other parts in order to exert their functions.

However, as a neurophysiologist, with no particular leaning toward any system of psychology, it seems to me that many of the Freudian "unacceptables" lose their tendentiousness and take on a matter-of-factness when interpreted in the light of this scheme of brain function. One of the biggest furors, for example, occurred when Freud insisted that every child falls in passionate (i.e., sexual) love with its mother. In the beginning "nice" people found the idea revolting and later on down-to-earth people found it far-fetched. But the Oedipus Complex need be neither. Once we realize that the early Freudian idea that sex is the goal of all endeavor was based upon an understandable confusion between peripheral and central nervous events, the idea becomes clearer. Usually, the sensory pleasures that first activate the newborn baby's limbic areas and become laid down as unconscious traces in the archicortex are derived from the mother. The child, to the satisfaction and approval of all, associates his mother with bringing about obedience to the ancestral command to activate his pleasure areas. So he smiles when he sees her, runs to her when things are amiss, and generally behaves with the close affection that anyone gives to a source of sensory pleasure. Much later in life, when the individual becomes aware of the great sensory input provided by sexual behavior, there must inevitably be an unconscious association of the mother with sexuality, just as she may be associated with music or painting. She will be associated with sex much more than with other sensory pleasures because her early offerings were heavily somatic—nipple, breast, milk, warmth, bodily contact. But there is no reason to believe that all children harbor an unconscious *wish* to do anything about it. The inner "push" is toward activating the pleasure areas and if sufficient ways of doing this are available the Oedipus Complex does not arise, except possibly in such diluted forms as buying flowers on Mother's Day (assuming it is done sincerely). If some other factors enter the individual's life, which in some way restrict his power to obey the command, he may well wish to turn to his mother for sensual satisfaction. Such a pattern in the female, especially when the mother is not around, could lead to lesbianism. But this does not prove that the rest of us are actively repressing a wish to become sexually involved in this way.

The Oedipus Complex is one of the many facets of Freudian psychology that arose from a misunderstanding of the role of sex in brain development, and most of the others can be explained in a similarly rational way, so that the concepts apply to normal people and are not entirely restricted to the mentally ill that Freud and Freudians take as examples of how the mind works. The suggestion that all children exhibit sexuality from an early age becomes more acceptable perhaps when we can see that Freud was really saying that all children are sensory creatures as soon as they can be. Whether the child is playing with his penis or the adult is surveying a sunset, they are both activating their pleasure areas, but the baby is not being erotic and the adult is not sublimating. It may well be that under the restrictions of Western society an individual does not experience as much sexual behavior as he would wish, and he may then seek to activate his pleasure areas with less effective sensory sources such as sunsets, painting, or even gluttony. It is said that modern society is greatly more sexually permissive than in the past, but there does not seem to have been a corresponding decline in artistic involvement.

The scheme put forward here does not claim to explain the whole of the highly complex and integrated set of doctrines that make up psychoanalytic theory. It certainly clarifies some of them and others will be discussed later. It may also serve for others to study the problem and find more acceptable rephrasings of the doctrines so that they may become better absorbed into the general body of accepted ideas and thereby enhanced in value. The difficulties lie largely in the dualistic approach of Freudians, pointed out by Professor Slater and Professor Roth in their *Clinical Psychiatry:* ". . . this dualism remains unresolved today, and is even now the greatest source of weakness in Freudian theory." If my theory helps to engender belief that mind is matter, then the way is open to strengthen the weakness.

Eventually Freud came much closer to the truth and substituted the concept of "libido" for that of uncompromising sexuality. He saw behavior as driven by a primitive, id-directed search for pleasure and avoidance of pain, with sex high and powerful but not apical in the scale of pleasure. But even this approximation to common sense was insufficient for Alfred Adler, who rejected libido as a fundamental drive, cast out repression as a motive force, and drew less distinction between conscious and unconscious minds. For Adler, the whole point of being alive is to acquire power and social adaptation. The inherent difficulties in bringing about these two aims lead to a "feeling" of inferiority, so the individual "behaves" as though he is superior. In this form Adler's school of Individual Psychology did not last long, but reverberations of it still exist, and understandably so, for such mechanisms are undoubtedly at work in some people at some times. They are seen clearly in children reacting against the frustrations of parental discipline, when the older child postures to a younger one; and they are seen in immature adults who are aware that they *are* inferior in power and status to others whose attributes they envy, giving rise to a way of life in which arrogance masquerades as "spirit."

How do these ideas fit into the present theory? The really fundamental drive in people is for activation of the pleasure areas, though the means of doing this may become remote and heavily disguised. We know that people can activate both the pleasure and displeasure areas by thinking processes in the higher brain regions. The neural apparatus is all there, for a person to compare his power and status with those of others, conclude that he has less than he wishes, and by such thinking send showers of nerve impulses into his displeasure areas. According to the ancient command this must not be allowed to continue, so the individual engages in behavior that stimulates the pleasure areas. Some people, because of the influence previously brought to bear upon them, will react in ways accepted and even admired by society—the ambitious, get-ahead type. Others, with less fortunate backgrounds, will exhibit arrogance, aggression, and snobbery, none of which, pitifully, is of the slightest use in acquiring power or status. This type of individual is an oddity in that he continues to take pleasure in his own estimate of himself, ignoring the very social devaluation he is trying to avoid. He is a perfect example of self-delusion fostered by the ability to direct his thinking in ways that activate the pleasure areas, thereby becoming relatively independent of critical environmental influences that can be repressed, that is forgotten by the archicortex (id). Sometimes the self-delusion cannot stand up to the overwhelming evidence of inferiority and the individual becomes temporarily or permanently neurotic, obtaining power and status (that is, pleasure) from such states as hypochondria, or protestations that the social scheme is intrinsically evil, or some other form of "dropping out." Thus the Adlerian approach has a good neurophysiological basis, but must be looked upon as several steps up from fundamental and, happily, a long, long way from universal.

Another theoretical approach to psychology was that of Carl Jung, who left Freud's flock to set up the school known as Analytic Psychology. Jung did not reject the concept of libido, as long as it was not thought to be primarily sexual, but he greatly modified the characteristics of the subconscious mind. Looking at the ubiquitousness of certain myths, beliefs, and legends, Jung decided that we all have the same subconscious mind, at least to start with, though we add personal touches from our own experience to the allocation of instinctive habits and attitudes with which we are born. The other key feature of Jung's psychology is that we are all predominantly either introverts or extroverts and become neurotic if we go to either extreme or try to switch from one to the other.

These ideas may be readily explained in terms of the present theory. Despite the enormous difference in detailed cultural patterns, newborn babies experience much the same sensory input. A real or artificial nipple, warm milk and warm skin, touchings and play, all serve as sensory pleasures. Occasional deprivations and noxious stimuli are bound to occur. Since, within limits, we all receive much the same sort of "brainwashing" during our very early days, it is not surprising that we construct similar ids or unconscious records, though we need not allow our whole lives to be dominated by them. The principle of intro-extroversion fits beautifully the present classification of people into sensation-seekers and thinkers—without at the moment attributing specific values to either. The reactive, objective extrovert is defined as "directing his libido outward" and the certain result of that process is sensory pleasure. The nonreactive, subjective introvert is said to "direct his libido inward" and this is tautologous—we might say he obtains his pleasures by internal brain events, thinking. As long as we do not overdo the distinction and recognize that we all have some of each category, but that from time to time we lean more one way than the other and that some people lean heavily one way, we can accept the Jungian doctrines as having neural reality. But they do not determine every form of behavior.

One of the first attempts to relate psychology to matter

involved a comparison of body form and personality. The rather crude efforts of Lombroso, with his category of "criminal types," were followed by the more precise measurements of Kretschmer, Sheldon, and several more modern workers. Briefly, it was found that people's bodies have three main features—mesomorphy, with predominance of bone and muscle; endomorphy, with large digestive organs and a marked tendency to roundness; ectomorphy, with thin bones, small muscles, large brain. All individuals possess these three characters in varying proportions and the "average" person has them in equal amounts, but frequently one or other feature is outstanding. When the outstanding types were investigated psychologically a very high correlation was found between particular body features and types of temperament. The mesomorphs are aggressive, active, and demand physical activity when upset; the endomorphs are inordinately fond of comfort, relaxation, and food, and when upset seek the sympathy of others; ectomorphs have fast reaction times, are capable of prolonged mental concentration, socially rather inhibited and seek solitude under stressful conditions.

No psychologist would press these correlations too far and they must be applied with great caution to individuals, but they appear valid for groups—they have statistical significance. Even given that the correlations are valid, no clues have appeared as to whether body form determines personality or the other way round. The theory of pleasure-seeking allows some speculation on this point. If a child is nurtured in an environment that emphasizes the reward value of sensation it might be expected that he would seek pleasures from physical activity so that his muscular system would become well-developed. He would also be likely to attach high value to food intake for gustatory pleasure and this would eventually produce large intestines. Such a physical, sensation-oriented individual might well spend a major part of his adult life involved with sports and athletics. This would lead to the superficially absurd expectation that sportsmen and athletes, taken as a group, are endo-mesomorphs—roundish, tubby, heavy-boned, and muscular. However, the popular myth that sportsmen and "athletic types" are long, lean, springy individuals has been shattered by such studies as those of Professor J. M. Tanner at the Institute of Child Health in London and Dr. Lindsay Carter at the San Diego State College. These and the other workers to whom they refer have measured precisely many hundreds of athletes, amateur and professional, and subgrouped them according to their sport. In every case there is, as would be expected, a high degree of mesomorphy, but the astounding feature is the emphatic endomorphy of these men. Ectomorphy is almost totally absent in every sport except Olympic distance runners.

On the other hand, a child reared under conditions where treasures of the mind are given their due weight might involve himself less in muscular activity and more in obtaining thinking-pleasure, with mere sensation low in value. He would be unlikely to overtax his intestines. As a way of life he would probably choose something that utilized the contents of his cranium. Thus the present theory would imply that seekers after human distinction rather than physical prowess would be predominantly ectomorphic with a dash of mesomorphy and practically no endomorphy. This is exactly what was found when nonsporting university students were measured.

I do not wish to push these speculations too far, but there seems to be evidence that in *some* people the overall influence upon their pleasure-seeking mechanisms has produced temperaments that propelled them into a way of living that develops easily demonstrated body forms. We can carry out our own oblique observations on the bodies and personalities of our acquaintances.

An outstanding feature of these approaches to psychology is that they are all homocentric, as though lower animals do not think and behave. This is partly due to the pervasive arrogance of mankind about its superiority, fostered by the religious bigotry that insisted that man was created as a distinct entity. Whether man was created at all is still a question for open minds, but the evolution of our species from earlier animals can only be doubted by those who believe in magic. Considerations such as these led a number of psychologists, headed by John Watson, to establish the approach known as behaviorism. Their viewpoint was that introspection on thought processes has limited value in understanding the dynamics of behavior, and that behavior itself should be studied. Free from what I call arrogance and bigotry, the behaviorists realized that much could be gained by observing the behavior of lower animals under controlled laboratory conditions as well as that of people in special circumstances. Since then a vast amount of dependable, objective behavioral facts have been collected. It was not the aim of the experimental psychologists to theorize and unfortunately few generalizations have been made from the wealth of information. However, as we shall now see, much of it is well in line with the present theory.

In 1936 an observation was made that has been confirmed many times since. It was based on the fact that many animals quickly learn the direct route through a maze in order to obtain food at the other end. A puzzling finding was that after rats were trained to use a short, simple maze and a longer, more complicated one, when given the choice they decided to reach their food by the complicated route. This was originally described as a desire for variety, but a more modern worker later came close to the truth when he said: ". . . the more complex path provided more to see and more to do." According to the present theory, we should say that the animals prefer to get some added sensory pleasure. Much the same behavior occurs at exhibitions such as Expos, according to Professor A. E. Parr of the American Museum of Natural History, New York. People avoid the "restful intervals" containing nothing much to look at and "empty space actually speeds the visitors on their way."

In 1925 it was shown that if an animal was placed at the entrance to a T-maze and it turned right, it always turned left on a second trial. This "let's see what's in here" response to the unknown arm of the maze has been established as the principle of "spontaneous alternation" and is the forerunner of thousands of experiments on what has come to be called exploratory behavior. Although it is an undisputed fact of science that animals have an exploratory "instinct," no one seems to have asked why this is so or advanced a neurophysiological explanation of it. We can now consider that exploratory behavior is the animal's attempt, under conditions of low sensory input, to obey the ancestral command to activate the pleasure areas by searching for sensory stimulation in the environment. D. E. Berlyne, a most accomplished worker in this field, has shown conclusively and quantitatively the role of novel stimuli and stimulus change in exploration. Rats who have seen a wooden cube for ten minutes on four successive days make significantly fewer approaches to it in a new situation than rats who have not seen it before. Many such experiments have produced similar results. Animals quickly "satiate" with wooden cubes, which can produce only minimal excitation of the pleasure areas; hence exploratory behavior takes the animal from place to place, from one stimulus to another with varying satiation rates. As observers we attach special importance to the stimuli of food and warmth that have quite long satiation periods, yet all stimuli have the same fundamental action; some are merely better activators of the pleasure areas and therefore take longer to get "fed up" with.

Repetition of this type of experiment, with only insignificant changes in the form of stimulus, enabled Berlyne and others to derive the same results from humans. Babies who were only a few months old preferred to look at checkerboard patterns rather than half-and-half black and white figures. Adults retained this primitive preference. Thus the basic neural mechanisms of sensory pleasure appear to be the same in man as in the rat. The subhuman desire for sensory novelty and stimulus change may be at least partly responsible for the rapid successions of fashions, hair styles, pop singers, pop songs; whereas the rather more enduring styles of classical art and music may testify to the existence of human people.

Experimental psychology has also, unwittingly, provided much evidence for the claim that the pleasure areas *must* be kept active by sensory input if the brain and its owner are to function properly. This involves research on "sensory deprivation" which can occur in varying degrees. The first experiments, which led to worldwide interest, took place in Montreal in 1951 under the aegis of Professor D. O. Hebb. College students were given strong motivation (high fees) to lie alone in a room with goggles over their eyes and muffled hands. They could stop whenever they wished, but then the daily fee stopped too. The students thought they could earn easy money, but in fact very few of them stayed more than two or three days despite being liberally supplied with food and drink. Not only did they withdraw quickly from participation but their behavior became quite abnormal. They were restless, made many random, purposeless movements, sang, whistled, and talked to themselves, often unintelligibly. They also had auditory and visual hallucinations and their intellectual functions deteriorated severely.

Similar experiments have proved conclusively that brain dysfunction occurs under these conditions in many species, and the degree and rapidity of onset of the dysfunction is proportional to the extent to which incoming stimuli are blocked. Obviously, it is not possible to produce complete lack of sensory input to the brain because much of it comes from organs such as the heart, lungs, intestines, and mesenteries. But when people are temporarily blinded and deafened, their whole bodies encased in yielding material, their limbs immobilized and then totally submerged in water, the deprivation is profound. Under these conditions they behave like an insane person within a few minutes and the experiment has to be terminated because they are incapable of coherent communication. Luckily, all signs and symptoms disappear extremely rapidly when stimuli are allowed in again and no trace of damage remains. Clearly the derangement is in brain function, involving processes, not structure.

Sensory deprivation occurs to all of us in different degrees and to some of us in very large degree. We are all alone from time to time and without the sound and sight of other people; it is then that many people start to sing or whistle or turn on the radio and they may even talk to themselves. It is perhaps not only reverberation that makes men sing in the bath. We deprive ourselves daily of sensation when we sleep, and several scientists have shown that we *must* dream; in my terms, we must create brain activity that activates the pleasure areas almost as though we were awake. Although many unfortunate people who have been deprived of one of the senses manage to lead accomplished lives that are an example to us all, a large proportion of the mentally retarded are also blind or deaf. This is when the sensory defect dates from birth. Today no scientists or clinician would raise serious doubts about the deteriorating effect of sensory loss upon behavior.

It is surprising that deprivation experiments started so late, for quite apart from Freud and his followers there have been psychologists who drew attention to the importance of sensation and pleasure in behavior. In 1911 Edward Thorndike insisted that all learning—building up of knowledge from stimuli—depended upon arousal of pleasure and claimed that mere repetition and practice were not enough. Clark Hull, around 1943, constructed elaborate mathematical formulas in an attempt to express such concepts rigidly. A number of the introspective theoretical psychologists such as William James also touched upon the role of pleasure. Unfortunately they all limited their concept of pleasure to a distinct, emphatic, conscious "feeling" and this led them to restrict the pleasure motive to only certain aspects of behavior.

There is now evidence that pleasure occurs whenever the limbic pleasure areas are activated and can exist in varying degree from one where it is consciously unnoticeable to another where it is almost the totality of consciousness. The "feeling" is not the prime aim of the behavior but is only incidental to neural activation. This emphasis on feeling, a state of mind, led to an almost total abandonment of such concepts when experimental, behavioral psychology became dominant. Even though the experimentalists were demonstrating what they called stimulus-hunger or stimulus-seeking, the framework of their thinking did not allow them to ask *why* animals seek sensations, still less to ask whether they *had* to seek them. A closer approach was made by Hebb. He tried to postulate brain events that were concomitant with stimulation, showing how some stimuli would be effective in motivation and others not. Hebb resurrected the old principles of Hedonism and attempted a thoroughly neurological explanation of the search for pleasure from sensation based upon reverberating circuits. Unfortunately this was heavily geared to cortical structure because the pleasure areas were not known. But the impetus for deprivation studies came from Hebb's laboratories, where the power of sensation was fully realized.

Another big step toward rationalizing pleasure was made by Benjamin Wolman in 1960, although it seems to have attracted little attention. Wolman formulated the "Antigone Principle" which states, in effect, that the human brain can reach such a degree of sophistication that a man will lay down his life for a friend or even for an idea. No neurophysiology was suggested for this behavior but Wolman was distinguishing between the selfish, sensory pleasures characteristic of subhuman animals and the selfless, altruistic pleasures that I have explained as caused by downward impulses from the higher brain regions.

This brief outline of points of contact between psychology and the pleasure-seeking theory cannot do justice to the myriad workers who have added to our knowledge and opinions of the roots of behavior. It is perhaps sufficient, though, to show that the theory may serve to unify many disparate ideas of thinkers of the past and to provide a material basis for much of their great work.

How may the present theory be applied to mental disease? If all behavior is concerned with the required activation of the pleasure areas, it would be expected on the one hand that defects in the pleasure mechanisms would lead to abnormal behavior, and on the other that abnormal behavior might be explicable in terms of defects in the pleasure mechanisms. I shall now try to show that this is in fact so. But I must emphasize that mental disease is even more complex than normal brain function and no relatively simple explanation such as the present one can sweep away the difficulties in understanding and treatment that have engaged the lifetimes of some of the ablest thinkers. But new ideas can spawn new work which can lead to progress and further new ideas.

A particularly distressing form of mental abnormality is early childhood autism. The most outstanding feature of the illness is the child's aloneness. People, even the parents, and many objects appear to have no meaning to the child, who shows a more or less complete indifference to the kinds of stimuli that give pleasure to normal children. They lack interest in the nipple, the milk, and the mother's arms. They are poorly oriented toward food, caresses, smiles, and similar sources of reward. On the other hand they will spend hours involved with peculiar stimuli, such as rubbing their carriage cover, pressing their eyeballs, pulling out their hair, scratching their skin. These and similar activities may be viewed as the child's attempt to obey the ancestral command by obtaining a sensory input for its pleasure areas in bizarre and harmful ways. If such lengths are necessary for limbic activation, it is not surprising that the normal mild stimuli of childhood produce no positive reaction in the child; when the feel of the nipple and the taste of the milk leave the pleasure areas untouched, the child simply ignores them. Some workers have drawn attention to the similarity in overall appearance of autistic children and men who have been sensorially deprived by a long experience of the desert or an arctic trek. The autistic child exhibits stereotyped repetitive movement and Dr. M. Rutter, an eminent worker with these children, pointed out that "these behaviours are similar to those exhibited in young chimpanzees reared in environments lacking in sensory stimulation." It is tempting to suggest, as I have done elsewhere, that the neural defect in the autistic child is a fault in the way in which sensory stimuli activate the pleasure areas.

I have even postulated a more primary cause, one that may apply, with change of detail, to several mental abnormalities. It is known that chemically the pleasure areas have an accelerator-brake system. A substance called noradrenaline is released from nerve cells in the pleasure areas when impulses arrive there, and by acting upon other nearby neurones this produces pleasure-seeking behavior and probably also the "feeling." Another substance, serotonin, is stored and released by yet other nerve cells in the pleasure areas and this has the effect of inhibiting pleasure-seeking. There is evidence that neurones in the autistic child cannot store serotonin, perhaps because of a derangement of membrane permeability. Perhaps in these children nerve impulses due to peripheral stimulation arrive in the pleasure areas and release normal amounts of noradrenaline but this is insufficient to overcome the blocking action of the high levels of extracellular serotonin, whereas certain abnormal stimuli can release enough noradrenaline to counteract this inhibition. Further research is still needed to prove that this is so.

I have claimed that learning and evaluation of the environment can only occur when stimuli activate the pleasure areas so that the sensory information is transferred to the brain regions involved in such processes as memory and association. In autistic children, the defect I postulate would prevent this transfer to a greater or lesser degree and as a result cause some mental retardation as well. Within the autistic group there certainly are many retarded children. But there are also many who are not, and who demonstrate that the higher mechanisms of memory and association may be intact. In the mentally retarded child, on the other hand, the central feature is intellectual impairment with no abnormalities of sensation. The child likes all the stimuli that normal children like, but does not incorporate them into a unified concept of the world around him. It would seem that in these children peripheral sensory activation of the limbic pleasure areas is intact but that some defect prevents the information from being processed by higher regions.

There are indications, too, that schizophrenics have a dysfunction of the pleasure mechanisms. In the early stages of Huntingdon's chorea—a disease of the motor nerve mechanisms—the patient is frequently misdiagnosed as schizophrenic and only later when the full symptoms develop is he properly classified. Even in the early stages there are degenerative changes in the limbic pleasure areas. Also, in patients who are undeniably schizophrenic, an expert has pointed out that those patients with organic brain lesions show damage in the pleasure areas. Even more relevant are the results of using electrophysiological techniques in examining schizophrenic patients. Implanted electrodes show a clear correlation between psychotic episodes and abnormal electrical activity in the septum, amygdala, and hippocampus, the three main pleasure areas. In 1964 these findings led Dr. R. G. Heath, who investigated the effects of self-stimulation in schizophrenic patients, to state: ". . . schizophrenic patients throughout their life-span are defective in their ability to display appropriate affect, more specifically, these people do not have the ability to perceive and integrate pleasure." Although there was no question of these patients being cured of their schizophrenia, there is also no question that while they were having daily sessions of self-stimulation they showed less intense and less frequent episodes of violence or depression. Thus at least a part of some schizophrenic abnormal behavior may originate on the one hand from abnormal electrical activation of the pleasure areas which is correlated with outbursts of violence, and on the other from a lack of electrical activation of the pleasure areas which corresponds with the depressive intervals.

Depression itself may be the only symptom in some forms of mental disorder in which the patient is effectively withdrawn from the environment, so that he is emotionally unresponsive. Such chronic depression can and does incapacitate a person for life. There is some evidence that a defect in the sensory pleasure mechanisms is involved. Professors Slater and Roth quote the following statement from a patient being treated with electroshock therapy (ECT) after a long depressive illness: "After the second treatment I could taste my food for the first time . . . after I got depressed I could not look at sweets, but just after the second treatment . . . a bit of chocolate tasted so good I just wanted more and I got better every day after that." It seems that the ECT enabled the pleasure areas to be excited by gustatory stimuli once again and this led to more general improvement.

We must always remember that when a new and important factor enters life the effect it produces is very dependent upon the kind of brain it is going into, that is, on the past experience of the individual. Few environmental influences are so powerful that they inevitably override the effects of experience. And so a factor that prevents proper activation of the pleasure areas by normal stimuli may produce depressive illness in some people. The same factor operating in younger, differently experienced persons could lead to delinquency. Long before the theory of pleasure-seeking was mooted, a group of American psychiatrists suggested that at least some forms of juvenile delinquency might be due to a defect in the central brain mechanisms of sensation. If normal living stimuli do not fulfill the ancient command, the individual may go out and involve himself in intense and vicarious stimuli that happen at the same time to be illegal and antisocial. Several sociologists have mentioned the possibility that the dreary sameness of environmental design in many American cities is an important contributor to the rise of teenage violence.

Violence is often self-directed in a number of abnormal mental conditions. Although the injuries are rather trivial in themselves, their frequent occurrence in any one patient is serious and worries the medical staff. It is now possible to look at this hitherto unexplained activity as a form of bizarre self-stimulation. One worker, Dr. B. R. Ballinger, has stated that ". . . it was my impression that environmental restrictions, boredom and frustration played a part in worsening self-injury in many patients." It is likely that one or more deficiencies are present in the sensory pleasure mechanisms in many forms of mental illness and therefore a common feature to all of them might be a tendency for the patient to seek peripheral self-stimulation in any easily available manner. Attempts are now being made to reduce or abolish this self-mutilation by the deliberate supply of bizarre but harmless stimuli such as electronic sounds and flashing lights.

More could be said about the psychiatric implications of the theory of pleasure-seeking but I shall concentrate on normal behavior, returning to psychiatry from time to time, since so much of what to many people is normal stands just a shade away from neurosis.

The
Search for
Pleasure

Part Two

Chapter 7

The Sensation-Seekers

SUBHUMAN BEHAVIORS

Activities are classified here according to the sensory channel used. It must be obvious that only very rarely does behavior involve only one of the senses. Even with a highly concentrated activity such as viewing television both sound and sight are involved. The press and radio are perhaps alone among the ordinary pleasurable stimuli in requiring only one kind of sense organ. So although each section of this chapter investigates a form of behavior much as if I am claiming that only one sense modality is used, this is, of course, the *dominant* sense in that activity and the use of any other senses is ancillary, even though important.

The case will be put for each form of behavior that it

arises out of sensation-seeking, utilizing the old, primitive parts of the brain that are all that is required for the basic mechanisms of animal behavior. It would be absurd to contend that no use is made of the higher brain regions in these activities; just as absurd as to suppose that such activities are based upon higher brain mechanisms of pleasure. For an activity such as baseball, for example, to exist in its adult form there must be rules and the organization of team fixtures. Such behaviors involve thinking on the part of someone, just as the actual playing of the game requires planning, forethought, and judgment. Nevertheless these mental deliberations are essentially subservient to the sensory activity. No one plays baseball for the intellectual pleasure of it.

It is a tenet of modern psychology as well as of common sense that no one does anything for just one reason. Man has a great capacity for extracting several rewards from any given piece of behavior. This is a constant feature throughout what follows, as is the fact that man seldom involves himself in behavior that has no social implications and interactions. Though he may be engaged in a physical behavior such as dancing, he is deriving more than the sensory pleasure of limb movements. He is, he believes, establishing prowess, making personal contact, exhibiting friendship, possibly even asserting dominance or submissiveness and several other subtle social values. The point at issue is not that man acquires solely a sensory reward from these behaviors; it is that he could acquire all the other kinds of reward in other ways, so that they are therefore incidental and extractable from the behavior. The specific form of the behavior is inextricably rooted in sensation.

How do we use our senses, voluntarily or involuntarily, consciously or unconsciously, unashamedly or hypocritically?

The sense of *touch* is a most primitive and fundamental external sense. It undoubtedly arose very early during evolution with the appearance of tactile sense organs in the outer layers of single-celled animals and plants. There is evidence to indicate that it is the first of the external senses to be of importance in the human even before birth, and it continues to play a large part in adult life. Two readable treatments of this sense have been published recently. One of them is *Intimate Behavior* by Desmond Morris and the other is *Touching* by Professor Ashley Montague. Many topics planned for this present chapter have already been covered in great detail by these authors, and I am also indebted to them for each raising some ideas that I had not thought of. However, they did not have much to say about the receptors.

Touch is mediated by peripheral receptors present in every external region except the hair, teeth, and nails. Sometimes they are merely naked, coiled nerve endings —really, nerve beginnings—such as are found wrapped around every hair follicle, giving the very finest sensitivity of all. Others are complicated little end organs called Meisener's corpuscles, found in large numbers in such places as the fingertips, lips, nipples, penis, and clitoris. These are not as sensitive as the naked nerve endings but they are much more discriminatory; they tell us not just whether we are being touched but *how* we are being touched. All tactile receptors adapt extremely rapidly, a fact that we may test for ourselves by placing a fingertip on a rough surface and not moving it even slightly. In less than a minute we will have no idea what kind of surface we are touching and will be only vaguely aware that we are touching anything at all. Even a small movement of the fingertip, causing other receptors to be stimulated, will bring perception back to full clarity. This is the neurophysiological basis for the continuous movements during stroking, caressing, and copulating. During gestation the "hair receptors" develop first and then the Meisener's corpuscles, but the important point is that both types of tactile receptor are well-developed at the end of the embryonic phase and are fully functional in the fetus.

Studies on premature children and those born after Caesarean operation suggest that the importance of the sense of touch before birth is likely to be the biological purpose of labor contractions in the human, which are much more prolonged and energetic than in the lower animals. In these babies there is, of course, minimal or no stimulation of the fetus by the uterine contractions. With premature children it was found that later in life they showed retardation in speaking ability and in manual dexterity as well as in more primitive behavior such as posture and walking. Emotionally, they were more inclined to be jumpy, anxious, and shy, and in general terms showed significantly more behavioral problems than did full-term children. With Caesarean babies a number of deficiencies were readily apparent. The mortality rate was three times as high as in children born normally; they were also more lethargic, cried more often, showed exaggerated fear of school, and a number of other personality difficulties. Even after the age of eight, Caesarean children can be distinguished by their high level of restlessness and frequent bouts of temper. It would be wrong to believe that all of these deficiencies are due to the absence of intrauterine tactile stimulation, but taken together with much other evidence for the necessity of perinatal tactile sensation, there can be no doubt that this is the main factor.

It could be justifiably claimed that there is an abnormal situation already afoot for a human baby to be born either prematurely or by Caesarean surgery. However, researchers at the National Institutes of Health in the United States investigated the problem experimentally by comparing Caesarean monkeys with those born normally after a normal pregnancy. They found that the Caesarean monkeys showed similar deficiencies to those found in the human.

But after birth one can make up for the loss of intrauterine touching. The stimulation during labor provides an activation of the pleasure areas more intense than has occurred but less intense than will occur after birth. It serves as a transitional period in which the brain is prepared for the large amount of sensory input it is about to receive. This "limbering up" stage is clearly of great importance, but it can be made to happen after birth. This is well demonstrated in veterinary medicine where Caesarean section is frequently performed. The chances of survival of an extracted animal are enormously increased if it is rubbed down very rigorously immediately after it is withdrawn, rather than pampered and left quietly in a warm place. Many farmers, zoo keepers, biologists, and veterinarians have recorded their belief that the licking and nuzzling of the young by the mother is of major importance in the proper development of even the animal born normally, with regard to its growth rate, feeding abilities, locomotor powers, and, later on, its behavioral reactions. Studies on the prime role of mother-child tactile stimulation immediately after birth have been carried out in chickens, mice, rats, cats, dogs, sheep, goats, cows, horses, dolphins, and monkeys. It is therefore not a species-limited phenomenon, and we cannot sensibly assume that it is inoperative in the human.

In general terms the results of these experiments are similar in all species to those obtained with rats. For a week or two, newborn rats are simply lifted daily from one cage into another, in addition to the usual feeding and cleaning. When these handled rats are adult they are compared with a group of rats that have not been so handled and some rather startling consequences of this mild tactile stimulation are revealed. The handled rats grow much more quickly, are practically unfearful in situations of stress, show no aggression, and exhibit a considerably greater ability to learn maze problems. Even more remarkable perhaps is that the life span of the rats who were handled is much greater than those who were not. The general behavior of the handled rats is better suited to survival as are some of their physiological reactions to stress, such as the mobilization of glucose stores and the release of hormones from the adrenal cortex.

When the brains of the handled rats were examined in adulthood, there were more nerve cells present and many more interconnections between nerve cells than in the brains of unhandled animals. Many other types of studies have revealed this tremendously important information: that the actual structure and function of the brain is determined by the sensory experiences of the individual.*

This knowledge of the great importance of tactile stimulation shortly after birth is a very recent discovery in the laboratory and the general tendency in Western society still is to remove the baby from the possibility of maternal tactile stimulation at the earliest opportunity. So it is rather mortifying to be told by Professor Montague that even in the 1920s the pediatrician Dr. J. Brenneman insisted that every baby in his wards should be picked up and handled for a while every day. He may have been looked upon as a crank but the handling

*See chapter eleven.

scheme in New York's Bellevue Hospital was rapidly followed by a remarkable decrease in infant mortality. There is no evidence available to show whether the children born into that environment exhibited advantages in adulthood, but it would seem highly likely that they did.

It is essential for the child to receive these various forms of tactile stimulation in order that the ancient command to activate the pleasure areas shall be obeyed, for the newborn is at a considerable disadvantage in obeying this command by its own efforts. Most of the pediatricians and child-care workers who have reported on these phenomena seem to have understood this intuitively, for they all speak of the child's need for the pleasure produced by the tactile input. These beliefs arose from observation of the babies' facial and other movements. Nevertheless, once we recognize that the subjective feeling of pleasure is merely incidental to the electrical activation of the limbic pleasure areas, we see that the child's experiencing pleasure is irrelevant to the argument, since the ancient command will be obeyed even within the uterus during labor. It is the postnatal period that requires attention. Despite the fact that large numbers of child physicians and child psychiatrists, including the former director of the World Health Organization, Dr. Brock Chisholm, share the view that was put into practice by Dr. Brenneman, the ready availability of technological expertise is leading Western women to relish the postnatal "holiday" that comes from having their babies taken away from them immediately after birth and placed in some kind of glass case. From just about every point of view of health and development and even the behavioral aspects of his adult life, it is of prime importance that the baby should remain with the mother so that she may stimulate the pleasure areas according to fundamental and widespread biological laws. We fly in the face of these laws at our considerable peril, perhaps producing a generation which, unlike the handled rats, will not be less aggressive in stressful situations and will not be able readily to learn the maze of civilized life.

The need for tactile stimulation does not cease in babyhood but under normal conditions there is usually plenty of it. Few people can resist stroking, patting, and bouncing babies or "rough-housing" with older children. Also most children obtain much tactile input from playing with other children. Controlled observations have been made on institutionalized children divided into groups, one group receiving extra touchings of various kinds and the other merely exposed to the standard routines of the institution. Under these conditions the manifold retardations well known to follow upon institutionalization were considerably reduced in the group subjected to extra tactile stimulation.

Even so, despite the undoubted devotion of institution staffs, there is always a degree of mental and physical retardation in comparison with children living within a family. Touching may be only a part of family life, but it is as important as any other, frequently because it is the neural basis of what many parents call love. This lends support to those social workers who insist that for healthy development of body and mind, for realization of full potential, the child needs to grow up among the interactions of a family. Such considerations give a scientific basis to the concept that the family unit is the root of stable society. We are able to see that the good intentions of social reformers, whose efforts result in easier divorce and similar arrangements for disruption and diminution of family endurance, are in sharp contrast to the recommendations that have to be made if the social structure is to be based upon the facts of biology rather than the freedom fantasies of social philosophy.

Breast-feeding can involve much the same kind of ramifying argument. It may seem at first glance that the necessity for the baby to receive touch stimuli via its lips in order to obtain food could be adequately supplied by an artificial nipple attached to a feeding bottle and to some extent this argument can be supported. However, there is much more to breast-feeding than tactile stimulation to the lips. More of the baby's face comes into contact with the warmth and smoothness of the mother's breast and this is important for the proper development of respiratory functions. Surveys on hundreds of children have shown incontrovertibly that children fed artificially have a high incidence of problems involving the development of facial bones and teeth and when tested they are shown to be both physically and mentally inferior to breast-fed children. They are demonstrably poor in nutrition, more susceptible to several diseases, and slower in learning to walk and talk. They are less likely to have an attractive face or a mind that sets them squarely among their peers. Though I may frequently appeal for the amount of sensory pleasure-seeking in advanced societies to be reduced, I am certain that the sensory pleasure-seeking of mother and child in breast-feeding is of the gravest importance for the satisfactory progress of the human race, physically and mentally. If when burning their brassieres for trivial freedoms women also metaphorically burn their breasts, most certainly the sins of the mothers will be visited upon the children.

In adult animals, if Dr. John Napier, the author of *The Roots of Mankind*, is right, touching has had the most profound evolutionary consequences for mankind. Touching as a social interaction seems to be limited to the higher mammals. Lower forms obtain their tactile pleasures by scraping themselves on objects and by manipulating their own bodies and although this too occurs in more advanced animals, including man, it is the manifold interpersonal touchings that are striking in the higher forms. The way in which we have made tactile sensation an integral part of our everyday lives is indicated by the fact that not a single organized activity has arisen in any human culture. Touching each other permeates so many general activities that it has not been necessary to devise a behavioral form that provides tactile pleasure while pretending to do something else. Perhaps this is partly due to the very intimate nature of touching, which allows this sense to be used not just for pleasure but also for signaling various degrees of friendship and intimacy.

In *Intimate Behavior* Desmond Morris has examined in detail the various ways in which we touch each other, drawing attention to the formal handshake, somewhat less formal pat on the arm, friendly slap on the back, chummy arm round the shoulder, fond stroke and caress, and all the great variety of closer, harder, private bodily contacts that are so much a part of human love affairs. Though Morris and others have pointed out the large amount of touching we do, and accounted for it by ethological and psychological principles, no one seems to have asked the question *why* we do it, why we signal lack of hostility by touching hands, why we signal love by holding hands. According to the theory of pleasure-seeking the answer is that touching activates the pleasure areas. Our handshakes and our cuddling have a straightforward neurological basis; they help us to obey the ancestral command and when doing that we feel a modicum of well-being. We do not have to devise complex explanations such as the need to show that we have no sword or dagger in the hand. We do not need separate explanations for separate touchings. It all comes under one simple heading, differing in form only because we have stratified personal relations.

Much the same is seen in the chimpanzee colonies, where grooming is highly prevalent yet subject to hierarchical controls. A chimpanzee is no more allowed to groom *any* other one than we are allowed to kiss whom we please. Certain relationships, certain experiences and interminglings have to occur first. In such subtle ways can we arrange for our basic neurological requirements to aid in establishing social *mores*. In more general terms, we shall find that *every* kind of social permission and denial is based upon the giving or refusing of pleasure, in low or high degree, by manipulating the senses.

The handshake is a normal part of ape behavior and is therefore unlikely to be related to swords. The fact that in men handshaking is a relatively modern innovation shows that the higher ranks of society have become less formal with each other; on the whole the lower ranks never did and do not now engage in this somewhat stilted behavior any more than do children. But grooming is both reflexive and transitive. It has its parallels in human scratching and rubbing and running of the fingers through hair. Dr. Napier has spent much time in precise observation of how the hand is used. His overall conclusion is that it can be used in two basic ways, the power grip and the precision grip. In apes the precision grip, using the thumb and index finger, is used almost solely for grooming. Dr. Napier's highly informed suggestion is that the great tendency toward grooming in our ancestors led to the evolution of the opposable thumb because of its survival value in the social strata of primate colonies. Since it is the opposability of the thumb that enables man alone to write, sculpt, play musical instruments, hold delicate tools and do all the other essentially human motor acts, we have to accept that much activity is only possible because our simian ancestors sought peripheral self-stimulation with their tactile sense.

Man's ingenuity is amazing when he decides to utilize this sense as a source of intense pleasure that long out-lasts the stimulus. It is inconceivable that any lower animal could construct such peculiar pleasure-pain activities as massage, the Turkish bath, and the sauna, although many of them enjoy a shower.

Another major source of peripheral self-stimulation giving subhuman pleasure is *taste* or the gustatory sense. No distinction will be drawn now between the tasting and smelling components of eating and drinking, for to do so would entail a lengthy discussion of neurological details that are complex, controversial, and irrelevant to the present issue.* Our ability to discern a multitude of flavors is now known to be due to a combination of oral and nasal mechanisms, but the neural details are still obscure. The fact is that we have powers of flavor evaluation, and it is in this broad and realistic sense that the term "gustatory" is used.

*Olfaction as such will be dealt with later.

One certain fact about these alimentary receptors is that they represent one of the oldest, and therefore most vital, means by which the animal organism has awareness of the environment. Studies on the protozoa, the single-celled animals such as amoeba, demonstrate unequivocally that even these simple creatures can accept or reject flavors. Apart from a supply of oxygen the most fundamental requirement for individual survival is an intake of water and suitable food. All biological reactions in the animal body convert matter into some form of energy, so a continuous supply of convertible matter is essential for continued life. There is a remarkable contrast between the simplicity of the biological demand and the complexity of man's supply.

No one who has ever fed an animal will doubt that the process of eating can elicit unmistakably pleasurable responses. No one, even in the most deprived parts of the world, lacks personal experience of gustatory joy. It would be unreasonable to doubt that nerve impulses originating in gustatory sense organs reach and activate the pleasure areas, and there is also a wealth of electrophysiological evidence that this is so. Animals enthusiastically press a lever for electrical stimulation of the olfactory neurones. From both the empirical and teleological points of view the generation of pleasure by the process of taking in nourishment has enormous survival value. Knowledge of patients suffering from *anorexia nervosa*, a condition in which eating is distasteful, emphasizes the essential role that gustatory pleasure plays in staying alive. Equally pathetic are the patients with a neurological defect in the taste mechanisms. For example, patients with mouth cancer are often treated with radiation therapy and this sometimes destroys not only the tumor but also the nerve fibers from the front and sides of the tongue. They can taste only bitter flavors and enormous effort is required by the nursing staff to keep the patients nourished.

This pleasure-producing aspect of food consumption is often lost sight of today with popular knowledge of calories and carbohydrates, and yet it is inherent in all ordinary eating. The problem of designing a successful slimming diet is not one of selecting foodstuffs that will insure no gain in weight; it is to choose food that will do this and also be pleasurable to eat, so that the patient will adhere to the diet. Under particularly demanding conditions, in war or on a flight to the moon, it is accepted that a few pellets and a bag or two of paste will satisfy the need for nourishment, and those involved have the self-discipline to forego the usual prandial pleasures. The search for food is one of the strongest drives among lower animals and yet they have not the slightest knowledge that eating does them any good. The ancestral command to activate the pleasure areas insures that animals explore every means available to stimulate their peripheral receptors and in doing so they inevitably take in nourishment. Eating and drinking behaviors are clear-cut examples of peripheral self-stimulation. Even in man the nutritional aspects are frequently only marginal in terms of conscious motivation. Much of what people eat and drink gives nourishment, but the true marginality of this is revealed when we remember the lengths man goes to in securing these vital materials and the time and money spent in supplying and devouring matter that does not fulfill a nutritional function.

Examination of humans' approach to the food supply shows an astonishing transition from the simple primitive technique of the Australian aborigine, who picks larvae from the cracks in bark and pulls fruits off trees, both for immediate consumption, to the gigantic complex of the modern restaurant and catering industry, including farms, supermarkets, and processing factories. One may still buy a steak and eat it as such, but this does not compare in preparation, pleasure, and price with what can be done to it by *haute cuisine*. The fact that the price of a complex dish includes the cost of many nutritionally inessential materials such as spices, herbs, and sauces, and the cost of the chef's long training, is accepted without question in order to obtain the extra pleasure.

The food processer and the advertising agency would never honestly deny that the consumer is only vaguely aware of nutritional value. It is obviously lucrative to build factories in which the nutritional raw materials of food, quite adequate in themselves, are colored, flavored, perfumed, pulverized, serrated, gasified and sculptured into end products that bear little resemblance to the basic stuff of life. The vendor rarely bothers to extol the nutritional virtues of a product; but tells us what fun we shall have eating it. One has to look below the surface to see this with respect to meat and vegetables but even a superficial view of the confectionery trade reveals its sensory basis. There is no doubt that a chocolate bar contains several kinds of nutritionally valuable items, but we are seldom exhorted to eat it because of that. Instead we may be told that when we munch the bar we shall experience an ecstasy so great that we shall want to eschew all other pleasures and run off into the woods alone for our gustatory orgy. Perhaps this is because there is so little to choose between chocolate bars nutritionally.

With regard to fluids, the essential demand of the body is for water. Except for very young mammals all the lower creatures manage quite well on this single fluid and so could people. Yet among humans even in primitive communities, the intake of plain water must be infinitesimally small. If we knew someone who insisted on drinking only water we might consider them distinctly odd. If we questioned wherein lay this oddity, we would see that their drinking is simply biological whereas ours, motivationally, is for pleasure. Drinking in lower animals is not for pleasure. Imbalance of the fluid arrangements in the body leads to highly unpleasant stimuli in the sensitive oral region, worse by far than hunger. Thirst causes activation of the displeasure areas and drinking removes the oral stimulus of dry membranes that causes the disquiet. In civilized communities thirst is a rarity. The required fluid intake is maintained by drinking liquids that are based on water but are chosen for their flavor.

Young mammals are an exception among the lower animals in that they drink milk. Milk is, of course, not just a drink but also a food, which is why it is supplied to a baby still unable to manage solids. But lower mammals do not go on drinking it into adulthood the way we may do. The dairy industry is vast and profitable and a large part of it is concerned with milk production, yet there is no vital need for milk among adults in advanced communities. Millions of gallons are drunk annually with no conscious awareness of milk's food value, showing that many adults continue to seek their sensory pleasures in much the same way as fish swimming through electrodes or babies at the breast. Similar statements, of course, could be made about cream, cheese, and butter.

With milk the cow has done a natural job of conversion but an objective observer, who was also a biological fundamentalist, would be profoundly puzzled by the lengths to which people go to convert water into something that will activate the pleasure areas. Vast plantations for tea, coffee, sugar, and cocoa form yet another complex and lucrative industry. Not only the plantations but also the great network of ancillary industry that goes with them—shipping, grinding, preserving, storing, packing, and advertising—has all been set up so that small quantities of raw materials may be infused, percolated, filtered, or in some other way made to transform water into a beverage. And the esthetic side of man has created the enormous pottery, ceramics, and plastics industries in order to have visually attractive containers for his drinks. Historically, some of the most shameful episodes of slavery, brutality, usury, and plunder were due to demands that humans' fluid intake should stimulate the gustatory sense and activate the pleasure areas. On such a foundation the British Empire was built.

Humans do not only flavor water but have managed to add a new dimension to oral stimulation. Using expertise denied to what are considered less intelligent lower animals, people charge water with a toxic gas—carbon dioxide. One may drink it as plain soda water or choose from a wide variety of flavored fizzy drinks. Here is the all-too-familiar realm in which man's search for sensory pleasure has become undeniably disadvantageous. Many millions of dollars a year are spent in voluntarily taking in this lethal gas as bubbles in flavored liquid. There is even the quasi fetish of taking health salts every morning, and from the popularity of these products there can be no doubt that the tingling oral sensation generates activity in the pleasure areas at the start of the day, giving a spurious feeling of enhanced good health in those prone to self-delusion. The same result can be and is obtained by standing under a shower for cutaneous stimulation or by carrying out exercises to activate the proprioceptors. None of these morning cavortings has the slightest medical benefit on those leading a normally active life but they soothe the uncritical mind.

Yet carbon dioxide is a poor runner-up to another

toxic compound that man repeatedly and regularly im-
bibes. He has set up a drinks industry without parallel
in any other field of gustatory intake, using ethyl alcohol
as its base. When man really puts his mind to it and can
make money out of his discoveries, he can enormously
complicate the simple matter of sensory pleasure-seeking. No one would claim that alcoholic drinks are consumed for the pleasurable taste of *alcohol*. Pure alcohol is
definitely distasteful to most people and the drinks that
contain nothing but alcohol and water, vodka for example, are drunk fast in small quantities or are diluted.
Dilute solutions of ethyl alcohol are in fact used in
laboratories to cause rapid death of tissue samples. Man
disguises the taste of alcohol by manufacturing a great

range of spirits, liqueurs, wines, and beers. All of these are drunk partly for the pleasure given by their flavors, and in this respect their consumption is not distinct from that of tea or Coca-Cola. But in addition to giving an immediate sensory reward via the taste buds, alcoholic drinks provide a delayed bonus due to the effect of the active constituent on the higher regions of the brain. Alcohol puts the superego to sleep; people relax the normal inhibitions of the higher regions, rapidly shed whatever adult traits they might possess, and the animated id reigns supreme.

There is a well-marked scale of gustatory intensity in both people and the dishes they eat. Some of the tastiest dishes in the world, which are frequently national dishes, are derived from the staple food of the peasant group. The life of a peasant was largely bereft of sensory pleasure so it is not surprising that people who spent most of their lives in particularly hard work arranged for highly pleasurable meals when their work was done, producing, for example, the paella in Spain, curry in India, rijstaffel in Indonesia, suckling pig in Hungary, kous-kous in Arabia, kebabs in Turkey, and the delectable dishes of China. Undoubtedly the peasants had a larger portion of rather tasteless carbohydrate than is served at more opulent tables today, but it is the intense gustatory pleasure value of the other constituents that has made these dishes highly respected in exclusive cuisines.

If we examine the range of dishes that we know ourselves, we will find that all levels of flavor intensity are catered for to suit personality or mood. Some people retain the immature preference for sweetness. Normally during the course of maturation the taste buds around the tip of the tongue, which are especially responsive to sweet flavors, disappear so that most of them are gone at the end of childhood. With increasing age and extended sensory experience most people develop acceptance of a much wider range of flavors, relegating sweetness to a minor position. For various reasons the general processes of mental maturation are delayed or inhibited in some people, and one feature is often an exaggerated liking for sweet flavors, and a desperate exploitation of the few sweet-sensitive taste buds left to them.

Today a gourmet who surveys or even bravely samples the myriad packets and tins of processed foods, whose sale seems to be increasing, might be pardoned for wondering whether our sense of taste is becoming slowly atrophied for so much of this "food," though by no means all, is relatively flavorless to the sensitive palate. There are in fact two influences operating. On the one hand easier long-distance travel and greater affluence in many communities have enabled many people to sample the attractive flavorsome foods of lands other than their own. Some approve of what they find and try to incorporate it into their "special meals." On the other hand, the rapid increase of technology has made so many more means of sensory pleasure available to everyone that for many people the pleasures of routine eating and drinking now rank low. For these people it is more important not to miss their favorite television program than to do some real cooking. Food processors have not been slow to take advantage of this mass decline in demand for food that requires even a modicum of culinary attention, and to substitute "instant" meals that, as one packet states, "are such fun to cook"—you put the plastic bag in boiling water for twelve minutes.

The shelves of "pretend" bread, pies, or fish dishes are part of the price we pay for television, transistor radios, discothèques, records, and even those orgiastic chocolate bars.

I do not mean to imply that food intake is a simple matter of sensory pleasure only. I have been describing the hedonistic aspects of taste, not nutrition. Several long scientific symposia have been devoted exclusively to food intake and still no general agreement has been reached, except that it bristles with uncertainties and anomalies. While there can be no doubt that in the physiologically and psychologically normal animal the search for and consumption of food is a matter of peripheral self-stimulation, very slight abnormalities can affect the situation profoundly. Since few people are free from such abnormalities the detailed picture for any individual is obscure.

The fact that we use our noses so much during eating and drinking is an accident of anatomy, the usefulness of which is attested by our relative loss of taste when nasal catarrh occurs. But we smell, transitively speaking, at other times, too, and as usual man has not neglected the pleasure input available from his nostrils. Far more scientific work has been done on the *olfactory sense* than on the gustatory sense. Much of it is described in detail in R. W. Moncrieff's *Odour Preferences*.

We now know, for example, that people agree almost unanimously about really bad or really good odors but that men are more sure about the pleasant and women about the distasteful odors. Children are unappreciative of flower smells but both adult men and women like them equally. Many artificial odors rejected by normal adults are fully acceptable to children. Interestingly, when the preferences of extroverts are different from introverts, they are like those of children. Men tend to retain their preferences into old age whereas women alter many preferences after the age of forty. The sex differences in odor-likings are detectable before the age of eight, although relative values change a lot during the first twenty years, mostly between fifteen and eighteen. Very old people do not notice even bad or dangerous smells. Usually there is no apparent reason for a person to like or dislike an odor, but quite often the preferences can be related to the emotional requirements of the individual. People vary enormously with regard to their association of odors with other things; for example, Moncrieff says, "The smell of vanillin may remind one subject of chocolate, another of his grandmother and yet another of a few bars of Chopin's music."

The role of olfaction in ordinary life is perhaps little noticed by the individual, but it has not escaped commerce. Quite a range of fabrics are now mildly odorized during manufacture. This follows the observation that when two garments identical except for the addition of odor to one of them are placed side by side on a counter, more "smelly" ones are bought. Women bought considerably more slightly scented stockings and brassieres than unscented ones, even though they were not consciously aware of the smell. Subliminal techniques do not have to be visual.

Less surreptitiously, artificial odors are added to artificial products, such as a leather smell to plastic handbags. In the United States there is an odorant spray for making secondhand cars smell like new ones. The smell of violets can now pervade our furniture polish, roses the sink cleanser, and almost the whole greenhouse can scent our toilet tissue.

These trivia indicate man's drive to use every possible sensory input to activate his pleasure areas even when the result may be a reduction in human dignity. Not only will he accept the most inappropriate odors on objects but he positively enjoys the use of odors by fellow men. One of the most lucrative of all industries is based upon the fact that many people, traditionally only women but recently also men, seem to value their intrinsic qualities so little that they seek to give pleasure by smelling like completely unknown flowers. Worse, their partners foster the belief that a person attains added value by sprinkling herself or himself with pungent fluid. None of this can be intelligently considered to be human evaluation, and there is now scientific evidence pointing to its subhuman nature, though the kind of smells may have changed.

Recent experiments have revealed that the sense of olfaction is of the utmost importance for mating in monkeys. At the time of sexual receptivity the female secretes an odorous substance called a pheromone and this is how the male knows for sure that she is ready and willing. When nasal plugs are inserted into male monkeys to block olfaction they show more interest in bananas than in receptive females, even though the normal postures and secretions are present. Such pheromones have been known for a long time among lowly creatures such as insects, where it was thought that odors wafted on the breeze are essential for the conjugation of creatures whose range of vision is only a few millimeters. But monkeys can see each other far off and, moreover, they are microsmic animals, that is, their sense of olfaction is poorly developed in comparison with macrosmic animals such as dogs. Man, too, is microsmic but in view of these unequivocal experiments we can no longer assume that olfaction plays no part in our personal interactions. Possibly the olfactory mechanisms play some part in the comminglings of people for whom personal hygiene is of little importance. Other groups expend considerable time and money in either removing the sources of animal odors or in applying manufactured concoctions. It is possible that because the human sense of smell is vestigial, animal odors are not strong enough to cause sufficient activation of the pleasure areas and that the worldwide production of perfumes is an attempt to utilize chemistry in this respect. Even though floral odors seem to be dominant in perfumes, any good quality scent contains musk or civet or both, and these are strongly odoriferous substances obtained from the sexual glands of animals. As with the stockings and brassieres, we must assume that unconscious, subliminal processes are at work. Are perfumes perhaps used by men and women who are uncertain that their masculinity or femininity is readily apparent by other signals?

On the other hand, even more subtle olfactory controls may be operating in us. The findings in monkeys will stimulate much research into human odors that may prove that we are in some ways similar to mice. Female mice isolated from males show very uneven sexual periodicity, whereas if they are exposed to male odors their cycles become absolutely regular. The smell of one male can counteract that of thirty females. There are even permanent olfactory effects. For example, the male odor to which they are exposed in infancy determines for life the kind of male with whom female mice will mate. They are usually exposed to the father's odors and will then mate only with animals of a different strain. If they are reared in the absence of a male they are entirely promiscuous in adulthood. When the father is sprayed daily with perfume they can become promiscuous and will even mate with him. There is the possibility, therefore, that man's search for pleasure through his nose has so deranged subliminal olfactory mechanisms that dysmenorrhea, sexual promiscuity, and even incest may have become frequent occurrences.

Moving now from the nose to the ear, we come to the

sense of *audition*. We share the ability to detect sounds in the form of vibrations in surrounding media with a vast proportion of the animal kingdom, certainly down to the Annelida (worms) and possibly lower. The ability to produce sound is more restricted and would seem to be the prerogative of the vertebrates, apart from devices such as the cricket's knees, though this assumption may have arisen because we have not yet designed suitable instruments to record invertebrate sounds. Deliberate production of sound by artificial means, not from the body but from external apparatus, is even more restricted and probably does not occur below the higher primates. Such activities as those of the woodpecker can be considered incidental to the task of finding grubs.

In contrast to most other senses, there has been a rapid and complicated evolution of the hearing apparatus from a small cluster of cells in an earthworm to the masterpiece of structural engineering of the mammalian ear, together with an extensively ramifying neural system within the brain. This testifies to the increasing importance of the auditory mode of sensation as animals became more adept at extracting pleasure from the environment.

In comparison with some animals man has a very limited range of audible frequencies. Modern electronic devices have shown that the animal world is a constant cacophony that is far beyond man's limitations. We are sensitive to vibrations from about twenty to twenty thousand cycles per second, so that if we enter a room filled with caged mice all we hear are a few squeaks now and then. In reality the air is filled with the vibrations from the rodents' squeaks. Newborn rats and mice may wriggle and open their mouths apparently without sound, but special equipment shows that the creatures are screaming at the tops of their voices. Even in post-prandial play, which is soundless to man, the animals are emitting many squeaks at twenty-four kilocycles per second. To communicate danger rodents are able to call each other at a frequency of over one hundred kilocycles. Similar findings have been made with other species and biologists now agree that our knowledge of sound production among lower animals is small. Evidently auditory communication and pleasure-seeking is far more important and extensive than we have envisaged by using our own ears.

Nevertheless, despite his narrow range of auditory sensitivity man has made full use of the whole available spectrum. Beginning with the sounds he hears in the womb and the sounds he makes after the first slap of his life, responding to the unwitting punishment for being born, man is continually hearing and making himself heard. Throughout human history the use of sound stimuli to generate pleasure has been known to all women who have crooned and hummed to a discontented baby, and it is found in every community investigated. The child itself soon learns that by making sounds he can generate signs of pleasure in those around him; the burbling of babies is pleasurable to all but the most insensitive people. Similarly, the baby learns that other sounds will generate displeasure or bring rewards such as food or fondling. For a baby, part of getting to grips with the environment is to find the right balance with unpleasant sounds so that the consequence is reward and not punishment. These sounds, though devoid of verbal content, are not without meaning. No one who hears them doubts the fundamental information they communicate.

Though it would be stretching the claim too far to say that sound production forms a major part of sensory pleasure-seeking behavior in man or lower animals, com-

mon observation indicates that sound is used for pleasure to some extent. It is difficult to doubt that the wide
range of sounds produced by birds, the barking of dogs,
wailing of cats, and the laughter of dolphins is unrelated
to pleasure-seeking. Sounds can have many functions
such as warning, attracting, marking territory, but many
would be called spontaneous and are usually associated
with motor behavior that indicates pleasure.

As with so many things that can be done with and to
the body, it is in humans that the production and hearing
of sound has been taken to the greatest lengths of complexity and discrimination in the pursuit of activating
the limbic pleasure areas. It is likely that any sound made
by an individual voluntarily, whether by word or deed,
generates pleasure or displeasure for the individual and
for the people around. But it is the human voice that is
most pervasive.

Manifold neuromuscular mechanisms are involved in
speaking the simplest word or hearing the simplest
sounds. At least six areas of the cerebral cortex and numerous interconnections with several lower brain regions are involved in the behavior to which most of us
pay so little attention. Several top-rank neurologists have
spent their lives studying the mechanisms of speech, yet
it is still one of the most obscure in the realm of brain
function.

The faculty of speech is basic to the functions of hearing, reading, and writing. Instruments have shown that
when we write we actually make very slight movements
of the laryngeal muscles that we would use in speaking;
similar unconscious movements of the vocal muscles
have been demonstrated when we are reading, so in fact
we "hear" and "speak" the words we read and write.
Speech no doubt evolved from the grunts, roars, squeals,
and screeches of our ancestral species. This capacity for

making one's own noises has been sharpened and refined to a greater extent than any other mammalian characteristic until it now represents the highest endeavors of man in the many forms of language that it takes. But despite its transformation into a sensory vehicle for precise, poignant, pregnant, and penetrating transfer of factual information, the human voice still retains pleasure-giving qualities distinct from the factual content of its messages.

Though the attractiveness of an orator is mainly due to the subject of his oration, it is not likely that he will be asked to speak again if his voice is strident or cacophonous. Most of us enjoy songs in languages unknown to us—it is sometimes an advantage to have the displeasurable effects of trivial lyrics removed. Obviously the voice and language are fully as complex as so many other topics I am covering, but what I am emphasizing is the profound importance of the noninformational part of language.

Although we discriminate among the voices of the people around us in terms of pleasure and displeasure, we all seem to enjoy our own. It is this pleasure generated by our voices that protects us under conditions of sensory deprivation. For some of us this is something of a rarity under ordinary conditions, but it was more common a century or two ago, giving rise to the wealth of shepherd songs, plowboy laments, and blacksmiths' ballads. The modern counterpart may be the widespread singing, humming, and whistling in the bath, which occurs from childhood through adulthood. Even when aural stimulation is being supplied by a radio many people will augment the broadcast music with their own voices. Musical historians claim that our orchestral instruments have been designed to imitate various properties of the human voice and that much classical musical form has arisen from the powers and limitations of human singing.

Quite apart from the personal features of his voice, everybody is able to evoke pleasure or displeasure in varying degrees by merely altering the way in which he speaks, from the sharp clipped "well done" through the smooth cadences of polite discourse to the long low murmur of words of love. Realists may claim that falling in love is a result of visual physical attraction, but they forget the very large number of couples who have never seen each other. Among the blind, surely, it is the voice that steals the heart. All these factors show that although the facility of verbal language is of tremendous importance in human affairs, the interchange has a significance quite distinct from grammar, it is lodged in the ability of the voice to stimulate the pleasure areas.

Considerations such as these cast grave doubts on the broad claims of some modern linguists who wish us to believe that the whole of human behavior could be explained if only we had complete knowledge of the phonemic qualities of language. It is less easy but perhaps more rational to recognize that the intricate tonal systems of the world's languages may well be built upon a common basic feature involving the pleasurable or displeasurable properties of self-generated sound. The linguists may demonstrate something fundamental if they will examine the myriad ways in which each phoneme can be uttered, and recognize that far from being the unit of language the phoneme is simply a highly flexible brick with which a hundred different messages can be built. We may test this for ourselves by seeing how many ways we articulate the phonemic "o" in the word "no." The essential error of contemporary mechanistic linguistics is that, virtually ignorant of physiology and psychology, it neglects the fact that a string of phonemes, whatever the deep structure, conveys only one factual message but also any one of maybe dozens of emotional messages. Such a sentence as "John is easy to tease" is hardly worth analyzing unless we know how it is said, for only then are we dealing with language rather than academic artifacts. In written language we can only derive the full meaning of a sentence by reference to the surrounding context. With the voice we know at once the full message, not just the verbal one.

Analysis of phrases in isolation from their use also leaves out of account the important matter of association. In carpentry the average man derives a modicum of pleasure from the sound of the saw working its way through the wood, mainly because he knows it is a step toward the final creation. To the craftsman cabinet-maker, however, the saw-sound gives pleasure in itself, if it is being used properly, and displeasure if it is not. The association here is complex, arising from the large number of exposures to saw-sounds during the craftsman's working life. Much less complex are the associations that are used in psychological tests and that formed the basis of the psychoanalytic technique of free association. Hundreds of thousands of testings have shown beyond doubt that to certain people certain words convey a meaning that is denied to others. Not only do certain words remind them of concepts and actions; they also produce varying degrees of pleasure and displeasure. *This* is the stuff of language, not grunts, hisses, and puffs. Viewed in this operational, functional manner we can see that despite the most erudite demonstrations of order and pattern in fragments of words, leading to the belief that language is innate and does not have to be learned, the actual use of language by ordinary people in their everyday lives is entirely dependent upon what has happened to their brains, with special reference to the pleasure areas.

Even so, man's predilection for manipulating his environment has led some people to seek beyond the voice for sensory pleasure. The human creations of this small group have now brought artificial sounds of excellent quality and great variety into the lives of everyone. A casual riffle through the pages of *The World Radio and TV Handbook* shows that even the smallest country has several radio transmitters. Twisting the knobs of a communications receiver reveals that high frequency electromagnetic waves are radiated for pleasure throughout the world all day. Technologically these criss-crossing wireless beams are far removed from the chirrupings of monkeys in the trees, yet essentially the broadcast bands represent a very clever way of doing what the monkeys do. Radio is not alone in this field. Discs and tapes are examples of technology that are little short of miraculous. They are produced by a very small group of human minds and are used mainly in the search for sensory pleasure. Hi-fi catalogs or exhibitions show the extent to which this auditory pleasure-seeking has been commercialized. The human qualities of mind found in the intricate abstractions of musicology that underly classical music are overwhelmed by the output of ephemeral popular jingles. A current complete catalog of one firm's music cassettes lists 361 pop items and 106 classical titles. There is evidence from the jungle that in a predominantly human society these figures would be reversed, for, as the following account shows, monotonous pop rhythms have exact analogies in the jungle.

From time to time in jungle clearings groups of chimpanzees come together and spend an hour or two jumping up and down rather listlessly while waving their arms about at random, as one of them stands by a selected tree and beats out a monotonous rhythm on a smooth root protruding above the ground. The scene and sound bear the closest resemblance to contemporary pop gatherings. It is perhaps not surprising that naïve intuition has led some exponents of this behavior to name their groups after lower creatures. The mere presence of chimpanzee music in our culture is no cause for great apprehension. What is more serious is that this subhuman form of pleasure-seeking has assumed such gigantic dimensions that it seems to pervade almost every medium of communication and almost every place to sit, as well as accounting for the transfer of enormous amounts of the world's currencies. The desire of many young people to spend several days at pop festivals, listening to jungle stuff at several kilowatts power, may well be considered a travesty of human brain mechanisms. But such behavior does not happen spontaneously; it is in some way due to deficiencies in the older generation's shaping of young minds.

In every human eye there are some 126 million light-sensitive cells, far outnumbering every other kind of sensory receptor put together. Sensitivity to light is present in the very lowest creatures and each step in evolution has led to increasing complexity of the visual apparatus, culminating in the prodigious acuity of the mammalian eye. Visual activity is not much used for pleasure-seeking in the lower animals, but there is some indication that, at least in some species, pleasure is derived from visual input on occasions. The domestic parakeet is a common example of an animal deriving pleasure from examination of its own image in a mirror, without supplying any homeostatic reward. Similarly, the elaborate and colorful courtship displays of many animal groups right down to fish appear to give pleasure in themselves. But it is humans who have deliberately and consciously abstracted *visual input* from homeostatic considerations.

It seems to have been one of his first acts when he came down from the trees, if the cave paintings are as old as evidence suggests they are. Early man cannot be distinguished from lower animals because he is a toolmaker, for quite a number of animals have tools. But only humans decorated them. It is in these useless but frequently beautiful grooves and knobs that we see the first sign of human evolution as promulgated by the pleasure-seeking theory. Some thirty thousand years ago an animal appeared which engaged in activities that were undeniably nonhomeostatic. The mutations of natural selection had produced a creature that could carry out the ancient command to activate its pleasure areas by using its thinking brain as well as its sensory brain.

Here then in neurological terms is the biological basis of esthetics, the beginning of art and of much else that is connoted by the term "spiritual life." What many have long suspected is now clear; human spiritual life may be considered no more supernatural or nonphysical than the practical life of eating and mating. The old controversy between monism and dualism can be resolved in the direction that much of modern science suggests, because it is now possible to align man's nonhomeostatic behavior under the same system of biological laws and neural interactions that have been established for the more lowly aspects of his life.

Cave paintings and sculpted pots served well as a beginning, but man's insatiable desire to improve and vary his sources of visual pleasure has led to a wide range of complex technologies, each with its set of ancillary industries, trades, and institutions. For centuries man has been discontented with the random order of plants as they occur in the wild and has set up his individual microcosms of vegetal design and color. Even the very form of natural plants came under his eye for modification in order to take their allotted place in the colorful blaze of botanical monstrosities that is his garden. Thus grew up the empires of plant breeders, seedsmen, and suppliers of weed killers, fertilizers, insecticides, and other garden requisites. Individual effort was paralleled by municipal endeavor so that nearly every civilized community developed park areas to engender the visual pleasure that is sometimes called peace of mind.

With so much attention paid to surrounding nature, it is not surprising that man also became embroiled in the shape and form of his dwellings. The contours of the cave gave way before the human esthetic onslaught and so arose that larger form of sculpture called architecture. Again a sharp distinction may be drawn between man and the lower animals, many of which build homes for themselves. Only man made a social institution and an art out of building, wedding his motor abilities and his desire for visual stimulation to the functions of his higher brain in such a way that the assembly of raw materials resulted in structures whose beauty is universally acclaimed through centuries. The recession of this diversity of form in buildings, in what have come to be called sprawling megalopolises or conurbations, has been enthusiastically cited as part of the cause of delinquency and violence, as well as of the less dramatic but equally undesirable anxieties and depressions of city life.

Man also turned the advance of technology to account in the preparation of pigments for painting and the substrates upon which they could be rendered. The tradition of cave painting was carried on by the churches, substituting their walls and ceilings for the caves, and saints and angels for saber-toothed tigers. More secular artists made portable pictures so that visual pleasures could be moved—and sold. There can be little else among men's chattels for which such enormous prices are paid. Ounce for ounce, the stuff of some paintings must be far and away the most expensive substance on earth, and yet suitable only for being looked at.

From such a simple beginning as the kaleidoscope came the worldwide colossus of the film industry. Obviously the charms of the cinema are not entirely visual, though they must have been nearly so before talkies came in, yet equally obviously it is the visual component that is decisive. The role of the cinema is that it can concentrate into a few hours the visual pleasures that would take months or years to experience under ordinary conditions. Much the same, of course, applies to television.

It is unlikely that many of television's devotees have even a slight inkling of the amount of laboratory work that had to be carried out before the first TV transmission could be made. Several hundred years of scientific endeavor have been concentrated into producing a device that can be looked at. In places this modern marvel of communication is being used to communicate. But the extensive, expensive, and wondrous machinery of television is mainly used to radiate programs that have more or less hypnotized into immobility, night after night, hundreds of millions, using the subhuman part of their minds to obtain mere visual excitation of the pleasure areas. Such is the power and importance of our optical system.

So powerful, indeed, that it does not even require meaning to be attached to the visual input. For quite a long time man strove to produce some sort of meaning in his pictures, sculptures, architecture, films, and, one must suppose, television. But eventually the magic appeal of the aurora borealis came to be understood by those who purvey pleasure and now there are several sources of quite meaningless visual input. Painting itself seems to have become largely nonrepresentational, or to show objects that hold little meaning for many people, as in pop art. Psychedelic light displays are now almost *de rigueur* in discothèques and are often used at exhibitions, and several magazines for electronics enthusiasts publish circuits for home construction. Rather similar is the trade in glass columns containing colored fluids that rise and fall in myriad shapes under the influence of heat from a lamp.

Moving from large-scale, commercialized visual pleasures down to the level of the individual, there are many more ways in which we use our eyes to activate the limbic pleasure areas, sometimes so subtle that we are not aware that this is what we are doing. Few people, however rarefied their spirits, are completely careless about furnishings and decorations. Yet none of these is in any way needed for survival. Even in the temples of the most intellectual religious sects of the Orient considerable attention is paid to the layout and décor.

As a portable extension to the domestic sources of visual pleasure, we pay attention to our appearance so that we can carry around an image of the visible self that is pleasurable to us and, we hope, to others. Quite apart from artificial aids with which people clothe, paint, and spray their bodies there are several means by which we derive visual pleasure from the appearance of others. We are greatly affected by the face. Standards of personal beauty certainly vary geographically, ethnically, socially, and temporally, but equally certainly standards of beauty exist in all cultures at all times.

It is quite usual for people of a certain mien to be delineated in popular fiction and drama as of correspondingly pleasant or unpleasant nature. We are all aware how arbitrary is such characterization by physiognomy yet we go on paying almost unconscious attention to the face as a guide to inner nature. It is accepted that the widest range and best-controlled muscular reactions are those of the manifold facial expressions during social contact. They are means whereby we may superficially inform the observer to what degree we are pleased, surprised, angry, or sad. Some of it is projected into the observer who also becomes a little pleased, surprised, angry, or sad. Experience is of great importance; early anthropologists were frequently made unduly apprehensive by primitive tribes who frowned in situations where we would smile. In several conditions of mental abnormality the patients are characterized by making facial expressions quite inappropriate to the overall situation or their mood.

The face is of prime importance but the rest of the body plays a part too, especially if it is female. Men may mostly wish to use the sense of touch with women, but they are tremendously gullible for the sight of them, too, hence the frequent occurrence of girlie calendars, saucy advertisements, and sexy magazines. In keeping with the modern desperate search for maximum sensory pleasure among the millions, commercial interests have not been slow to supply the visual aspects of sex as pictures or even live shows. Perhaps the inability of reformers to demonstrate a connection between pornography and sexual behavior is because these are in fact poorly related. Pornography may be viewed as simply self-stimulation by the visual channel, having no deeper or longer lasting effect than the visual pleasure of looking at a sunset. If pornography were increasing while other sensory pleasures were not, there might be cause for alarm. At present the alarming situation is that so many forms of sensory pleasure are mounting rapidly. No permanent good can come of focusing attention on only one symptom of any disease, physical or social.

Possibly because so many primitive communities are colored there is among many people an antipathy toward members of the colored races, red, black, brown, or yellow. Despite intensive research by scientists in several branches of biology, no conclusive or even weighty evidence exists to demonstrate any essentially unfavorable characteristics of colored people. Yet it lends itself to argument, at all levels from violence to vitriolic philosophy. What is not arguable is that the antipathy of white for black, or black for white and the sympathy of black for black or white for white is fundamentally based upon a visual input. The visual pathways to the pleasure and displeasure areas have been utilized by prejudiced, ignorant, or clearly aggressive people to inculcate ideas that have no basis in evidential proof. Just as the uncritical person may absorb the conditioning to enjoy perfume, so he can absorb the incantations of those around him to produce preferred pathways to his displeasure areas when a particular racial visual input occurs.

The thesis of this book implies that all men are most certainly not equal, as a fact, and gives the neurological and behavioral reasons why this is so. The inequality, however, between acceptable and unacceptable, between human and subhuman, is not to be made on the same sort of spurious genetic basis as the Hitlerian shibboleth of Aryan grandeur. If we are to have segregation this can be achieved most profitably by treating race as irrelevant and concentrating attention upon what people do. The yardstick for human value is human behavior. Should extermination of one kind or another be invoked, it is the subhuman sensation seekers who should go, whatever color they are, for it is they who retard the proper development of humankind.

* * *

There are activities in which large parts of the body are used but very little mind. Most people are fully aware of their exteroceptors but are only vaguely knowledgeable about their interoceptors. Exteroceptors are the obvious sense organs, eye, ear, skin, nose, and mouth. Interoceptors are sensory receptors in internal organs.*

It is the proprioceptors that are involved with movement. These tiny, specialized nerve endings are placed very neatly in parallel rows and columns in the ligaments and membranes of all the junctions between two movable bones. They are sensitive to stretching or some other kind of distortion and as a joint is moved, for example, the lower arm flexed at the elbow, proprioceptors in the joint discharge nerve impulses which are sent into the brain. In this way, the brain receives a coded message that tells it precisely where a limb is going and how fast it is moving. These nerve impulses pass along specific tracts to the cerebellum, but on their way they meet with many synapses (nerve junctions) and so have the opportunity to go forward in many directions. As with the other senses there is every reason to believe that impulses in the kinesthetic modality reach the limbic areas of the brain. Indeed, proprioception is second only to pain in causing the most intense and widespread electrical activity in the brain.

It is not surprising that the activity called play has developed. Due to inexperience the young animal in most species is at a distinct disadvantage when it wishes to elicit sensory pleasure from the environment. But the young animal has the same ancestral brain program as the adult; it *must* keep its pleasure areas active or it will not survive. It is reasonable that it should do this on

*There are many of these. One group, those in the viscera, is discussed on pp. 202–209.

occasions by engaging in the physical romps that constitute play and so obtain activation of its pleasure areas by
its own proprioceptors.

A pointed comment on the nature of play behavior is
made by Irenaeus Eibl-Eibesfeldt of the Max Planck Institute for Behavioral Physiology, West Germany, in his
book *Ethology; The Biology of Behavior*. He points out that
from brain stimulation experiments and from behavioral
observations it can be concluded that play is musculoskel-
etal activity that is *"independent of the normally involved
superior centers"* of the brain. Some may feel that these are
hard words, but they draw attention to the scientific
basis for much that is implied in my discussion of play.
All the scientific indications are that physical activity
unrelated to immediate homeostatic needs is a function
of only the lower, ancient parts of the brain. My own
researches show that these are the pleasure areas of the
limbic system. Obviously, the higher regions *can* be used
during physical activities, but they are not *necessary*. We
can see, then, that the organized forms of physical activity created by people are simply ritualized versions of
play behavior. They are engaged in predominantly for
kinesthetic pleasure and require little more neural
equipment than that possessed by a rat. They therefore
represent subhuman behavior.

In its simple romping form play is not present in normal adults, but is the prerogative of the child, a sensorially oriented creature whose higher regions are not yet
in use. When an adult indulges in simple play behavior
—rolling on the floor, kicking his legs in the air—we
immediately suspect mental abnormality. But in many
people this particular aspect of maturation is delayed
and society allows for it by establishing a varied choice
of play behaviors—sports and athletics—each of which
has a superficial complexity of organization that renders

it recognizably distinct from romping. Mentally normal people accept these forms of play and reject simple play behavior because the organized forms allow the pretense that something adult is being done. When the mind becomes unhinged there is no longer the social need to appear different from the child, so the trappings of sports and games become superfluous and romping supervenes.

The physical activities themselves and the people engaging in them may be classified according to the amount of proprioceptive pleasure involved. The really enthusiastic sportsman, professional or amateur, stands at one end of the scale as an individual whose personality requires a high proprioceptive sensory input; he wishes to spend the major portion of his life in the infantile pursuit of play behavior. At the opposite end of the scale is the person whose makeup demands that he avoid sports and games, and in between these two extremes comes the great mass of the population with widely varying amounts of muscular activity in their lives. From what has been said, this scale is also one of mental maturity, and multiple testing of people asked to take up a sport has shown that the rapidity with which a sport is learned and the extent to which it is engaged in is directly proportional to the individual's degree of extroversion and immaturity.

Within the framework of acceptable play behavior for adults it is possible to discern a pattern to suit varying degrees of desire for proprioceptive pleasure. For the immature person whose predilection for kinesthetic pleasure is allied with a gregarious personality there are the team games, ranging from cricket through the slightly tougher baseball to the rough and tumble of soccer and the all-out furor of rugby. For the less gregarious, society provides the range of two-man encounters, which go from the serenity of golf, through table tennis, badminton, lawn tennis, and squash to the slash-poke of fencing, thumping of boxing, and limb-wrenching of wrestling. When the childish impulse to play is coupled with even greater self-centeredness, the individual may choose to walk, run, jump, or throw things about. The mental deficiencies of ardent sportsmen are discussed more fully in Dr. A. R. Beisser's psychiatric monograph, *The Madness in Sports*, where it is shown that such deficiencies are present continuously, not only when the individual is actually engaged in sport.

In larger social terms these behaviors stand in marked contrast to the muscular movements found in activities like carpentry with which something endures beyond

the movements, even if it is only a simple pipe rack. This type of muscular activity is engaged in primarily as a creative effort. The higher centers are used as a source of pleasure while the muscles are only ancillary. It needs no emphasizing that the whole progress of human society has been a sequence of creations, although not all of them are universally acclaimed as advantageous. Nor should it need emphasizing that sports and games are entirely noncreative; no game yet played has had any lasting effect on human well-being. The Olympics create no enduring benefit for the world; they simply represent a gigantic organized and commercialized playtime. One might understandably form the view that such events are taken with too great seriousness when it is realized that in them people are doing very badly what lower animals do very well. One might wonder whether the assessment of human value has become distorted when there is so much fervor and acclamation involved in the award of a medal to someone who cannot swim as well as a penguin, run as fast as a cheetah, or jump as well as a kangaroo. The medal is awarded because everyone else is even worse at these accomplishments. One might question whether the dire events and profound problems of the modern world are intelligently consistent with an average of four to five pages of national newspaper being devoted to the ephemeral phenomena of parochial athletics. One might consider deeply the fact that the day after the first successful moon drive the first news item on every New York radio station was about a football player's ankle. In the overall view, one might well conclude that playtime has been very much overdone.

What is both pathetic and serious is that the pretensions and preciousness of commercialized professional (and highly organized amateur) sport have taken this proprioceptive pleasure away from the masses, who now almost consider themselves to be sportsmen if they look at and read about sporting events. Obviously it is easier to be a football player sitting in an armchair in front of a TV set, but biology makes clear that it is not as much fun. The loss of a sensible modicum of this physical brain-pleasure may have untoward repercussions. As Professor G. M. Carstairs has pointed out in the *British Journal of Psychiatry*,* the physical fitness of college students has been steadily declining while sport has become increasingly commercialized. Given the present undeniable situation that a childish propensity for proprioceptive stimulation is widespread up to middle age or later, the reduction of this input to a small minority of the population might well be a decisive factor in social unease. If the spurious values of professional sports were exploded and proprioceptive pleasure became a part of most people's lives—*at the end of a period of human work* —perhaps other more harmful sensory inputs would be reduced. This would only be the case if sporting events were not used by the uncritical mind to assess human value; kicking a ball through goal posts accomplishes nothing, but is tremendous fun; winning a sporting contest does not make a person a better man, only a more joyful animal.

A popular misconception about these physical activities is that they represent an essentially masculine way of life. This idea neglects the observed fact that some women engage in almost every kind of sport, and it bypasses the fact that play behavior occurs equally in the young males and females of all species. Predominant involvement in sporting activities represents a lack of acceptance of an adult role in society. Such individuals always exhibit during that involvement (and frequently

*114(1968): 1049.

at other times, too, on the evidence) neither masculinity nor femininity; they have the neuter mental state of the child. Quoting from Professor Carstairs again, men may arguably find an outlet for aggressive drives in sport but "only at the cost of regressing to a relatively puerile attitude of dependency and egocentricity, and if the popular idealization of the athletic hero is allowed to go unchecked quite serious distortions of value-judgment may develop."* This is only one of many pieces of evidence that by and large, women are more mature than men, that is, they are more likely to obtain activation of their pleasure areas by adult means.

Rather less competitive and pretentious than sport is dancing, a widespread physical activity unrelated to homeostatic needs and requiring a minimum of help from the higher regions. Undoubtedly the modern dance hall, ballroom or pop, may lead on occasions to combat or coition or both. But so do many other activities not connected with dancing; they are not the objects of the dance. In dancing the sensory reward is the barrage of nerve impulses from joint receptors. The impetus to dance is no different from the impetus in a crocodile to crawl for an electrical kiss. Although this is perhaps not as obvious in classical styles of dance, it must be very plain in the random gyrations that constitute the contemporary pop scene and are reminiscent of the "chimpanzee hop."

As with the superfluous rules, techniques, and uniforms of sports, attempts have been made to incorporate the higher regions into dance, resulting in the ritualized patterns of ballet. Here, too, actual participation is limited and most ballet lovers are watchers, but ballet is really a part of multiple sensory activities.

* *Op. cit.*

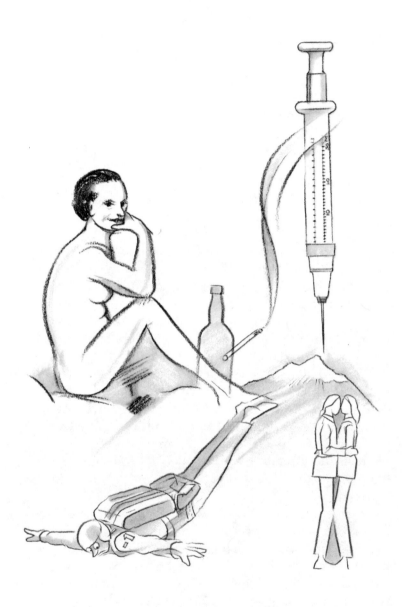

Osborn

Chapter 8

The Search for Multiple Pleasures

TOURISM, TOBACCO, DRUGS, DRINK, SEX AND FEAR

The acquisition of pleasure by using more than one sense at a time is rare in lower animals for it is more or less limited to sexual behavior. With humans, however, many activities are plurimodal and in these the higher regions may play a considerable part both in the thinking out of what to do and of how to do it. Simple and obvious examples are the theater, cinema, and television, where the visual and auditory senses are the determining factors in the form of entertainment, but in which creative thinking may have a major role. Activities such as swimming are also plurimodal, for proprioceptive pleasure is added to the bodywide cutaneous stimulation of the water, but the activity is essentially bereft of higher region pleasure. Swimming for the mere fun of it is found only in mammals at quite a low level; our relatives among the primates avoid it whenever possible. When man gilds the lily of sensory pleasure he descends profoundly in the evolutionary scale.

It is possible that this search for heightened sensory pleasure, carried out in ignorance of the way in which our body works, has led to some of the ills of society. A well-known principle of psychology and neurophysiology is "stimulus overload" and there is a neural "stimulus barrier" that is unconsciously and involuntarily dropped like a "safety curtain" when the stimulus situation becomes too intense. It is likely that under conditions of unimodal sensory pleasure-seeking an appropriate level of excitation of the pleasure areas is rarely exceeded. The fact that intense unnatural stimuli in a single mode *can* cause dislocation of brain mechanisms is emphatically demonstrated in the loss of consciousness that occurs when a bright light is "flickered" at a person. Few people can withstand such light; when flashes of about six per second enter the eye, the great majority become mentally disoriented in a minute or two, then become convulsive as disruption spreads to the motor system and finally the stimulus is blotted out by a temporary coma. But the stimulus barrier is more likely to be in use, albeit less dramatically, as a result of multimodal stimulus input.

It is perhaps not too far-fetched to wonder whether, when thousands of people have experienced several hours of the intense multimodal sensory input of a ball game—with its visual cavortings, auditory shouting, proprioceptive waving and jumping, and the autonomic excitement reactions, the stimulus barrier is at least partially lowered at the end of the game and under those conditions a very slight displeasurable sensory input may provoke exaggerated aggression and even violence in some people. On the other hand, individuals may experience a feeling of depletion when the game is over and are impelled to commit unprovoked acts of vandalism on their way home so that activation of their pleasure areas is not suddenly reduced but gradually attenuated to their ordinary living levels. Vandalism and violence seldom follow the unimodal experience of concerts of classical music.

Although there is a demonstrable tendency for people and lower animals to seek more varied and more complex routes from one place to another, in long-term conditions, especially when the sensory input is not under the control of the individual, the principle of stimulus overload can be seen in operation. The stimulus barrier mechanisms could be proposed as the neural basis for the overwhelming preference that people are showing for the short-time stimulus barrage experienced with air travel. Many people, traveling by the more traditional and much more time-consuming train and ship, arrive at their destinations in what they describe as a fatigued state, but in fact they have used up very little energy during the journey. It is not fatigue of the muscles but fatigue of the pleasure areas due to protracted bombardment with unselected stimuli. This can be so strong that often they seek sensory deprivation by a few hours in bed. The gradual demise of railway and shipping lines, which developed partly to provide greater sensory input, may be attributed in this way to the electrical activities in the pleasure areas.

The enormous increase in car ownership cannot readily be explained in terms of the need for travel, since various alternatives are available. The vast majority of motorists enjoy driving for they do not drive for purely utilitarian purposes. Here again one can see how the subhuman propensity for multimodal stimuli, in this case visual, physical, and autonomic, fight or flight, has fostered a giant industry that seems as though it may crush the very source of pleasure it set out to produce. Much driving is professional and necessary but it is the amateur motorist who clogs the roads, pollutes the air, and creates one of society's biggest unsolved problems.

Another related form of multimodal pleasure accounts for the multimillion-dollar holiday trade. Travel brochures have little to say about the intellectual pleasure that will be obtained at the various resorts, but are eloquent in their description of the gustatory, tactile, and visual stimuli provided. If it seems to be stretching the present theory too far to claim that tourism is based upon activating the pleasure areas sensorially, one has only to guess the degree of success that would be obtained by a resort which advertised only one form of sensory pleasure, for example the unremitting sunshine of a mid-Sahara oasis.

The current increase in multisensory pleasure-seeking is also seen in boating, said to be the second most popular outdoor activity in the United States. In boating, especially when sails are used, the vestibular sense of balance is stimulated by the rolling and pitching motion, the proprioceptive sense is activated by the ritualistic rope-handling, and there is much visual and auditory input. Coupled with these sensations is the strong autonomic input with much boating that, judging from the tales of derring-do in yacht club bars, is an integral component of sailing pleasure for some people. But with boating, too, man is overdoing it and this particular search for plurimodal sensory pleasure is steadily crowding out the sailing areas with moorings and marinas. There is much criticism of the great size of some marinas and the small amount of boating done from them. Clearly there are people who can transfer easily their wish for subhuman pleasures from actual boating to the multiple sensations offered by a thriving marina. In such a way can commercial interests manipulate the physiology of the brain and thereby behavior, without using a single electrode.

The repetitive and in some degree obsessional manner in which devotees engage in multimodal sensory behaviors, often exhibiting frustration and discontent when prevented from doing so, is reminiscent of addiction and raises the subject of drug-taking. It is an extremely complex one that cannot be explained by a single cause. However, it seems likely that at least part of the mixture of factors that lead to addiction is the subhuman search for multiple sensory pleasures. Despite the differences between the effects of various stimulant drugs, they have the common feature of increasing the person's awareness in all sensory modes. With drugs such as the amphetamines, the pep pills, this increased sensitivity in several modes applies to the natural external stimuli of the environment. Stimulant drugs increase the rate of lever-pressing for intracranial self-stimulation and indicate a lowered threshold of response in the limbic pleasure areas. This simple neural feature of heightened awareness of the environment has led to philosophizing that such drug-taking in some way sharpens the intellect and confers greater brain power. The spuriousness of the argument is obvious, once one recognizes that the drugs simply render sensory pleasure more easily available from trifling stimuli. Some people's minds are adept at convincing themselves that what they particularly like is also of value to them, and they may well be right on occasions, but it has little to do with brain power. This view would have to be changed, of course, if a drug-taker ever produced something of enduring worth with his brain power that could not be produced any other way.

Drugs such as LSD have the power of causing distortion of perception so that ordinary objects appear absorbingly interesting. They also enable completely new sensory stimuli to be manufactured by the brain in the form of visual, auditory, and tactile hallucinations—a sort of delirium tremens. They are so potent in causing activation of the pleasure areas that animals will stop pressing the lever for intracranial self-stimulation entirely when dosed with LSD. It seems that people, too, rarely engage in useful activity when "on a trip."

An individual constructed in a way and leading a life such that his pleasure areas are adequately stimulated and his displeasure areas largely inactive is hardly likely to seek the phenomena provided by drugs. Whatever the personal and social problems of drug addicts, they reduce to a situation of unacceptably low levels of activation of the pleasure areas. Pleasure then is sought on the subhuman sensory level in a way that makes the participation of others unnecessary. At first sight it is a strange paradox that young people are now presented with a wider range of more intense sensory pleasures than ever before and yet distressingly larger numbers of them are becoming involved with drug addiction. One may wonder whether the problem would have arisen if technology and commerce had applied itself to providing a wealth of nonsensory pleasures for young human beings with the same vigor that it has used in capitalizing on their subhuman features.

Tranquillizing drugs come into a different category and are in many ways similar to alcoholism. Small quantities of alcohol have a stimulating effect, accounting for the major fraction of its use, but large amounts, as taken by alcoholics, have an anesthetizing action on the brain. In large amounts it can even be used in emergency surgery. Personality studies on alcoholics bear out the neurophysiological basis of their addiction. Far from seeking subhuman sensory pleasures, the alcoholic is attempting and often succeeding in reducing the input to his displeasure areas, mainly from his higher regions. With many highly active executives, alcohol is used as a kind of chemical stimulus barrier that shuts out the pressures. The methods of Alcoholics Anonymous when treating alcoholics reveal an intuitive understanding of the need to reduce unpleasant stimuli rather than supply pleasant sensory input. The close connection between alcoholism and the pleasure areas has been clearly indicated by studies at the Brain Research Laboratory of Syracuse University. Solutions of alcohol are normally avoided by all animals but when the lateral hypothalamus, which contains highly potent pleasure and displeasure areas, was electrically stimulated in rats, the animals drank inebriating quantities of alcohol daily for as long as twenty-five days. Interestingly, they did not become addicted for they refused alcohol on all occasions when brain stimulation was not occurring. This strongly suggests that "compulsive drinking" requires specific events in the environment that cause neural activation of limbic brain regions.

Addiction to tobacco, once exclusive to primitive tribes with few sources of pleasure, is now a routine feature of the highest technological communities and is no longer restricted to periods of quiet meditation. There can be no doubt that there are several sensory components to smoking. There is stimulation of the lips, of the buccal cavity, and of the lung membranes and in addition there is the proprioceptive input from the movements of assembling the materials of smoking and of the smoking process itself. When a person is marginally worried about his work, the down-going impulses from his higher regions to the displeasure areas can in

some degree be ameliorated by up-coming sensory impulses, produced easily by smoking, and work does not
have to stop as it might with other sensory pleasures. It
would not be socially acceptable for a person to deal with
deep anxiety, for example in regard to a relative undergoing an operation, by going to the cinema or playing
football, but smoking would be and so here, too, the
multimodal input from smoking helps to keep up activity in the pleasure areas. It is significant that many
people who try to give up smoking by eating sweets fail
dismally; clearly the unimodal gustatory pleasure of can-
dies is insufficient to compensate for the more embracing
pleasures of tobacco.

A process of selection has operated in those who
choose to go to the cinema or watch television or sail or
become a tourist or smoke or drink. The particular pattern of multisensory input chosen must depend upon a
great many influences, but we may accept that the ones
dealt with so far are dependent largely upon external
factors, such as the kind of parents and friends one has.
This is not the case in the selection that occurs in the
widespread multisensory activity of sexual behavior.

Although there are some common components for
both male and female in sexuality, nevertheless there are
also very sharp and distinct filters for the sensory pattern
which is acceptable in normal heterosexual behavior,
and these filters are an intrinsic property of the nervous
system. It is not possible to show under the microscope
or on the dissecting table the difference between the
male and female brain, but it can easily be done in other
ways.

In most mammals very clear quantitative observations
can be made to show the sharp distinction between male
and female in such matters as hormone levels and physical activity. The female is cyclic, she has periodic rises

and falls in blood hormones, and also in the amount that she turns an activity wheel. The male is acyclic, he is relatively steady with both these parameters. For many years it has been known that hormone levels are controlled by the anterior pituitary gland, situated at the base of the brain and connected with it by a set of short blood vessels. Experiments conducted by Professor G. W. Harris and Dr. Dora Jacobsohn showed that it is not the kind of pituitary gland an animal possesses that determines whether it behaves in a male or female fashion with regard to hormones and activity cycles. They found that when male pituitaries were transplanted into females, they did not stop cycling, and that putting female pituitaries into males did not make them cycle. These experiments were performed with rats, but have been confirmed in several ways on many higher species. Much other evidence now proves that the pituitary is the same in both male and female but that the brain above it, the hypothalamus, is not. Chemicals formed by nerve cells in the hypothalamus pass down the short blood vessels to the pituitary gland and exert a controlling influence upon it. In this way the brain controls the endocrine glands all over the body. This was first theorized by Professor Harris and has now been amply proved. Harris and I isolated the hypothalamic chemical that controls, via the pituitary, the functions of the ovary, including release of the egg. Other workers have extracted similar materials which control the other glands, and some superb biochemistry by Professor Andrew Schally at Tulane University has resulted in their analysis and synthesis. These compounds will become of great importance in human glandular medicine.

Some American research has shown that a single dose of one microgram of male sex hormone administered shortly after birth to female animals affected the hypothalamus in such a way that the animals were permanently sterile in adulthood, that is, they did not show fluctuations in hormone levels or regularly release eggs. Professor Harris took these experiments further by removing the source of male sex hormone from newborn male animals and showed that when these became adult they cycled in terms of physical activity and also, when provided with a transplanted ovary, released eggs periodically like any normal female. I worked with Harris for some years on this type of research and my own published findings indicate that in fact the male hypothalamus cycles for a short time even when the animal is untreated and then ceases to do so. Thus, in terms of brain function we are all girls for a while and then in some of us male hormone changes the brain into the male type. This is assuming that the findings in lower animals apply to man, but this is likely because they have been duplicated in a very wide range of species from rat to monkey.

There is no reason to suppose that the changes in the brain which result in distinct patterns of hormone and physical activity behavior do not also affect behavioral mechanisms. Some of my other experiments have shown that the chemicals formed in the hypothalamus which control the pituitary gland, also have an influence upon pleasure-seeking as seen by intracranial self-stimulation. Unlike so many of our other pleasures and displeasures, it seems that for the majority the kind of sensory input we find acceptable in sexual behavior is entirely dependent upon what happens to the chemistry of our brains around the time of birth, and this neural selection is infinitely more incisive than with any other form of pleasure-seeking. For example, many surveys show that, whether talked about or not, it is perfectly normal for the standard type of male to indulge in tongue kissing with a woman and, at a later stage of acquaintance, to engage in cunnilingus. Similarly, the standard female is said to enjoy tongue kissing with a male and also fellatio. On the other hand, the standard gender would find great revulsion in much the same sort of sensory input obtained homosexually.

The development and working of the pleasure area mechanisms can give rise to mental disease. Though the genesis of homosexuality is as complex as any other form of human behavior, it is possible that in at least some cases this pattern of sexuality has arisen because of a fault in the chemical environment of the brain during development. Clearly, the homosexual is not to be pilloried for something that happened even before he could talk, or perhaps even breathe. Noting the manifold problems that arise from gearing satisfying heterosexuality to the arbitrary demands of the social pattern, the homosexual is perhaps to be envied for the simplicity with which he arranges this form of multisensory pleasure. Whereas heterosexuality is an essential survival device among the lower animals, it ceased to have this function in the human long ago; procreation in its present unlimited form could prove disastrous to our race. Homosexual men and women, even if initially subject to abnormal brain chemistry, seek their bodily pleasures in ways that can do no harm to society.

On the basis of this experimental evidence attitudes that we consider to be personal and private are in fact accidental consequences of what happened to our hypothalamus about the time of birth, although the precise form in which we exhibit sexuality may be conditioned by the environment, especially with regard to the degree of overtness or covertness. Nevertheless, with regard to sexuality, the distinctions between male and female have long been clearly defined. As Desmond Morris points

out in *The Naked Ape*, the human body, unlike that of
many apes, is virtually bereft of unequivocal signs of
gender, and so man created artificial signals such as costume, hair styles, cosmetics and jewelry. All these insure
that there shall be no slip-up in providing an individual
with an appropriate sexual sensory input that will activate pleasure rather than displeasure areas.

Such artifice must be of great value to the unsophisticated mind, which needs to define its attitudes and
intentions blatantly to other equally blunt mentalities.
The current tendency of equalization of appearance,
often referred to as "unisex," is a splendid example of the
enhanced sophistication among young people to which
I will again refer. It suggests that sharper intellects are
now at work, who reject the anachronistic symbols of
gender and recognize that true masculinity and
femininity are not to be revealed by dress or hair style.
This is one example of how the younger generation dem-
onstrates clearly a closer contact with some aspects of
reality than many of their elders.

With this neurological orientation to our sexual mechanisms it is not surprising that the idea of substitutes for
sex has arisen in those societies in which the "substitutes" are available. Once it is recognized that the unique
value of sexual behavior resides in the widespread and
intense multimodal sensory input that accompanies it, it
can be seen that any activity that can result in a similarly
intense multimodal input is a candidate for the epithet
"sex substitute." However, it would be invalid to believe
that every time a person engages in multimodal stimuli
he is substituting for sex; he may be simply enjoying the
activation of his pleasure areas from the activity in its
own right. It is still not uncommon to find people, especially those of an unquestionably physical kind, who
claim that behavior involving the arts and sciences, for

example, are sublimations of the sexual urge. But several of the creative figures of the past demonstrated undoubted sexuality, sometimes to an exceptionally high degree. It does not seem reasonable to believe that the creativity of mankind is in any way a refined and transmogrified type of copulation, since most creative enterprises are not multisensory or greatly intense. On the other hand it could be argued that many *physical* activities are sublimated sex; sexually frustrated young people are often advised to go for long walks or play games or take up some other multimodal activity.

What is much more interesting is the reverse of sublimation. What appear to be forms of sexual behavior turn out upon analysis to be nothing of the kind. Much seemingly sexual interaction is only marginally concerned with sexual pleasure and is predominantly engaged in because of the need of the individual to convince himself or herself of inordinately high masculinity or femininity and to have this idea confirmed by others. Unfortunately, this is *human* behavior, as defined here, for such people derive their main pleasure not from the sexual sensory input but from the descending impulses from higher regions. Somewhat similarly, an individual who is not receiving an acceptable amount of limbic excitation from any cause, sexual or otherwise, may indulge in behavior that remedies the deficiency. Thus it can be seen that masturbation is by no means always a solitary form of sex. Many cases are recorded where masturbation is an afterthought of almost accidental stimulation of the genitals. Just as under some conditions people will suck the end of a pencil, play with their earlobes, or tug at their mustaches, so under favorable circumstances they will absentmindedly touch their genitals. After a while they become consciously aware of what they are doing and it occurs to them to continue but with more attention. If they had not been playing with their genitals they may well have simply stopped whatever they were doing and turned on the radio or TV.

Although in many cases of rape the offender is seeking sexual relief, this is not true with many others. Frequently the rapist is not in a situation that can sensibly be described as sexually impoverished and the likelihood is that he is seeking autonomic stimulation.

Briefly, the autonomic system is the branch of the nervous system that looks after automatic processes such as heartbeat, respiration, movements of the intestines, diameter of the pupil, erection of hair and sexual tissues, changes in blood pressure, and the voiding of urine and feces. Some of these functions are partially under voluntary control, but all of them are largely carried out without much thought. Since 1929 physiologists have been saying that the autonomic system is concerned with "fight or flight" because the bodily changes involved are easily evoked by these behaviors. It is common knowledge that when we are afraid our heartbeat increases, respiration speeds up, and a whole series of other responses occur, especially those that are described—quite incorrectly from the anatomical point of view—as being "in the pit of the stomach." Much of the total autonomic response is due to adrenalin which the autonomic system causes to be released from the adrenal gland. Teleologically, all these reactions have evolved in order to prepare the body for some difficult effort of aggression or defense.

However, in the relatively peaceful framework of human life in advanced communities, they have taken on an additional, quite different function. Certain regions of the limbic system, close to the pleasure areas, are concerned with the control of rage reactions and there seems little doubt that autonomic responses cause nerve impulses from various internal organs to pass into the brain and induce activation of the pleasure areas. Behavior that is involved with matters that rationally must be considered unpleasant in actual fact gives pleasure.

Pathologically, the extreme of this situation is found in the masochist and sadist but many common behaviors fit into the same category. Seldom is the average man called upon to fight or to flee but when this happens as in war, there are myriad examples of violence and danger evoking pleasure. The ebullience of Battle of Britain pilots and of members of the German Luftwaffe has been copiously documented but it is perhaps no very exceptional example of how some men derive pleasure from conflict, that is, in situations in which the autonomic system bombards their brains with nerve impulses. Many believe that, whatever is written upon the banners, some young people join in virulent protests because they enjoy the clashes with authority. Some have pointed out that it may be no coincidence that the current rise in civilian violence roughly corresponds with the time that a third world war might have been expected.

Apart from violence, people have found many other ways of experiencing autonomic pleasure, of deliberately seeking fearsome situations. The roller coaster at a fairground is a common example of human technology applied to a device for producing fear on payment of a fee. Essentially, these fairground devices are designed for the immature personality, for as Professor Eliot Slater and Professor Martin Roth write, " . . . children can derive keen pleasure from experiencing fear . . . the physical accompaniments of anxiety, the toning up of the nervous system, the prickling of the skin, the shiver down the back, even the sinking sensations in the belly, both attract and repel." The repulsion is clearly a minor component in many of these "stop-it-I-like-it" behaviors.

But the pursuit of fear as a source of pleasure is by no means limited to the fairground and battlefield; the same kind of immature pleasure-seeking is found in a number of activities which at first sight, rather like sport, have a spurious aura of adulthood. Professor David Klein of Michigan State University has recently drawn attention to the fact that the riders of the 1.4 million snowmobiles in the United States deliberately seek danger to offset the tedium of their working lives. He believes, and I agree, that a way of preventing or reducing this environment-damaging activity is simply to make the activity absolutely safe. Mountain climbing, according to my definition, must also fall into this category of immature seeking after autonomic pleasures, for nothing of any material use is accomplished by scaling high rocks. Though the attractions of mountain climbing must be manifold, including sights and smells and proprioceptive input, what permeates the whole unproductive endeavor is the difficulty and danger involved, and despite its apparent masculinity it reduces to the fairground mentality.

Only rarely does the search for autonomic multiple sensation produce some real benefit for mankind, as with aviation for the early pioneers who must have enjoyed the tremendous risks they ran. The same yardstick of benefit finds other activities measuring short, as with skydiving and parachute jumping for the fun of it. Skiing down sharp slopes and across wide crevasses may look spectacular but its only dubious value is to give autonomic pleasure to the participants and the observers. Even the single-handed, long voyage sailor must be placed in this category for it is unlikely he would wish to become involved in a similar voyage on totally calm water. His sense of achievement, albeit prolonged and adulated, is little different in its effect on the pleasure areas from the girl who manages to ride on the roller coaster without demanding to be let off. The perils at sea may account for the major quantum of many sailors' pleasures; the fun of reliving and recounting the dicing with danger can last longer than the sailing trip itself. This love of danger is odd when one remembers that civilization has been seriously concerned with making man safe from the attack of the elements. Some people seem just to insist on retrograde evolution!

However invidious it may be not to mention other immature minorities who seek their pleasures from receptors in the viscera I shall concentrate on what affects nearly all of us. There must be few people who cannot recall their sexually unsophisticated youth and how in their earliest physical encounters with the opposite sex the emotions generated were largely autonomic and only slightly sexual. This is not surprising since the adolescent is only aware of sexual emotions as an idea, talked about and read about but not experienced. The pleasures of early sexual interactions are largely composed of the physiological responses to the fear of being discovered and to the fear of what the partner will do or say if some limit is transgressed. The acuteness and intensity of the pleasure in such encounters diminishes autonomically with each sexual experience, and this may well account for the fact that the majority of human, long-term sexual relationships are unsatisfactory. The persons involved, unaware that the initial exquisite pleasure is predominantly autonomic rather than sexual, continually try to recapture the intensity of pleasure they once had, not realizing that this is impossible neurologically because the fearsome situation no longer exists. In this state of ignorance of basic neurophysiology, it is not surprising that partners blame each other for a "cooling off" of response and seek to renew their adolescent rapture with someone else. At first this is successful because the fearsome conditions are back again, but inevitably it fails after a while because the same brain mechanisms are inexorably at work. Thus we may explain materialistically the multiple marriage pattern that has unhappily exposed the United States to much criticism. In just such a way can electric charges in circumscribed brain regions, in a culture too technological to admit biology as the science of life, almost make a laughing stock of a nation on whom the whole world depends for its future well-being.

In those fortunately not too rare long-term sexual relationships, which continue to give pleasure of a sexual kind, which sustain and fortify the participants against many vicissitudes, the simple, easily acquirable feature is that neither partner is searching for immature autonomic sensory input during sexual congress. They are not afraid of each other's reactions. They simply conjoin to enjoy togetherness rather than apartness. They exhibit, without morality, religion, or philosophy, the only sensible, rational distinction between love and lust.

Considerations such as these raise the probability that much of the sexual permissiveness, which is said to be a feature of the current adolescent scene, is not so much sexual but rather behavior that utilizes the trappings of sex in order to obtain autonomic pleasure, as some behavior uses the trappings of ideologically induced violence or crime for the same purpose. The problem is that although the protestor and delinquent may well recognize the autonomic font of their actions the person engaging in sex does not. A large number of repetitions of violence or crime are needed to dull the autonomic input, because danger is ever present in these pursuits, but only a relatively few sexual encounters with the same partner are required to reduce drastically autonomic sensation. The continued search for renewed autonomic pleasure is one cause of promiscuity.

The ready availability of women for sexual relations without much trouble and expense makes the frequent occurrence of rape at first difficult to account for. However, some such cases become understandable when it is realized that they are essentially nonsexual in their motivation. A person who yearns for autonomic pleasure and equates this with sexual activity rather than, say, sailing, may well, when for one reason or another deprived of his usual source of multimodal pleasure, avoid straightforward consenting sex and become involved in rape. Sexual encounters with new partners, even when consenting, do have some of the features of rape. Often, too, the female allows advances to be made in order to experience autonomic responses and only begins to resist when the affair takes on an undeniable sexual aspect. There are many instances in which the male has confessed to utter astonishment when the female has abruptly terminated an interlude that he thought, from her reactions, had been going to schedule. If on the other hand the male is the one in pursuit of autonomic pleasure, the fun only really starts when the girl begins to object, and the scene is then set for an ugly rape.

The search for autonomic pleasure is present at a very early age and may well become one of the dominant forms of pleasure-seeking in some children. The small child who raids the larder and steals something to eat is seldom hungry and is not usually seeking gustatory pleasure. He is enjoying the fear of discovery and possible retribution. As with Professor Klein's technique with the snowmobilers, one way to drill out such behavior is to make larder-raiding and similar naughtiness quite safe

autonomically, by treating it with emotional indifference and applying a negative reward by withdrawing
the nonemotional pleasures the child obtains.

This awareness of autonomic sensory pleasure makes
it possible to formulate a clear concept of the anatomy
and physiology of courage. Courage is no longer an idea
or a mere state of mind; it is behavior controlled by brain
function. Some people consider that courage is demonstrated when a person deliberately enters upon situations of danger with no apparent anxiety, such as the
lone sailors and many servicemen in action. These individuals are simply seeking pleasure and therefore cannot have courage attributed to them. Courage, if it is to
have any human value at all, is found in those whose
displeasure areas are activated by the autonomic input of
fearsome circumstances and yet whose morality,
maturity, and responsibility—their human use of higher
brain regions—induces them to inhibit the natural aversive behavior. In these individuals their behavior causes
pleasure from the activity in higher regions associated
with the knowledge that their risk-taking is for some
rational good. Courage is never found in people who are
not afraid, for they are engaged in subhuman behavior.

To some it may seem a misfortune to see the disappear-
ance of these activities based upon autonomic pleasure.
The "sense of adventure" would have gone, the "spirit"
of physical accomplishment would be missing. If one
values that kind of adventure and spirit then the argument is tenable. But if mankind no longer sought autonomic pleasure it is unlikely that such large numbers of
men would agree to take up arms against another body
of men about whom they know nothing. If the pursuit
of fear as pleasure were not present, perhaps the crowds
involved in riots would be smaller or even nonexistent.
Social workers would have no difficulty in knowing to

what extent the spirit of adventure (another name for fearsome pleasure) plays in the genesis of young delinquents. There are many other examples to indicate that in the absence of deeds of derring-do, although life for some would be less flamboyant, it would also be more peaceful, more dignified, and more mature.

Although it can be predicted that the inexorable forces of evolution will eventually remove the childish forms of autonomic pleasure-seeking, there is every reason to believe that fearsome situations will continue. For eternity there will be plenty of occasions for courage, as there are now, only not so much hullabaloo is made about some of them. The average person can have little emphatic awareness of the great anxiety and acute fear which besets a surgeon during an operation of any magnitude, or to conceive the courage and determination needed to amputate a limb. Only by men bringing the displeasure of fear under the control of higher regions, rather than enjoying it, can they perform surgery that is responsible for so many people being alive today.

It would be interesting to see how many racing yachtsmen, mountain climbers, or parachutists could bring themselves to separate a man from one of his limbs or from his stomach. Some, I am sure, could do this. But even then I wonder whether they would enjoy it, and whether they would make conversational capital out of it later. When autonomic pleasure is the mainstay of a person's pleasurable life, there is little room for human behavior.

The Thinker

Chapter 9

The Thinkers

ROOTS OF HUMAN BEHAVIOR

The essential feature of all behavior which can be classed as human is that the limbic pleasure areas are activated by nerve impulses generated in the higher regions of the brain. These higher regions are not simply any part of the cerebral cortex but comprise the tertiary association areas, those areas of cortex which are especially large in the human brain. It is here that thinking occurs and it is in these thinking brain regions that the descending nerve impulses are generated that mediate human behavior.

It is most important to understand that the proper functioning of these regions depends upon the brain having received a large, long-term input of all kinds of sensation. There is no evidence to indicate that the higher brain regions have any significant degree of independent function. Various brain areas, in the hypothalamus for example, have an intrinsic ability to maintain such vital functions as heartbeat and respiration, beginning long before birth and continuing through life irrespective of, though influenced by, experience. But in this respect as in many others, the higher cortical regions are utterly different from lower brain structures.

Our thinking regions are to all intents and purposes nonfunctional at birth. With the passage of time, provided the time encloses sensory experience, nerve cells in the higher brain regions make physical and functional contact with each other and with nerve cells in nonthinking parts of the brain. The most essential contact to be made is with the pleasure areas for without it, according to the theory of pleasure-seeking, human behavior cannot occur. Given this prime requirement, the next most important neural process during development after birth is the establishment of interconnecting pathways within the thinking regions so that intermodal information may be dealt with and, even more important, so that the gigantic storehouse of memory may be stocked with readily available material. At every point along this line of development sensory information is of the utmost importance. Gradually, as brain maturation proceeds, the importance of sensory input declines. It never becomes irrelevant but eventually the higher regions are sufficiently developed anatomically and informationally so that interchange between the thinking regions and the pleasure areas can become largely self-sustaining. When that happens, a mind is present and the highest, in the neurological sense, form of human behavior can occur.

The phenomenon of obtaining pleasure from thinking in the total absence of apposite sensory input is not, as many people seem to believe, the prerogative of an elite with high income, high education, high intelligence, and highbrow attitudes. It is a feature of every person's life. But the common view of thinking pleasure as elitist is based on good evidence if we observe only those forms that come to wide public notice, because the dominant behavior of the vast majority of the population is subhuman. Those who derive their major pleasures from thinking stand out in sharp contrast, targets for admiration or ridicule depending upon the viewpoint (the phylogenetic position) of the observer.

One of the earliest forms that thinking pleasure took was thinking about thought, which is sometimes called philosophy. Although the etymological meaning is "lover of knowledge," this only arose historically because there was so little else to know about. Until a few men began to examine the environment by doing something about it, men merely wondered what it was all about and thought about their own and others' cogitations. A man of learning had little to learn in the modern sense of the term, so although he was a sophist his mental application was almost entirely directed to examining how his own and other sophists' thoughts related to nature. This nonempirical method of questioning the fabric of existence has continued for many centuries of recorded time and is represented now by the many departments of philosophy in the world's universities and the abounding schools of philosophy to one of which we all, wittingly or not, owe allegiance. With the gradual recruitment of effective manpower, the subject has become fragmented so that there are now subdivisions such as moral philosophy, scientific philosophy, educational philosophy and, most pervasive, political philosophy.

Those who hold the widespread belief that philosophy and philosophers are rarefied, out of touch with reality and not to be taken seriously, have something to be said for their view. Some philosophers must inevitably be as ludicrous as some engineers. But every political system the world has ever known is based upon philosophical considerations. This should be obvious in the case of Communism, which sprang from the well-publicized ponderings of Karl Marx, which were based upon a profound knowledge of academic philosophies. Less obvious perhaps, but no less publicized, the policies of Adolf Hitler arose from a highly garbled and distorted understanding of philosophical systems. Hitler must have been one of the least sensorially oriented individuals who ever lived, obtaining his pleasure from the rambling, disjointed constructs of his intellect, and yet his behavior, neurologically speaking, was human. I do not claim that human behavior is necessarily of enduring value; only that sensory behavior cannot be.

While few would doubt the harmfulness of human behavior as exhibited by the Hitlers, Khans, and Caesars, millions applaud and live by the intellectual pleasure-seekings of Marx, Lincoln, Cromwell, Mao, and Franco. The philosophical realm of "pure thought" pervades all our lives to some extent. We are all philosophers in what we think about the form and content of our thought processes, constructing a more or less stable and well-defined "personal philosophy." We differ from the serious philosophers in that we take no great pains to remove incompatibilities in our thought systems and use no rigid tests to determine their relation to the truth. The yardstick for the serious philosopher is consistency with fact; for the common man the criterion is expediency, which is an abbreviation for "arranging things to activate the pleasure areas."

Somewhat similarly, the field of abstract thinking called theology has impinged upon the majority of the world's populations. All religions, even the old pagan ones, have a theological basis—they are the practical aspect of history. The evidence in Frazer's *Golden Bough* suggests that man began to derive pleasure from thinking about gods very soon after he stopped thinking so much about bananas. It reflects, no doubt, his early concern about the causes of effects in the environment. Despite the eventual recognition and subsequent definition of many physical causes for effects that were hitherto attributed to gods, some individuals retain the ability to derive pleasure from crediting the as yet unexplained phenomena to gods. They then go on to describe the properties, personalities and propensities of these totally undemonstrable entities and their imaginary interrelationships with man. In order to deal adequately with god-man relations, they even find it necessary to ascribe to gods some effects whose causes are perfectly well understood. When metal fatigue causes the tail of an airplane to crumple and results in the total destruction of an airliner and its human cargo, it is not infrequently attributed to "God's will," which, believers admit, is a little peculiar.

Clearly a major attraction of theology is that one's beliefs and explanations cannot be shown to be false. For those who are uninterested in being proved right, the theological field is wide open for the application of a fertile imagination. It can provide all the activation of the pleasure areas that can be obtained by constructing systematic dogma which is untestable and in which the inconsistency of elements is even considered to be a virtue. Further intellectual pleasure is then obtained by long-term discussion of the interrelations and incompatibilities of the various imaginary subsystems of omnipotence, based on scripture, tradition or reason. Oddly enough, for an area of thinking which is supposed to be concerned with the font of goodness, tolerance and kindness, contrasting theological views have led at different times to extreme degrees of cruelty and violence, as seen for example in the Spanish Inquisition, the papal-inspired tortures, and the holocaustic religious wars of the sixteenth and seventeenth centuries.

The intellectual pleasures of deism and political philosophy have the common feature, not shared by other abstract systems, of being readily combinable with distinctly subhuman autonomic inputs to the pleasure areas. An agnostic could be pardoned for wondering what a sensible god must think of his earthly champions and their devilish behavior.

Those who have labored through texts of philosophy and theology will know that in these subjects man's powers of intelligent communication through language are stretched to their limits. Indeed, with some authors it almost seems that language has not yet evolved sufficiently to be a vehicle for their complex ideas. Considerations such as this may prompt some people to become involved in yet another prolific area of nonsensory pleasure, linguistics. The limbic pleasure areas are activated by thinking about the form, structure and interrelationships of the world's languages. Linguists are not usually overly concerned with what is being said but with how it is said. It may be thought that this means of pleasure-seeking is remote from the real world, but here too the case is different. Though linguistics has dawdled along for a century or two with nothing much to show for its existence, the modern linguist, basing his ideas on that stockpile of doctrine, has made himself noticed by workers in many disciplines, including neurophysiology, psychology, psychiatry, and sociology. What will eventually emerge from this unexpected collision of hitherto unrelated intellectual disciplines is difficult to predict, for opinions are still sharply divided; but what is beyond doubt is that everyone involved will learn more about his own subject and it is highly probable that whole new schools of thought will appear, and inevitably affect the general population in various ways.

Even "purer" than philosophy and theology is logic. While philosophy, broadly, concerns itself with such matters as why we think, how we obtain knowledge and what we do with our concepts, logic tries to determine the proper methods of thinking. The deductive branch of logic establishes the rules by which separate thoughts must be interrelated if "rational" conclusions are to be reached, with little interest in what relation the conclusions bear to reality. At first sight, it may seem that any individual who obtains most of his limbic activity by engaging in deductive logic plays little part in continuing man's world. This is far from being true. The fact that deductive logic is unconcerned with what is being thought about allows its principles to be expressed symbolically. For example, very simple logic tells that "If all Xs are Y and this Z is an X, then this Z is Y," without bothering what X, Y and Z really are or even if they exist at all. This statement has an algebraic aura because algebra and the whole of all mathematical systems are simply particular forms of deductive logic in which the Xs, Ys and Zs have quantitative value. A moment's consideration of the roles of algebra in engineering, geometry in building, and arithmetic in commerce shows the degree to which deductive logic, that area of pure thinking-pleasure, manipulates our lives. And yet these examples only scratch the surface of the great mathematical edifice that overhangs the human scene.

I have mentioned only areas in which deductive logic is concerned with tangible matters, which are obviously useful, but if he cares to look in the right places the skeptic will find that initially totally unrealistic mathematical systems, for example, non-Euclidean geometries or Boolean algebras erected for the sheer intellectual pleasure of it, have later been found to be of inestimable value in practical matters that are part of the skeptic's life. Some men, too, have derived great pleasure from contemplating the idea of the square root of minus one, symbolized as i. Unlike gods, this nonexistent entity has been vital in the development of radio, television, and space technology. All in all it is likely that there is not a single person on earth who has not benefited, and benefited greatly, from the fact that some individuals have activated their pleasure areas by playing with deductive logic.

The other branch, inductive logic, is not so much concerned with the rationality of thought interrelations as with the relation between thoughts and objects. It is concerned with such matters as how to make reliable observations, how to seek primary causes and rule out interfering factors, how to construct hypotheses founded on known facts and how to verify or disprove them by discovering new facts. Broadly, inductive logic formulates strategic rules by which the tactics of discovery may be most confidently, effectively, and profitably carried out. As with deductive logic, induction can play an important part in our everyday lives; it is even used to discover why the car will not start. But its greatest impact upon mankind comes from its systematic application in the fields of science and technology.

When the Aristotelian approach to understanding the universe was complemented by experimentation, science came into being. A new way of seeking intellectual pleasure had arisen in which the seeker no longer sat and thought but used his motor and sensory systems and went out and did things. He differed, and still does, from other people who use these systems in that to the scientist the activity and the sensory input were not the final goals of his efforts, nor indeed were they always pleasurable. The scientist, like the philosopher and theologian, obtains his greatest amounts of activity in the pleasure areas as a result of thinking activity, largely in the form of solving self-imposed problems, whereas most people try to give problems a wide berth or find someone else to solve them.

Currently, the abrupt distinction between science and technology has become greatly blurred as a result of the impact of applied science upon everyday life. People will speak, for example, of scientists trying to find better ways of storing meat, or of beating pollution, when in fact scientists could have nothing to do with these endeavors. If a person wears a white coat, works in a laboratory, and is involved with technical matters, such as what chemical to put into bread to keep it softer for a few days, he is falsely presumed to be a scientist. The essentially different pleasure goals of scientists and technologists have been almost lost to sight, so that intelligent people are led to recommend university training for entrants to industrial laboratories, with increasingly deleterious effects upon university function, industrial expertise, and student well-being. The scientist, traditionally, is an individual whose pleasures come from finding out how things work, or more elegantly, unraveling the laws of nature. He has in fact little professional interest in the things themselves. The zoologist, for example, will not work up any emotion about a single animal, as does the naturalist and pet-lover. The chemist will not enthuse about the uses of saturated hydrocarbons, so much as about how their physical and chemical properties fit into the broad scheme of substantial interactions.

The technologist, on the other hand, does not demand such unadulterated intellectual pleasure. Obviously he needs a higher than average requirement for thinking-pleasure in order to acquire the knowledge of the basic sciences which he applies. But the technologist's main pleasure comes not from finding out how the natural universe works, but rather from how to make an unnatural universe work, how to utilize the findings of pure science to create productive changes in the environment. The technologist's aims include sensory pleasure-seeking and in his general life he is likely to lean more toward the sensory than the intellectual. His "lifeline" from the pleasure areas is not so much a concern with ideas for the ideas' sake, but with ideas for man's material, sensory sake. He certainly requires a different training from the scientist, though some areas of study will inevitably overlap. No single course of instruction can adequately supply both these needs. Thus a realistic understanding of how pleasure-seeking mechanisms operate can provide neurophysiological bases for the higher education in these disciplines and perhaps reduce student discontent at the same time as providing the community and commerce with appositely-trained graduates.

By separating clearly the preparation of scientists and technologists, people might be a little better able to distinguish between their different effects upon man's life and environment. The human behavior of the scientist produces knowledge, which the rest of us may enjoy for its own sake or which we may exploit for our material pleasures. It is a fact of nature that no scientific discovery has in itself caused harm. Nor, of course, has any scientific discovery in itself caused any good, other than the intellectual pleasure it may have given. The very manner of life of scientists, the kind of pleasure-seeking role of science, precludes pervading advantage or disadvantage to mankind in general. Where there have been consequences stemming from scientific discovery, as in the cure of disease or the design of weapons, neither praise nor blame can sensibly be attached to the scientific community. The responsibility lies squarely on the shoulders of those who have applied the new knowledge to human affairs. To make recommendations along the lines of stopping scientific research or demanding that scientists themselves should exercise some kind of social control over the natural directions of their research, is to acknowledge total defeat by the general population in the control of its own pleasure-seeking proclivities.

When the findings of science are so abused that artificial meat fibers are placed on the market, it should honestly be recognized that some people, free from governmental intervention, are applying science in order to make money out of the sensory pleasure-seeking of the masses. There is nothing new in this. Castigating science and scientists for the ills produced by mindlessly-administered refined sugar or mindfully-administered cyclamates is to confuse the basic causal mechanisms. For reasons of prejudice it is a refusal to countenance the exact analogy of commercial exploitation of science in many other sensory fields, so that fortunes can be made by pushers of the auditory dope called pop and the visual dope called television. Even worse, the concentration of antiscientific vilification against weapons and military affairs in general obscures the basic cause of human conflict—the subhuman desire for competition, an indelible hallmark of the jungle. Despite the unfortunate ways in which some of them express their views, the younger generation's almost universal proclamation of antimilitary sentiments must weigh heavily upon governments inclined toward conflict. The older generation may have much rightly to deplore in young people, but at least the young do not seek animal pleasure in quasi-patriotic slaughter. Their vociferous complaints against the technologists of war may well eventually reduce the travesty of human brain function that results in napalm and poison gases. It is to be hoped that soon the young will turn their concentrated attention upon the manufacture of processed foods, some of which are almost certainly having a greater long-term deleterious effect upon the health of humanity than a major war might do. They can count on the hearty cheers of practically every scientist in their nonviolent protests, sit-ins and blockages of mass-produced, chemically loaded, artificially flavored, profit-making robot fodder. Just so long as they recognize that science is innocent of both war and toxicity and that technology exploits subhuman desires.

Scientists, then, are free from the taint of evil and the halo of good, which, incidentally, makes awards in the basic sciences such as the Nobel Prize irrational, even if this were not so for other reasons, such as the impossibility of attributing any significant discovery to one or two researchers. However, this anomaly probably does little harm. But with scientists as with sportsmen there is a stratification of degrees of sensory pleasure in the work, which probably reflects the evolutionary level of the individual. Least sensory of all is theoretical physics, in which the scientist need have no sensory contact with anything but reading matter. As with logic, the apparent rarefication of theoretical physics is no indication of its practical possibilities. Albert Einstein, probably the world's greatest theoretical physicist, never handled any of the sensory phenomena he studied. His major pleasures were completely independent of sensory input; most activation of his limbic pleasure areas, except that involved in merely staying alive or relaxing with his violin, was derived from thousands of hours of concentrated thinking about what other people had done with magnets, electric currents, light, clocks and measuring instruments. When this pure human behavior was combined with the powerful tool of deductive logic, Einstein summed up his cogitations with the equation $E = mc^2$. A few symbols, which most people cannot understand, do not seem much to show for all that effort, and yet this equation and the reasoning behind it opened up a completely fresh approach to the whole range of physical phenomena. It showed clearly the acute limitations of many previous concepts and led inexorably to atomic weapons, atomic power, space flight technology and many other less spectacular innovations. The general concept of relativity has permeated most other sciences, too, and is now used even in human psychology. Einstein is a particularly dramatic example of what pleasure-seeking in theoretical physics can do, but there are many other lesser minds dotted through time and space whose pleasure-thinking has affected and will affect the lives of us all.

The practical branches of physics are still rather impoverished in terms of sensation, for apart from experimentation with light, the phenomena being studied are invisible and can be made apparent only with transducers, such as oscilloscopes and meters, which can hardly be considered as among the most enthralling sensory sources. Even the drama of modern high-energy physics, which uses cyclotrons, is sensorially weak. Physicists, in their professional lives, are among the most human creatures, receiving only an insignificant amount of sensory activation of their pleasure areas. Their joy comes from establishing the numerical relationships between physical quantities. They are like Galileo, who it is said could not derive subhuman pleasure from the ritual and spectacle of the church service he was compelled to attend, but did enjoy watching one of the sacred lamps swaying on its chain and pondering upon the interrelating factors. Eventually he showed that it all depended on the length of the chain and earth's force of gravity, yielding the equation, $T = 2\pi\sqrt{1/g}$, a set of symbols that has given much pleasure to many generations of physics students and has enabled accurate clocks to be made. Modern man's radio, television, tape recorder, camera, automobile, boat, airplane, lighting, heating, water system, drainage system, and even the very structure of his house, are all derived from the fortunate fact that some people have considered that a life spent in sensory pleasure-seeking is unsuitable for a human being. To grind the ax still sharper, count up the objects around the house that have resulted from the proclivities that follow sensation-seeking.

Next in order of history and fundamentalness is chemistry and here, too, there is a higher order of sensory pleasure. The chemical laboratory is characterized by a wide range of unusual odors and many chemists recognize how much they enjoy these smells, most of which are objectionable to most people. Also, the operations of chemical research involve much visual pleasure, with fluids going through filters or being distilled, substances changing color and forming crystals. Even the simple process of weighing substances has a sensory appeal, whether by the swinging pans of the balance or the illuminated scales of modern digital devices. An ancient natural philosopher said that "the chemist is a strange class of mortal who seeks his pleasures amid soot and vapor, smoke and flame, poisons and poverty, yet among all these evils he seems to live so sweetly that he would not change places with a Persian king." This predilection for manipulating substances, observing their interreactions, analyzing and synthesizing them, clearly has sensory appeal. I remember it well from six years in pure chemical research and I remember, too, the eerie feeling of humility when one has synthesized a totally new compound, watching crystals form and knowing that this substance exists nowhere else on earth and probably not anywhere in the universe. The pleasure and the humility come from knowing that this event is the result of one's true understanding of at least some of the intricate laws of chemical combinations. As with physics, application of this understanding has resulted in, literally, substantial changes in human life until we have reached the point now where practically everything we touch, wear and, deplorably, eat is an artifice of chemistry. Thinking-pleasure amid soot and vapor seldom reaches the headlines unless something has gone amiss, but it contrasts most humanly with surmounting Everest or England winning a series of cricket matches against Australia.

A science which is rather difficult to define in sensory terms is astronomy. It has broad fronts in chemistry, physics, cosmology, radio, and, recently, biology. Not all of these disciplines are notably sensory but the traditional form of astronomy must have great visual appeal. Even nonastronomers derive pleasure from surveying the stars with the naked eye and most of us thrill at the sight of the moon through a telescope. Even when photography has removed the necessity for much personal inspection of the sky, there is still a large input from the photographic plates themselves and from the beautiful telescopes. This is all missing from the most recent division of radio astronomy, whose instruments are frequently unprepossessing lines of wires and whose observations are auditory pips and squeaks or penjerks on moving paper. While all astronomers are united in their preference for the intellectual pleasure of pondering on the features of the extraterrestrial universe, some of them have brains which demand the particular form of visual pleasure derived from scanning the visible celestial bodies, while others are prepared to forego even that small amount of sensory pleasure in order to derive the thinking-pleasure from remote space, from which light has not yet reached us and perhaps never will. This factor of colossal extramundane periods of time and amounts of distance is clearly central to the fascination of astronomers. So far, nothing of universal utility has come out of this form of pleasure-seeking, though it has been essential to space flight technology. Astronomy is very much a science that may show its teeth, so to speak, in the future when man's vehicular and communicatory probings reach into really deep space far beyond the solar system. Eventually, if it is true that the sun will one day blow up, astronomical information may be the decisive factor in the continued existence of the human species.

Once beyond the physical sciences, the whole range of biological disciplines opens up, revealing the most sensory of all scientific pursuits. The very objects of study provide a lucrative source of pleasure even for nonbiologists and there can be little doubt that a biologist, who spends his days dissecting plants or animals, observing their behavior or investigating their tissues, is obtaining significant amounts of sensory pleasure. Much of the equipment and instrumentation of biology has visual and tactile appeal, too. Marine biologists are even able to work under conditions that many people would call a holiday—studying octopuses in the Bay of Naples or dolphins under Californian sunshine. The marine biologist must derive great sensory pleasure from his surroundings and yet his behavior is very different from the sport of most skin-divers whose subhuman pleasure-seeking beneath the sea is totally sensory and unproductive.

This example highlights the essential difference between scientists and laymen in terms of their pleasure-seeking methods. Almost everyone is involved in some way with plants and animals. The average person, when confronted with fungus in the woodwork or maggots in the apple, shows all the signs of activation of the displeasure areas. The botanist and zoologist, respectively, while noting without emotion the inappropriateness of position, evince an immediate interest in the living things themselves. Again, the layman slavers over the aurora of the florist's wares and the chiaroscuro of his garden with little interest in the plants themselves, but the botanist wishes to slice them up for microscopic study to find out what they are made of and how they function. Large divisions of the plant kingdom are thus entirely beyond the experience of the average "plant lover."

Much the same situation occurs with animals. The "animal lover" often turns out to be someone who knows a little about one or two species and interacts with a tiny number of animals for a very small fraction of life, usually to the animals' detriment. The zoologist, on the other hand, extends his intellectual pleasures to the entire animal kingdom and does not "love" any particular species or example of a species. He may well specialize in a particular group but his interest is not the reflexive, sensory kind exhibited by the pet owner. The biologist, therefore, is not concerned with how the plants or animals relate to him, but with how they relate to each other, structurally and functionally. His pleasure-seeking has an intellectual, scientific quality as opposed to the essentially sensory pleasure-seeking of laymen. The layman's dealings with plants and animals serve the temporally limited purpose of activating his pleasure areas during his lifetime, and that is all he requires of them. The scientist's interactions with living things always add to knowledge, which may or may not prove useful but which endures. It would be difficult to establish who planted all the pretty little gardens of suburbia over the decades and how they did it. In the volumes of scientific literature, together with those of other similar intellectual disciplines, there is tangible evidence that certain men at certain times did certain things. This heritage of knowledge, aligned with that from the arts, is perhaps what some of the messiahs meant when they spoke of behaving like a human being and attaining life everlasting. We all live by seeking pleasure but sometimes our limbic activation takes a form that can last into eternity; we can be sure that if this has happened then the pleasure was not sensory.

It is clear, therefore, that the belief that scientists are ascetic, emotionless, unpassioned people is nonsense. Scientists have to keep their pleasure areas activated like everyone else, and their work is done for the fun of it. It is as false to consider them lacking in emotion with regard to their pleasure-seeking as it is to believe that they are dedicated to the good of mankind. An important difference, though, is that scientists do not allow emotions to control their significant behavior. Their training puts them constantly on guard against arriving at courses of action based on feelings rather than facts. In this fundamental way they differ, or are supposed to, from many laymen; their actions are not predominantly controlled by the old (or id) parts of the brain. Perhaps this is partly why the scientific community is one of the most liberal and tolerant collections of people in existence. Even the frequent controversies of science, conducted with vociferous verbal artillery, are mostly without personal rancor or petty pride. This is not to deny that within the confines of scientific establishments there are those who do not fit this description; this is an excellent reason for branding them as nonscientists, and other, better reasons are sure to be found.

Nonscientific "scientists" also comprise those who tinker with the various pseudo-sciences, sometimes called occult sciences. Astrology probably takes pride of place as being historically the oldest and probably the most widespread delusional doctrine. It has a small number of perpetrators and a vast army of dupes; most of the dupes do not even recognize the quaint anomalies of reading about *planetary* influences in "what the *stars* foretell" and subscribe to a system of celestial influence that excludes the most numerous celestial bodies except as a misnomer. Palmistry seems to have existed for a long time, too, although it does not possess either the systematic formulations or the extensive literature of astrology. It is largely restricted to fairgrounds and, like tea-leaf predictions, to the tea parties of some emotionally deprived suburban housewives. But at least palmistry has some sort of bodily basis and so there is the very remote possibility that some of the palmists' outlandish correlations are genetically determined in the form of general tendency toward disease conditions. Hand prints are being taken from thousands of newborn babies and research workers are attempting to keep detailed health records of these children right into adulthood. This scientific factual approach contrasts with the opinionated basis of the occult sciences. In the true sciences when an assertion is made one can demand to know the evidence and this is forthcoming. With the pseudo-sciences one is simply referred to an authority, a book or pamphlet; the occult sciences are Aristotelian in structure, but lack the rational background of that approach to knowledge.

Also, like most religious doctrines, they are irrefutable and this must make them highly attractive to the inferior mind. It is as impossible to prove that a gastric ulcer is not caused by Jupiter's position at the time of the patient's birth, as it is to prove that the ulcer was not caused by a flash of lightning. Orthodox science can trace the genesis of a gastric ulcer, or any other effect, through a chain of cause-effect relations only so far, and then has to stop due to limitations of methodology or of available knowledge. After the stopping point, any postulate at all can be made without fear of evidential contradiction. In science, such postulations of undemonstrated causes are the hypotheses on which further experiment is based; in the occult sciences such postulations are the principles of belief.

It is sometimes said that we should respect a person's avowed beliefs. This is not a sensible maxim for intelligent living. While we should respect the right of any person to hold any belief, we must all be completely free to express the highest disrespect for the beliefs themselves and for the mind that holds them. No one of reasonable intelligence and honesty can respect occult beliefs, nor could such a person sincerely hold such beliefs. Openmindedness is one thing, belief is another. A simple yardstick for the sincerity of any belief is to examine the extent to which the belief influences the person's life. Few "believers" in the occult sciences will shrug off a nonstarting car as due to the conjunction of Mars and Venus. Even less would they stoically accept their surgeon's refusal to remove an operable tumor because Saturn is not quite in the right place. The devotees of magical phenomena demand the mechanisms of orthodox science in an emergency. If, as occasionally happens, they are sincere, they are usually to be found in institutions for the insane.

A similar argument can be adduced against the supporters of those nonevidential extensions of natural science called extrasensory perception. The telekinesists use their hands to move objects, the telepathists reach for the telephone, the precognitionists are not the world's greatest gamblers and the spiritualists are as scared of death as most of us are. This tedious intellectual mess has been scientifically scrutinized in detail by a number of workers, most notably and completely by Professor C. E. M. Hansel in his book, *ESP: A Scientific Evaluation.* After reading this splendid work of demolition, as one sophisticated reviewer said, ". . . the unbiased observer can dismiss the whole topic; there is no need for him to concern himself about it any more."

Though discussions about ESP and the occult sciences are a form of mental contraception, it is of interest to consider the possible intellectual deficiencies which lead to involvement in them. It is a prerogative of man to activate his pleasure areas by thinking. The fact that many people consider man's outstanding feature to be rationality reflects the universal tendency of people to activate their pleasure areas with thought that is cast in rational form. By "rational" I mean deductive systems of thought, sets of interrelated concepts forming a doctrinal hierarchy with premises and conclusions. The orthodox, useful, fertile, evidential, factual systems described earlier can only be learned to the point of participation by the application over a period of years of tremendous self-discipline and intellectual stamina, which must continue at lesser intensity throughout the remainder of thinking life. With the great majority of people, intellectual curiosity and the desire to learn about things is seen as one form of pleasure-seeking in early childhood, but as the pressures mount with increasing complexity of subject, the mental effort of dealing with vast quantities of uninteresting but essential material and the attenuation of sensory pleasure-seeking that is required activate the displeasure areas more than the acquisition of rational knowledge activates the pleasure areas. So the learning of legitimate disciplines, for most individuals, becomes a distasteful activity which is dropped as soon as they leave school.

But the intrinsic desire to be part of rational systems is satisfied in several ways. Almost every trivial activity concerned with play has an unnecessary complexity of rules and principles which enables the participants to activate their pleasure areas with the spurious impression that they are "using their brains" in a validly systematic and admirable way. An extreme example is the pseudointellectualization of American football, where the actual movement of the ball is spasmodically over tiny distances and the largest amount of time during a game is spent in both sides discussing the tactics for the next tank-man attack, while thousands, millions perhaps with TV, watch to see the six-second outcome of these deliberations. The desire to obtain pleasure by being rational forces man to "dress up" activities with an apparent intellectual aura which can be arbitrary, anarchical, dogmatic and dreary to those not involved. How many millions of wives must have had their intelligence tampered with by their husbands' "intellectual analysis" of the match, the fishing, the poker game, the sail? For this is very much a masculine feature. When women wish to activate their limbic pleasure areas by the thought of being rational they tend to choose either the legitimate intellectual disciplines or systems which at least are not arbitrary and are productive, such as cookery and dressmaking.

Exploitation of the human desire for rational pleasure is seen in the floods of popular books on science, many of which contain more pictures than words. These enable some people to feel that they are knowledgeable without actually having to go through the displeasurable process of acquiring the knowledge. The scientist, in conversation with such people, finds that they have a most garbled understanding of nature without the redeeming feature of recognizing their own ignorance. On occasion this "little knowledge" can affect adversely both health and nutrition.

With the current drive of some reformers to reduce university entrance requirements and swell the ranks of students, it is inevitable that large numbers of ill-qualified entrants will find the process of learning a potent activator of the displeasure areas; these no doubt are among those science students who clamor for the abolition of examinations and the award of degrees with no test of scientific competence. This permissiveness would rebound unmercifully on the student later in life, for he will make no progress as a scientist if he cannot apply to his work the very tenacity and self-discipline that is required to pass examinations.

I have come a long way from ESP and the occult sciences, but when the human desire for obtaining limbic activation by rational thinking is allied with archicortal dominance of behavior, it is reasonable that the individual will become entangled with the occult, thereby displaying "knowledge" of the principles and "reasoning" of the consequences in a field that is easy to assimilate, unassailable on deductive grounds, and delightfully magical. When the person has a greater smattering of knowledge and a leaning toward the natural sciences, he is likely to eschew magical explanations and take his pleasure from the unknown, undemonstrable extensions of natural phenomena in ESP.

Pathetic as these examples are at a time when men are walking on the moon, they testify to the claim that people can activate their pleasure areas by thinking and will do so even when their environmental background has made them predominantly sensory pleasure-seekers. The mechanisms and intentions are all there for truly human behavior in even the most subhuman people. Their subhumanity lies in the way in which they have been encouraged to use their brains, not in the brains themselves. The cult of such pursuits as football, astrology and telekinesis, have the same pleasure-seeking neural basis. All their followers *could* apply this basis to topics that would prove their humanness, though of course wishing will not make it so. I am not suggesting that everyone should become a scientist; there is much to be said for the arts.

Artists and scientists, as many have pointed out, have some common features. They tend to be more dedicated than most to their work, rating its requirements higher than their own. More importantly, these two groups differ from all other sections of the populace in that their prime concern is with truth—some would say Truth. They both believe themselves intuitively aware of truths, but from that point on they diverge. The scientist tests his beliefs experimentally and is commanded by fact, though he is also guided by informed opinion. The artist goes ahead and tries to express the truth in which he believes in the way in which he is best able, regardless of any factual systems or doctrines. From time to time both scientists and artists change their minds about what is true, the scientist as a result of conflicting new facts and the artist as a result of conflicting new concepts. All this applies to the individual and to the group, so that generally held scientific and artistic views undergo transformations at intervals, each one being a little nearer the truth being aimed at. In just such ways do scientists and artists share the same mechanisms of activating their pleasure areas by use of the higher regions. In art sensation necessarily plays a much larger part since the intellectual principles of art can only be expressed and communicated sensorially, whereas scientific dogmata are best made available through words, graphs and tables, which are not outstandingly sensual, although they possess a kind of beauty for the scientist.

It would seem that sculpture is the oldest art form, judging, for example, from the carvings on bone. We must not assume, though, that sculpture did not follow some other art form involving less durable materials, and the present neurophysiological theory of behavior would indicate a sequence for the development of the arts that is different from the usually accepted one.

We shall probably never know, but I would hazard that man's first activity which could be considered as a primitive art form was some kind of dancing, which used the proprioceptive pathways. This seems likely in view of the ubiquitousness of dancing among primitive groups today and its presence in chimpanzees. No traces would be expected to remain except perhaps as graphic depictions. Certainly some of the stances of people in ancient carvings and bas-reliefs seem remarkably like stylized dance positions. Since dancing can be a purely sensory pleasure, as in the apes, it is an excellent candidate for the transition from subhuman to human activity, eventually becoming refined and intellectualized in ritual dances and ballet, where there exists a pleasure beyond that of mere movement.

One can reasonably postulate that vocalizations occurred spontaneously during man's early cavortings and that pleasure from the human voice, utilizing the auditory sense to activate the pleasure areas, was a close second to proprioception in the genesis of art, gradually becoming transformed with the development of language into oratory and singing. Then, just as the chimpanzee uses tree roots for pounding out a rhythm, we can imagine that early man's concerted utterings during the dance sounded better when in rhythmic unison, and so induced our ancestors to fabricate drums of some kind. Since the potentialities of physical movement are severely limited, man's desire to extend his artistic pleasures would naturally focus upon the auditory components of his dancing sessions, so that in time pleasure from the ear would greatly predominate over movement. Hence audition in the form of singing and music is today one of the two major sensory modes of art.

The other major sensory mode is vision and this, in the form of carvings, may only appear to be the earliest art form because dancing and singing leave no enduring physical remains. Nevertheless, latecomer though it probably was, visual artistry must very soon have made a strong impact on early man, for every archaeological site surrenders examples of visual art. Now pleasure by vision is the common feature of sculpture, architecture, painting, commercial art, ornamentation, costume, jewelry, typography, photography, furnishing, landscaping, and all else to which the principles of design are applied. In a sense, too, the cinema and television are probably to be looked upon as visual art forms which have yet to reach any consistent degree of maturity as media, though there are plenty of isolated examples.

All the art forms so far mentioned are heavily imbued with a subhuman sensory component. Though transfigured over the centuries, modern examples of these arts are different in form but not in kind from the efforts of early man. Henry Moore is recognizably another type of Michelangelo; some of Picasso's works are not so different from the cave paintings; pop art existed even before cave decoration. I am not suggesting that these arts are ideologically static, but simply that they comprise many ways of using a very few, very old methods of expression. In this they differ from the linguistic art forms. Literature in all its aspects is a qualitatively different field of art in which sensation plays no part except as a vehicle for ideas, to be taken in through the eyes and ears (or fingertips if we are blind) because we have no other way of communicating. Even though it has existed for only a fraction of the time that other arts have been extant, literature is the most evolved of them all in that it represents an entirely human means of activating the pleasure areas. This no doubt reflects the profound importance of the development of language upon which so much of human affairs depends.

The playwright, the poet, and the novelist, together with some nonfiction writers, purvey an art form that has come into existence as a result of the authors' intellectual pleasure-seeking and is intended to evoke a similar essentially human response in the reader or hearer. This is not to deny the observable fact that the content of some literature and the concepts it is meant to engender are arguably human, hence the disparity of opinion on obscenity and pornography, but in this respect literature is in no different position from the other arts and indeed from the sciences, all of which can be abused. Literature is similar to the other arts also in that it does not have to be entirely fictional. Some paintings are deliberately realistic, some sculptures immobilize a vision of a real object, even some music is intended as an

aural description of natural scenes and events. There is
a convincing school of thought which suggests that artistic phenomena must necessarily in some way reflect the
artists' conceptions of reality. Much factual literature,
including some sources of journalism, attempts to interpret the real world in a verbal way which will excite the
pleasure areas ideologically. On a not too high level this
is found in travel brochures and advertising copy; rather
more altruistically it is found in biographies, histories,
and travel books.

It is found, too, on a far larger scale in our own personal writings and readings. The vast majority of people,
like the lower animals, do not go to the ballet, look at
pictures or listen to *serious* music. Only a tiny fraction of
the population actually creates commodities in the sensory arts. But just about every literate person is involved
in literature of a sort. Even the most humbly composed
letter or memo is a minor creation, a diminutive work of
art in which the writer strives to use the symbols of
language to consign nerve impulses from the thinking
regions to the pleasure or displeasure areas of his corre-
spondent. The ubiquitous newspapers and magazines
are all designed to generate thinking activity, leading to
human pleasure or displeasure, and since they at least
claim to be dealing with the truth they must fall into the
category of art. Also, literature is only a more enduring
form of speech, so that when we speak to each other a
spark of human art flashes. And this, surely, is the basic
difference between animal noises and human speech.
Noise communicates emotional states, evoking activity
in only the lower, primitive brain regions. Lower animals can hear and respond to noises even after the higher
parts of the brain have been removed. But speech conveys ideas, and even very slight damage to some human
cortical brain regions causes profound disturbances of

language function. Not that this is all speech does. Any view of language which does not take account of its emotional content is incomplete and inadequate. But even when highly charged with emotion, human speech transmits, in varying degree of efficiency, a set of ideas upon which emotion is based. Every attempt at language interchange is an essay in dealing with truth, albeit distorted on occasion for personal pleasure as, for example, in boasting or flattering.

While painting, sculpture, music, and the other sensory arts are affectionately affianced to human life, literature has been wedded into the daily limbic activation of everyone, and in differing ways plays indelible roles in the structuring of our personalities. In the field of art the process of intellectualization is readily apparent.* Until recently the purely sensory way of living had to be conducted with limited sources, but with the great upsurge of technological expertise over the last few decades there has been a plethora of new sensory sources. With the inevitable opposite reaction, creative people bridled against mere sensation and began to incorporate the laws of physics and mathematics into their art. Representationalism went first but initially the abstract art which followed was chaotic, formless or without internal cohesion. Gradually, some artists began to insist upon precise geometrical relations, specific juxtaposition of light frequencies. Rejection of tonality and its replacement by algebraic rules of musical composition, even traditional instruments and sounds were put aside by some composers in favor of electronic sound, and they cast primitive rhythms, time signatures and harmonies to the prevailing wind of technology. Some of those artists who were

*In chapter four I hinted that people will eventually use their brains in human fashion as an inevitable result of evolution and I discuss this at length in chapter eleven.

unable or unwilling to encompass the principles of physics and mathematics did what they thought was the next
best thing and made some of their creations by crushing
automobile engines into odd shapes, or sticking bits of
ordinary objects on canvas or taking great pains to re-
produce precisely the commodial mundanity of a super-
market window. It seems they would do anything to
eschew mere sensation and to comment on technological
reality without relying on the old artistic notions of
beauty and rhythmic form. Artists depend upon their
higher thinking regions more acutely than ever before
and the pace is quickening.

This alliance of science and art is not restricted to the
galleries and the concert halls. It has impinged upon our
daily lives in architecture and city planning. Many
voices have been raised against the overcerebrative approach to urban design and none more eloquently than
that of Professor A. E. Parr, Director Emeritus of the
American Museum of Natural History. His articles in
Landscape, Art and Architecture and other journals have
drawn attention elegantly to the stultifying, mind-dep-
leting, understimulating mediocrity of modern conurbation schemes that drive receptive people from the disqui-
eting towns into the intellectual stupor of suburbia.
Thinking-pleasure, like all others, can be overdone.
Soon, if not already, the average man will be unable to
understand the creations of artists unless he agrees to put
his "feelings" aside and bring an informed, rational
mind to bear, just as he cannot understand the immediate output of a scientist. Unfortunately, the majority of
people are not yet able to put their feelings aside in many
matters. Subtly and perniciously the science-art around
us has deep influences that we can be aware of only
vaguely, and we react accordingly.

One reaction, of course, is that the ephemeral popular

arts coterminously become more sensory and more plebeian in order to be understandable without intellectual effort. Commerce steps in to exploit the situation with a plentiful supply of sensory sherbet, often in pseudoclassical guise so that those who activate their pleasure areas by feeling modern and intellectual have no trials keeping up with the Carmen Jones's. But self-deception and faulty personal evaluation in human behavior are by no means confined to the popular arts.

So far I have dealt with human behavior in circumscribed areas, intellectual activities to which class labels can be given. Only a small minority of people belongs to any one of these, and vast numbers belong to none of them. Yet every person behaves as a human to some extent, not by choice but of necessity.

Every one of us is not only capable of thinking, we all think. It seems that carrying out thought processes is an unavoidable consequence of the metabolism of our brains, once the connections in the cerebral cortex have developed after birth and when plentiful sensory information has been provided in childhood. Given suitable anatomical substrates and proper nutrition, the brain exhibits continuous electrical activity wherever recording electrodes are inserted. The degree and type of electrical activation depends upon the overall circumstances, but it ceases only in death. Indeed, cessation of detectable brain electricity is frequently taken as the only positive sign of death. This electrical activity is brought about by a combination of nerve impulses continually traveling from one place to another and a vast series of complex chemical reactions occurring in the brain cells. Thought is one of the consequences of this physiochemical activity, which can never stop while mental life remains. If we try to stop thinking about anything we discover that thinking is completely involuntary and totally continuous. None of us can choose whether to think any more than we can choose whether to breathe. Nor should we make the mistake of believing that we are conscious of all our thoughts. Even though on occasions we seem to be "daydreaming," thinking in an undirected way, we still know what we have been thinking about when called to order. But in addition to all this, large numbers of mental processes occur below the level of consciousness. This can be made apparent by "truth drugs," hypnosis, psychoanalysis, or less arcanely by ingeniously devised psychological tests. Sustained self-criticism, resulting in varying degrees of what has come to be called "insight" also reveals the extent and directions of unconscious thinking, but never the thought itself. Most psychiatrists have abundant evidence in their case records of mentally healthy, average people to show that the actual behavior of many persons is guided by these unconscious mental processes; in them their conscious thought is frequently superficial rationalization to provide justification for their actions. As trenchantly expressed by Professors Slater and Roth: "Men are indeed moved by drives and motives of whose nature they have little awareness and understanding, by which they may be pressed towards a goal which means the destruction of all they would claim they valued."

Thinking, conscious or unconscious, can activate the pleasure or displeasure areas of the limbic system and is therefore human behavior. This is fact, but whether specific forms of the behavior are good or evil, acceptable or unacceptable is a matter of opinion. They are terms used by people. An interesting distinction exists between this generalized human behavior of everyday thinking and some of the special forms previously dealt with. While there is protracted controversy about the good or evil of philosophical systems, theological dogma, scientific discovery and artistic attitudes, we are all basically agreed on what is right and wrong in the individual human behavior of people. Unfortunately, this has precious little effect in practice.

Almost every normal person will agree that thinking that gives rise to kindness, tolerance, honesty, assistance to others, love, and affection is good. And almost every normal person nods agreement to the assertion that thought processes which generate hate, cruelty, intolerance, dishonesty and self-centeredness are the hallmarks of evil. Unfortunately, this universal agreement about the classification of concepts breaks down when these ideas take substantive form. Social workers, domestic counsellors, psychologists, priests and policemen (and even husbands and wives) will all testify to the difficulty of trying to convince a person that he or she is selfish or dishonest or cruel. And I am not referring only to that minority of the population who are demonstrably thieves and villains but to the great mass of ordinary, average people. Accusations of kindness, honesty and helpfulness are received without demur.

Because one consequence of our thinking is activation of pleasure or displeasure areas by down-going nerve impulses, we make sure that our thoughts whenever possible route these nerve impulses to the pleasure areas. We learn how to do this by experience. We come to know that only displeasure can come of thinking that we have been selfish or cruel. So when on occasions our pleasure-seeking leads us into cruelty, if we lack good insight as most of us do, we mentally attribute our action to other motives, and similarly for all the other behaviors that we have all agreed are evil. We buy another car, bigger, faster or flashier, because, we "tell ourselves," that the previous one was beginning to fall apart. The fact that our old car will be bigger and flashier for someone else is "repressed." Our neighbors, especially those who do not somehow get on well with us, are under no illusion about what we are up to. Indeed, we know just how selfish, envious and snobbish they are. And yet, oddly, their friends naïvely accept those neighbors as good, friendly people!

Sometimes unconscious or semiconscious self-deception of this kind is commercially exploitable, as it is with the model-a-year pattern of the automobile industry. Fat profits must be made from the millions of birthday, Christmas and get-well cards that ritually ricochet through the postal machines every year, the majority of them hypocritical greetings of no serious import to the sender or receiver. The sender may pat himself on the back for being such a prolific well-wisher and the receiver may congratulate himself on the mantelpiece panorama which, he insists on believing, testifies to his own popularity. He cannot consciously accept the fact that his cards are merely the result of his name being kept on a list by the people he sends cards to. The propensity of some people for hypocritical gestures is also seen in such commercial exploitations as Mother's Day and the charitable exploitation in the various collections of items that would normally be destined for the trash can. Individuals are able to activate their pleasure areas very well by bringing their niceness to the notice of friends and relatives by continually asking for used stamps, cigarette foil and other trivia, probably basking in the smug glow of charity and adulation, when in fact a few cents or a few hours of assistance a week would help to transform the charitable organizations involved.

Much of the violence and protest marching that occurs

with tedious predictability is based upon the strong autonomic sensory input to the pleasure areas produced by
it. But few of the participants would admit to this. Their
thinking processes are so arranged that they can, with
the aid of the mechanisms of group psychology, establish
chains of thought that generate pleasure by self-descrip-
tion as "Fighters for a Cause." When the need for autonomic stimulation has passed, the fighting stops too,
though the Cause usually remains. Such is the neurophysiology of sayings like "evil done in the name of X."
Of course, there are other reasons that determine why
certain individuals choose demonstrations as a source of
autonomic pleasure.

Even more rife is the distorted human behavior involved with many parents and their children. Under the
self-righteous guise of being kind and pleasant to the
child, punishment which would be distressing to the
parent is withheld; rewards are given which are mostly
beneficial to the parent; moral values are taught which
simply consolidate the parental mode of behavior. These
parents have not acquired the human sophistication
which enables a person to allow his displeasure areas to
be stimulated for the sake of truth and honesty. Put
another way, these parents do not have the kind of brain
in which truth and honesty activate the pleasure areas.

Frank appraisal of the majority of human behavior as
here defined reveals that our universal agreement on the
eternal verities of goodness is simply an overriding hyp-
ocrisy with which we protect our displeasure areas and
coddle our pleasure areas. It also reveals that the basic
fault is in our misunderstanding of the concept of selfishness, for it is from this that all other human misdeeds
arise.

Neurophysiologically there cannot be an unselfish act

or an unselfish process of thought. Everything we do or think is consciously or unconsciously arranged to activate our pleasure areas or avoid activation of our displeasure areas. Only in this way can we survive, as animals like any other animal. The very structure and function of our brains insures that we can do nothing, if we are normal, that does not accomplish one or both of these ends. We cannot distinguish among various human behaviors or among the people involved in them on the basis of selfishness and unselfishness. All we can do, and what we must do, is learn how to distinguish in impersonal, unemotional terms between selfish thinking which generates pleasure solely for the thinker, and thinking behavior which activates the pleasure areas of both thinker and others, on a *long-term* basis.

The parent who takes his child swimming all the time and never tries to help it with homework, is certainly giving pleasure for a time, but he should have the sophistication to know that later the child will pay a big price in lack of pleasure. The husband who gives his wife a day out by taking her to the automobile exhibition is likely to be behaving entirely selfishly. The wife who decides to give her husband a salad because it is such a hot day, thereby enabling her to spend another hour sunbathing, is equally selfish. There are those who behave like this consciously and deliberately, knowing the culpability of their thinking, yet not caring. They are on such a low developmental level that nothing much can be done about them; we must just hope that they die off soon. But many more people engage in deceptive thinking with such expertise that they deceive themselves, and even feel unjustly berated if the deception is brought to their notice. Religious missionaries stamping out the joyful customs of sacrifice, cannibalism and head-hunting by

*The findings of science
abused by the pleasure seekers*

diverting the natives with medicines, food and apparel, while glowing with the pleasure of Christian virtue must be placed in this class. The psychiatrist who enjoys the professional success of curing his patient's gibbering madness and sends him back to a strife-torn life fits in here, too. Sometimes, even the accusation of selfishness is selfish. The man who claims that his wife is selfish because she spends so much time on voluntary social work instead of darning his socks is clearly being self-centeredly selfish. He is also right.

Our real problem, then, is not to live by some vague moralistic concept that selfishness is bad, but to recognize that selfishness is an inevitable result of our brain function, beyond our control entirely, and to fix our attention on the pudding in which the proof lies—the consequences of our behavior in terms of other people's pleasure areas. The missionary and those who evaluate him must accept that this kind of "God's work" is as selfish, that is, pleasure-producing, as any other human activity and can only be determined as admirable or not on the basis of its long-term material results in terms of the limbic nerve impulses in those affected by the behavior. The psychiatrist can only justify his actions, which are thoroughly selfish, if they result in more pleasure for his patient or less displeasure for those who have to deal with him. The husband is selfish wherever he takes his wife out for the day, but his behavior may be considered more admirable if the place they go to give her pleasure, too. In this type of behavior it is necessary of course to avoid the form of selfishness known as mock martyrdom, deriving pleasure from the idea of self-subjection, especially when the real motive, that is, unconscious thought, is to resurrect the episode later as evidence of goodness.

The matter of arranging our thinking behavior so that

predominantly we use the content of our neocortex (superego), rather than the subhuman propensities of hippocampal (id) regions is a tall order for a species which has only partially evolved. Carrying out the ancient command in ways which are both human and socially desirable is the essential problem that faces us. This has been known intuitively by some people of the past.

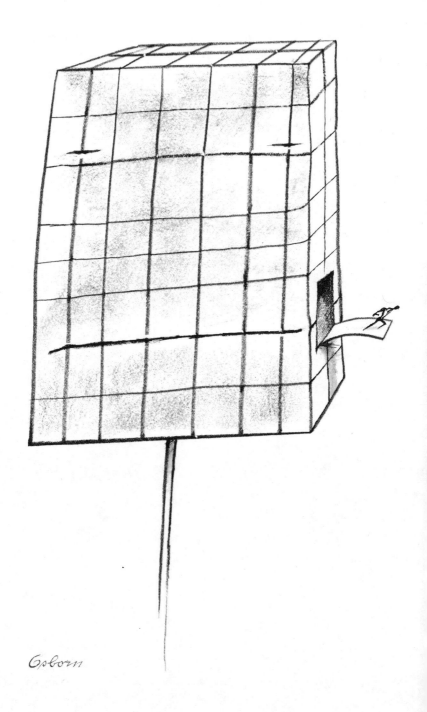

Osborn

Chapter 10

Human Institutions

RELIGION, LAW AND THE FAMILY

Social interactions are not exclusively human. Numerous writers have described the organization and patterns of social living in ants, bees, mice, rabbits, elephants and monkeys. Most ethological studies suggest that sociability of a sort may be much more widely distributed in the animal kingdom than most people think. But however widespread the animal interminglings, there is one clear, incontrovertible difference between the societies of the human species and those of lower animals. It is neglect of this difference, perhaps, that has led some behaviorists into drawing too close parallels between the behavior of apes and of humans. From the neurophysiological point of view we should not be overawed by the morphological

similarities between humans and apes. There is evidence now that the ape's behavior is made up solely of sensory pleasure-seeking in various forms, and therefore in terms of behavioral evolution the ape is hardly different from the fish. Although he is tremendously more efficient at finding sensory sources to activate his pleasure areas and has a vastly greater range and discrimination of sensory stimuli, the ape uses his higher brain regions only as a top-quality organizer for subhuman pleasure. If we could give the ape an opposable thumb he would use it in some form of sensory pleasure-seeking, just as would any other lower animal if we could provide it with a more efficient bodily tool, for that is the meaning of the evolution of bodily tools. As I wrote in the *Smithsonian:**\
When a man is drinking bourbon he is no nearer the ape than to the fish. And whatever the ape does, he is no nearer man than the fish.

When the ape or any other lower creature is involved in social commingling, it is for the purpose of sensory pleasure-seeking. The sight, touch, smell and sound of like-kind activates the pleasure areas through peripheral receptors, and is therefore indulged in by the lower animals for the same reason as eating and mating. Quite incidentally, as with eating and mating, social behavior confers biological advantages. It shows everybody where the food is, where the enemies are, provides concerted action against adversity and allows family units to exist, with protection of the young and transmissions of knowledge from one generation to the next. So, again like eating and mating, social behavior is a form of sensory pleasure-seeking that has survival value and withstands the test of natural selection. One of the features

*October, 1971.

of "the fittest" is the ability to derive pleasure from social interaction.

It is likely that this kind of sensory-sociality character- ized early humans and is clearly an important feature of many groups in modern humans, such as dancing soci- eties, sports clubs, jazz clubs, and is surely an essential ingredient in organizations such as the Rotary Club and Freemasonry where parties and dinners are part of the routine.

But despite the fact that much of human sociality, though heavily disguised, is as primitive and subhuman as that of the apes, lower animals do not have institu- tions. Among lower animals the social sensation-seeking is largely random, and that which is not is generated by simple biological requirements such as the predictable interaction between mother and child, husband and harem. With humans, attempts have been made since very early times to modify and control random social behavior for the common good. Some people have used their thinking regions in setting up systems of social living that require other people to use their higher re- gions. Thought-controlled behavior rather than sense- controlled behavior has been their object, and every one of us has come under the influence of one or more such systems. The early "leaders" of the human species knew from simple observation that no incentive or pressures were needed to induce people to seek sensory pleasure, and they also knew that no advances could be made to social organization while such subhuman behavior re- mained the sole driving force. In every primitive com- munity there arose a few people who could see beyond their peripheral receptors and who drew the attention of others to the efficacy of thought processes, not always correctly. Each generation has included people who saw as their purpose in life and obtained their pleasure from trying to foster *human* behavior. It is from these people that we derive our social institutions.

In the beginning plain magic was understandably the basis of behavioral control, arising from almost total ignorance of the natural causes of effects such as rain, disease and famine. Magic enabled people to answer questions about these events, and that is always a good activator of the pleasure areas, whereas inability to answer questions always causes disquiet. The majority are not overly concerned with the truth of their answers, so long as they are part of a system. Magical explanations still are predominant in the most primitive modern societies and with the most primitive minds in advanced societies. Some people were not content with a mere answer and strove for behavioral rules that could be seen to work, and so arose political systems stemming from the considered wishes of the boss-man. It was but a short step to strengthen human authority by adding the concept of powerful supernatural entities with earthly representation and paving the way for the biggest boss-men of them all, the gods and their priests.

Totally lacking in formal biological knowledge, people could only explain the inactivity of death by postulating departed spirits, always lurking in the offing ready to do the dirty deeds they had done when in a body. It is easy to see in general terms—or read about in detail in Frazer's *Golden Bough* and Freud's enthralling *Totem and Taboo*—how much of the old, primitive, mind-groping concepts have lingered on, modified, modernized in some respects and offered as the standard major religions.

All religions have two fundamental features in common. Firstly, they draw attention to a need for the use of the mind in communal behavior, with sensual, private gain reduced to low levels. Thus the essential deep message of religions is the same as that to be drawn from modern biology; people, in order to take their proper place in the evolutionary scale, should predominantly activate their pleasure areas by means of the higher thinking regions, rather than by concentrating their efforts toward stimulation of their peripheral receptors. Secondly, the other common feature of religions has no points of contact with biology or with any other science. Religious principles of action, the dicta by which the particular form of human behavior is to be selected, have all been stated as certainties arising from revelations of various kinds, among which are documents, visitations and miracles. There is no question of probable truth as in science and no appeal to observation and fact. Perhaps this is why there are so many distinct bodies of opinion in religion but only one body of scientific knowledge. Universal acceptance of the main body of scientific knowledge occurs for two reasons. On the one hand, the truth of scientific principles is daily attested in almost every department of everyone's life, and on the other, each person is entirely free to examine whatever scientific evidence he wishes and to accept or reject it as he sees fit, without pressures of any kind. Conversely membership of a religious group is almost one hundred percent the result of brainwashing by influential individuals who use carefully selected portions of the revelations to support their edicts.

The last sentence, I am acutely aware, may cause pain and anger in many who read it, for there are still many millions under the spell of this kind of brain control. I should therefore expand the statement in order to justify it. Those who want a more detailed analysis of this aspect of religion will find, if their churches allow them to do so, clarity, brilliance and, if they are rational, conviction

in Dr. B. P. Beckwith's *Religion, Philosophy and Science,*
one of the few easily readable books on this subject.

Taking up my claim of brainwashing, it is the case that
the enormous majority of Christians are the children of
Christians, and the same can be said for all the other
adherents of religions, Jews, Moslems, Hindus, Bud-
dhists, and indeed for the adherents of the subdivisions
of religions, Roman Catholics, Protestants, Anglo-Cath-
olics, Baptists, Mormons, Jehovah's Witnesses, Christian
Scientists, and all the others. This is incontrovertible
proof that almost all religious people have adopted the
revelational views that were taught them by their parents and by the priests selected by their parents. With so
many religious systems from which to choose, the very
reverse would be the case if individuals used their reasoning powers to determine their religion. From birth
onward the incessant reiteration of revealed "truths,"
the constant suggestion that faith is an adequate substitute for knowledge, the repetitive invocation of penances
and dire threats of vengeance here or after death, the
continuous emphatic enmity to other systems of belief
are all features that characterize the slow process of induced beliefs which has come to be called brainwashing.

There is abundant scientific evidence to prove that the
very structure of the higher regions of the brain in terms
of number of cells and cellular interconnections, the informational pathways, is absolutely dependent upon environmental influence. This is also true of the informational content of the brain, its ideas, beliefs, values, and
its conditioned ideological responses. The environmental influence of scientific teaching inculcates a refusal to
accept beliefs from an authority and demands that each
individual examine the demonstrated facts for himself
before coming to a temporary, workable conclusion;
where this cannot be done, he is encouraged to keep an

open mind about the ultimate answer. Religious teaching, on the other hand, demands belief because "I say so" —it is true partly because I know it is true, partly because it is in the Bible or some other document. When no external influence designed to foster independent thought and appeal to facts is brought to bear, it is neurologically inevitable that the child adopts the religion of the parent. The particular worth or worthlessness of the denominational beliefs has no relevance to the situation.

Religion is by no means alone in this respect, of course, which is why most democratic people live in democratic countries, most Communists in Communist countries, most fascists in fascist countries. It is also the reason why paella is eaten mainly by Spaniards, curry by Indians, roast beef by the British, and spaghetti by Italians. It is why Indians wear saris and Japanese wear kimonos. Control of our minds has existed ever since we started to use them.* It is unrealistic to cavil at mind control, because there is no way of avoiding it. What we have to do is distinguish between the different kinds and decide which are best for mankind, a task of great magnitude and enormous difficulty, especially when, as with political systems, there is much evidential basis for several of them.

But at least the modern sophisticated mind might decide against systems of mind control which are based upon arbitrary sources and have no evidential basis whatever. The arbitrariness of religious systems is rarely made apparent to devotees, even though they must be aware of the plurality of main sources, the Bible, the Koran, the sermons of Jesus and Buddha, each of which is believed to be certain truth despite their incompatibili-

*See p. 288.

ties. Yet relatively few Christians, for example, are aware that the "scriptures" have been carefully censored by mortal Church authorities, so that only some of these ancient "God-inspired" truths have been allowed to form the basis of the faith of millions. Roman Catholic churchmen have probably been outstanding in this form of control of the environment leading to control of the mind, rejecting among many other divine revelations the gospel according to the Egyptians, which tells the "truth" that the main reason for Jesus' coming was to destroy the work of the female, turn the sexes into one and make marriage sinful for Christians. Millions have been prevented from considering the desirability of these "truths" through contrived ignorance of them. The mortal leaders of the Protestant Church took it upon themselves to throw out fourteen books of divine revelations. From the plethoric potpourri of "God's commands" it would appear that in the main the priests have suited themselves and that Roman Catholic, Protestant, Coptic, Greek Orthodox and Abyssinian Bibles exist, each demanding different allegiances and different forms of holy conduct.

This can happen only because the "truths" are selected for purely mind-controlling purposes and because they are entirely unverifiable and imaginary. If one wishes to learn about chemistry, it matters little which of the many texts one uses because they all tell the same story and they tell it in order to acquaint the reader with facts rather than to control his mind. They have to, for the statements in them are readily testable. When the Jew and the Moslem learn chemistry they are given the same system of beliefs. This is also partly due to the fact that life would soon become intolerable if there were arbitrary systems of chemistry, whereas today, with some exceptions, the existence of several religious systems is a matter of relative indifference to how life goes on.

This was not always the case. Although manipulation of neural traffic between the higher regions and the pleasure areas by churchmen today is happily without too much material effect, history abounds with examples of cruelty, oppression, torture, murder and misery arising from the bigoted insistence upon universal acceptance of arbitrary and undemonstrable beliefs, involving collectively many more millions than have suffered in a political war. In addition religious leaders have steadfastly attempted and often succeeded in preventing or delaying progress in the arts, sciences and social reform. Unequivocal evidence is on record, for example in Joachim Kahl's *The Misery of Christianity* to show to any rational person of average decency that the churches and their priests have been the greatest sources of evil the world has ever known. At the same time, I am not claiming that no good at all has come from their existence.

Clearly this is a matter of brain function and its abuse. Man can activate the pleasure areas and avoid activation of the displeasure areas. His thinking can be geared to reality, which is time consuming, effortsome and only fractionally rewarding, or it can have no contact with reality; it can be wishful thinking. The brand of wishful thinking that constitutes religious faith is obviously a most potent activator of the pleasure areas, for this is the only way to explain the massed millions who indulge in it. From the witch doctor to his modern counterpart, ecclesiasts have recognized the widespread propensity to believe nice things, and there was no problem in selecting nice things from the abundant supply of revelations or even digging up a new set of pleasant "truths" as with the Mormon Bible. The unsophisticated mind generates activity in the pleasure areas by contemplating life in paradise, and few religious people believe that *they* are destined for the less amenable environment provided by the good kind God who loves us all. On the other hand, many people of low intelligence can be kept better in line by the activation of the displeasure areas that sinful thoughts or behavior generates. Fate after death, this simple piece of nonsubstantive doctrine, has alone been sufficient to deter much personal evil. Again, during the inevitable tribulations of realistic living, activation of the pleasure areas in the form called "comfort" is derived from the belief that an all-powerful father figure in the sky is watching through even the darkest clouds. The fact that he so often holds only a watching brief is an uncomfortable thought that is either passed through the hippocampal suppressive mechanisms or is explained away as a result of God's devious ways, ways which in a mortal would inevitably brand him as what is sometimes called a screwball. The pleasure called peace of mind is generated by the prayers which God needs to hear before He realizes we are in trouble. We can say and ask things of God that would be absurd addressed to another mortal. We may request magical intervention on our behalf and ignore the natural laws of cause and effect. We may fob off any self-centeredness by dropping in a word for lighthouse keepers or some other worthy cause. These and other thinking pleasures like them are very real for those who indulge in them, but the mechanisms of operation belong to the realms of psychology and neurophysiology, not to faith.

In their most primitive form, these beliefs are of great sustaining value to ill-educated people of low social status, who may also believe in magical matters such as astrology and palmistry, without even realizing that such heretical beliefs may cast them into hell if their religious systems happen to be true. As such, the religious systems have played an enormous part in maintaining order among the vast peasant communities of the past by utilizing the most facile means of reward and punishment there is—manipulation of the mind. Religious affiliation does occur too among well-educated people of high social status, but these are a minority. Also, it is not always possible to determine the sincerity of belief. In most advanced societies today it is still unfortunately the case that pretense to religious principles can be materially advantageous, especially where public appointments are involved. However, sincerity must exist in places, and this is a clear indication that one of the biggest problems facing mankind is the eradication of wishful thinking as a source of pleasure and its replacement by inductive rational pleasure-seeking.

Luckily for the future, there is ample evidence that the evolution of man's brain is inexorably increasing the amount of inductive rational thinking and reducing the amount of religious faith. Many young people in several parts of the world are coming to understand and reject the mental tyranny of revealed "truths." Surveys have shown that the percentage of college students who believe in God is greatly less than among noncollege people of similar age and background. This percentage is also gradually reduced as the process of factual education unfolds—in one study from 20 percent in freshmen to 5 percent in seniors. The psychologist J. H. Leuba, whose *The Reformation of the Churches* contains much data of this kind, has shown that the average percentage of college students believing in God dropped from 69 percent in 1912 to 21 percent in 1933. Using the star of eminence in Cattell's *American Men of Science*, Leuba was also able to produce factual results of interest to all young scientists today. The average percentage of lesser scientists believing in God dropped from 38 percent to 29 percent from 1914 to 1933; among top-rank scientists the equivalent figures were 21 percent to 13 percent. One may reasonably guess that comparable figures today would be insignificantly low, testifying to the liberating effect upon the mind of scientific indoctrination. In view of the current campaign for greater freedom among women, it is curious that every survey of which I know reveals a significantly higher level of religious affiliation among women than among men. Perhaps some of them will soon give attention to this particular manner in which their minds have been controlled by an almost exclusively male priesthood.

There are two major reasons why the yoke of revelationary "truths" has been steadily dropping from man's shoulders. One of them is the continuing ability of scientific methods to solve man's practical problems and provide intelligent, testable answers to his questions about the universe, one corollary of which is that people are asking sensible questions rather than logically meaningless ones such as where do I go when I die, does God object to cunnilingus, can I eat meat on Fridays if fish makes me sick? More and more the ability and desire for rational thinking-pleasure is proving a greater activator of the pleasure areas than mere wishful thinking. People now read about, see on TV, and ponder realistically many topics which a few decades ago they would not even have allowed themselves to admit to conversation or introspection. Use of the higher brain regions in bringing their own earthly experience and knowledge to thrash out the most successful approach to abortion, divorce, contraception, drug-taking and political impasses, is generating true human pleasure in many more brains than ever before, especially among those highly emancipated younger people. This is no guarantee that correct solutions will be found immediately, but at least there is the chance that they will come. This would be impossible with the stultifying staticism of arbitrary religious edicts from however exalted an eminence.

The other reason for the steady reduction in religious pleasure-thinking over the years is the development and spread of legal systems. They form another social institution that has no parallel among the lower creatures. Certainly a kind of cuffing and ostracism is seen in some subhuman societies, especially those in which there is a hierarchy of dominance from chickens to chimpanzees. But these can be seen as simplified versions of the arbitrary and despotic religious tyrannies that have sometimes served as law or the driving force behind it in the dark times of human history. The baboon retains his "big stick" legislation but the stick of cardinals, archbishops, rabbis and other unitary oppressors has been continuously whittled down by the rise of secular law, though by no means to matchstick size. The power of religion in establishing undemocratic law is evidenced by the plentiful reasons Dr. Beckwith gives for his statement that ". . . the Roman Catholic Church, the closest Western equivalent to the Russian Orthodox Church, markedly resembles the Russian Communist movement."* It is the methods used, not the doctrines taught, to which attention is being drawn.

There can be no question that much of the ethical recommendations of the churches has been incorporated into useful secular law, using different methods. The idea that the behavior of individuals and small groups should not prejudice the overall pleasure of the community has been one of the large number of valuable and practical precepts of most religions. Like every valuable

*Op. cit.

principle, belief in them does not require anything in the nature of revelation or the supernatural, but is amenable to common sense and scientific demonstration. We need not be told that stealing is immoral. We can demonstrate that this idea has a perfectly real, substantive basis once we realize that the only sensible way of defining "moral" is in terms of the effect of specific examples of conduct upon the social order, represented by communal freedom of pleasure-seeking. The proper behavior of people in relation to society is a matter for science, not religion, for the factual effects of improper behavior can be shown to be the case. At the moment this is not entirely so, for the search for actual truth takes longer than finding "truth" by revelation. But at least the rational, secular system of laws can be constantly subjected to change as new facts come to light, which indeed has been the case, so much so that astonishment may be produced when a law of, say, 1750, is invoked. In the religious community no eyebrows are raised at the invocation of a revealed law of virtually unknown antiquity, reliability and intelligibility.

The use of the higher brain regions that is essential to produce, enforce and comply with secular laws recognizes that gray exists. Revelationary principles know only black and white. "Thou shalt not murder" leaves no room for the application of human intelligence to the manifold situations in which common sense may teach that killing is required, leading among other things to cabalistic condemnation of abortion and contraception. "Thou shalt not commit adultery" is easier to grasp by the lazy mind than "Thou shalt not commit adultery unless there is a reason that most of us would consider valid in your particular circumstances." Secular law, with its courageous attempts to come to grips with the gray areas of human conduct as it actually happens, exemplifies the "mercy" that is totally missing from religious bigotry, except perhaps as personal priestly dispensation in the communally sacrosanct confessional. In the law courts we can all see justice trying to be done, and thereby step in and try to make it nearer to our own ideas of earthly, realistic, workable justice. Hence, law enables all people, not only members of the legal profession, to activate their pleasure areas by using their thinking regions to deal rationally with the uncertainties of human interaction.

The essential feature of all legal systems can be seen as the reduction of displeasure to others produced by the unbridled sensory pleasure-seeking of the individual, as seen by its actual effects. In this way, law is much the same kind of human behavior as science. Law seeks by inductively rational methods to provide a framework of conduct that will best insure that peripheral sensory stimulation is not harmful to the community or its individual members. This ideal has obviously not been reached, but in the last few decades enormous progress has been made in removing from law the anomalies in control of pleasure-seeking which are not demonstrably harmful in this way. Enlightenment has come in stages, so that, for example, the sensory pleasure-seeking involved in certain kinds of private heterosexual acts is no longer subject to legal interference. Where consenting adults are concerned, homosexual behavior was recognized as a matter outside the domain of law.

As in science, there will inevitably be errors of judgment and of observation, but there will be overall advance. The thinking-pleasure of legal man, quite bereft of subhuman sensory input, grappling with the wishes of increasingly sophisticated communities, is gradually evolving a system of mind control that will eventually safeguard society and injured individuals and yet leave harmless individual pleasure-seeking to the individual's own assessment. With the steady increase in the number of people who opt for thinking-pleasure as a predominant means of activating the pleasure areas, greater numbers will be involved in the making and acceptance of our laws. All this is part of human brain evolution, which insures that every new generation brings slightly more people who value their ability to think above their ability to feel. The more we recognize that secular legal systems have a neurophysiological basis, the sooner will we remove the arbitrary, puritanical, tyrannical rules of despotic faith.

This gives no guarantee that immediate solutions to legal problems will be found, and we must expect that some measures, inevitably based on the present insufficiency of evidence, will be either popular and effective, unpopular but effective, popular and ineffective, or unpopular and ineffective. It is necessary in law as in chemistry to experiment in order to determine the truth. Sometimes, especially when the law impinges upon very old, very personal customs, there will be severe disagreement until the truth appears. This is no more evident than in the human social institution of marriage.

Among the lower animal groups we may or may not find male-female relationships of enduring character. The evidence is incomplete but it is likely that most people who study this phenomenon would agree that "marriage" in the lower groups is a rarity. In all human groups, on the other hand, however primitive, we find the social institutions of marriage and the kinship relations which follow. Indeed, in the majority of human groups the canons of kinship prove equally strong, if not stronger, than either religious principles or secular law in maintaining social behavior. The idea that the family is the unit of a stable society is not sociological wishful thinking; it is a statement of biological fact. Anthropologists and sociologists have found that, in the words of Oscar Lewis, Professor of Anthropology at the University of Illinois, ". . . most of the categories traditionally used in describing an entire culture could be used effectively in the study of a single family." The human family is a microcosmic representation of society, which, according to the theory of pleasure-seeking presented in this book, must be able, on the whole, to serve as a source of activation of the pleasure areas, for only if this is so would it exist. Further, since marriage, the family and kinship ties are essentially limited to the human species, we may reasonably believe that their pleasure-giving features arise from the use of higher brain regions, even though, as with so many other behaviors of man, they have obvious sensory components. The ubiquitous presence and great antiquity of the family and marriage testify to their potency in producing pleasure. Whether this will remain so is arguable.

If all pleasure is based upon producing activation of the pleasure areas and deactivation of the displeasure areas, then marriage must be a distinctly human way of arranging these matters, and divorce is a step back to the jungle. The particular form marriage takes, whether monogamy, polygamy, or polyandry, is the incidental result of being born in a particular community and having certain preferred pathways set up between the pleasure areas and the thinking regions by parental and general environmental influences. As with religion and political systems, very few individuals are as autocratic in their marriage pattern as they wish to believe. Studies have shown that each person in a Western culture now has a limit of about five hundred people from which to choose a mate, and that most people choose someone who markedly resembles one or both parents mentally. In social psychology this particular form of brainwashing is called "internalization" and has been shown to be the most potent mechanism by which people acquire their familial and social beliefs. As each individual grows up, that is, as the mind develops, he internalizes the marital and familial outlook of the people with whom he comes in close contact. The behavior of parents to each other and to siblings facilitates the formation of specific neuronal pathways and informational stores in the brain of the developing child which are close copies of those in the parents' brains. This automatic mechanism of early mind control obviously has a biological survival value because it insures that the small society of the family will be composed of relatively homogeneous members rather than of individuals who differ so much in their motives that stable living is precluded. Much the same process goes on in the interaction between different families, producing relatively similar individuals in a tribe or nation. In a family or a tribe attention is called to and criticism is heaped on the person who is "different."

As the developing individual's range of contacts increases through school, college and the outside world, so new patterns of thinking become available for internalization, for copying into his own brain structure. The selection of new patterns will depend upon the extent to which they activate the person's pleasure areas or the extent to which, perhaps by conflict with parental copies, they activate the displeasure areas. Alteration of internalized concepts, rearrangement of preferred pathways and stored information, are an inevitable result of brain function; no one can avoid it. For biological survival this alteration must be delayed until the individual is capable of independent living. In the traditional pattern of the family this is catered for; there is no other sensible reason why family life should have arisen. During the individual's period of dependency upon other people, he derives within the framework of the family the conditions necessary to structure his brain in a way which enables him to accept the benefits on which life itself depends. It is this neurological mechanism which explains the observed fact that, other things being equal, individuals who grow up within a family become better citizens than those who are orphaned or abandoned. No institution staff can provide the unity or precept that is present in even the most disturbed family. As his dependency slowly decreases with greater control over his body, greater size of body and steady increase in his knowledge of causation, the necessity for the child's brain structure to be a fairly exact copy of his parents' also decreases. At adolescence, with the as yet obscure action of hormones on the brain and other parts of the body, there is a critical period of extensive recopying, so that old internalizations are pushed into the unconscious and new brain pathways are opened up under the influence of friends and propaganda media.

Psychologically, at this time the adolescent is more than ever acutely aware of his own separate existence and the degree to which parental indoctrination has overwhelmed that separateness. Because it is an intrinsic feature of his brain that he should want to activate his pleasure areas by use of his own higher brain regions, the adolescent is likely to reject much of the principles which parents have put into his brain, irrespective of the particular meaning of those principles. This is the neurophysiology of teenage rebellion; brain mechanisms cause the adolescent to rebel so as to provide himself with new ideas. He is usually quite unaware that his rebellion is not in any way his own decision based on the inadequacy of parental ideas. Nor is he usually aware that the new ideas from new friends or new heroes are being internalized just as automatically, that is without his volition, as when he was a baby. This is what is meant when some adults claim that adolescents who defy convention simply replace one set of conventions by another. It happens to be neurophysiologically true. Nevertheless, far more parental ideas and values remain in his brain structure than the adolescent ever guesses, and after the battle of adolescence is over, when he begins to live according to those ideas and values, he is likely to believe that he thought them up himself.

Thus the mechanisms of brain function insure that each person incorporates some new behavioral directives that might be of advantage to himself and to society, while retaining sufficient of the parental principles of action to prevent cataclysmic destruction of the established order. In this way, biology insures slow, safe changes in social organization, even when superficially there appears to be a sudden mass alteration of outlook as in the French, British, American, Russian and Chinese revolutions. Historians can trace the long development of these upheavals, and such history can be readily interpreted in terms of brain function. The necessity for this slowness, this fractional admittance of new ideas to the brain, can be seen when it is remembered that not all of the new ideas can be advantageous. We cannot afford the risk of a sudden influx of new ideas in case too many of them are harmful; that way extinction lies. Rebellious adolescents must try to realize that it is not radical adherence to old ideas that prevents their solutions to the world's problems being put into operation, but inexorable biological laws over which no one has the slightest control. Patience is not merely a virtue; it is common sense.

One important result of the adolescent's greatly decreased dependency upon parental care is that he has greater opportunity to select the quality and quantity of his sensory pleasures. However much humanness the parents have managed to inculcate, the adolescent usually takes several steps backward toward the jungle. Once again as in babyhood, he places predominant value upon stimulation of his peripheral receptors, in the guise of attaining adulthood. Commercial interests exploit this propensity to the full, supplying a wealth of sensory sources in yet another form of mind control. Most of them, though often degrading, seldom cause lasting harm, but during adolescence one source of sensory pleasure-seeking has enormous potential for causing later displeasure to many.

It is in adolescence that sex becomes a major source of subhuman sensory pleasure-seeking. It has all the trump cards, for it is new, it is multisensory, it is relatively cheap, it has been shrouded in taboos of some kind by most parents and it is a sensory pleasure specifically reserved for grownups. It is an ideal activity for those who wish to demonstrate to themselves and to others that they have passed into the phase of independence. So much so, in fact, that many people retain the adolescent attitude to sex long after the other trappings of this transitional stage have been lost. None of this would matter too much if it were not for the fact that so many marriages result from predominantly sexual motives.

There is much evidence to prove that no one marries a particular person for just one reason. There is also plenty of evidence that people do not necessarily marry the sexiest person they come in contact with in adolescence. Indeed, there is much evidence to show that the adolescent who eventually becomes an accomplished citizen actively avoids marrying a person well-known to be promiscuous or even highly sexed. Nevertheless, tradition in all societies lays emphasis upon the idea that the salient feature of marriage is social license to engage in sexual behavior. In this respect modern society has made practically no progress or advance on the most primitive human groups. Obviously, these official *mores* have arisen because sexual behavior has been so much identified with reproduction. The well-known fact that sexual behavior very frequently occurs in the absence of procreation has been largely ignored, mainly due to oppressive religious doctrines which have no use for facts. Mankind could take a significant step forward by exercising rational powers to reject all the "revealed truths" about sex and accept the incontrovertible fact that sex is not inextricably involved with marriage or any other social institution. It is simply a form of sensory pleasure-seeking.

Steps are being taken along these lines by some modern reformers who advocate sex before marriage, sex outside marriage, sex with many partners. But it is naïve to think that the problem is solved by rejecting the old collective misunderstanding about sex and marriage and replacing it with the collective misunderstanding that sex should be unrelated to anything except desire. Sex with everything is as potentially harmful and degrading as sugar with everything or any other form of preoccupation with peripheral stimulation.

As well as the neurological basis of waning sexual desire between any two individuals, there is also the very frequent finding that broken marriages have a history of sexual disharmony. Whether the sexual difficulties came first or arose out of other interpersonal problems, the fact that sexual joy is supposed to be an unquestioned feature of successful marriage will inevitably cause each partner to consider the marriage void for this reason alone. If sex were clearly seen to be quite unrelated to marriage as a social institution, the real reasons for divorce might be less easily hidden. It is possible, too, that if people did not look mainly upon marriage as the only socially acceptable means of activating the pleasure areas by sexual behavior, they might not derive the false conclusion that marriage is an institution established for their personal benefit. The demand for personal happiness in marriage, arising from the very structure of the marriage, is one of the most damaging pieces of irrationality extant. Unfortunately, the mass media, the churches and all the conventional tribal ritual of the marriage ceremony exert a highly efficient piece of mind control, giving rise to the demonstrably false belief that marriage is a kind of passport to paradise, so that each partner expects the other to be a life-long source of pleasure, rather than a collaborator in establishing a unit of society. It is curious that an institution whose sole social reason for existence is to add to the collective good by producing a family, is often so personalized that people marry without the slightest intention of having children. Even when progeny result from a marriage, the vast majority of parents still seem to consider that *they* should necessarily derive pleasure from the institution rather than that they should steadfastly exert their efforts to rear their children in the most appropriate manner.

There can be little doubt that the steeply climbing divorce rate results from the gradual loss of all the essential biological features from most people's concept of marriage. More and more, people are looking upon marriage as an arrangement that will provide them with sensory pleasure. When it fails to do so, they feel quite justified in breaking a social contract for personal advantage. I have stated earlier that some religious principles are valuable. I have no hesitation in endorsing the religious principle that divorce is not an acceptable form of human behavior. This is unrelated to gods or morals. It is good biology, rooted in the demonstrable functioning of the brain. The well-intended efforts of some reformers to increase the sum total of human happiness by making divorce as easy as possible are not rationally based, but are founded upon emotion. Although all behavior is pleasure-seeking, as human beings concerned with the future of our species we must exercise the greatest care in the methods we select to obtain pleasure. Happiness itself must never be the sole criterion of action or we are biologically doomed.

What is required is well-financed investigations into ways of making entry into marriage less accidental and less self-centered, and new ways of structuring marriage so that its vital family-rearing purpose is not swamped in a welter of emotional self-pity. For this it is essential that people at large should have greater freedoms and powers of pleasure-seeking, especially in the sexual field, so that marriage ceases to be looked upon as the key to personal joy and becomes the door to social responsibility that it rightfully is. For those who do not wish to shoulder this responsibility and wish to remain childless, there should be some other form of conjugal living that is not confused with marriage. If such partnerships break up, no profound biological requirements are negated.

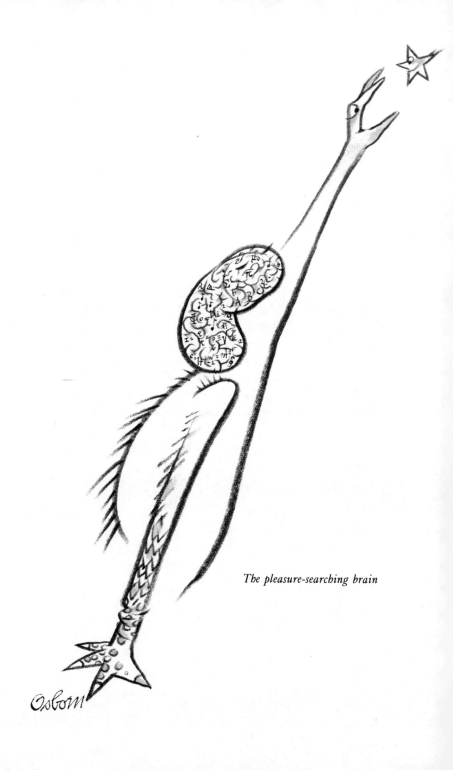

The pleasure-searching brain

Chapter 11
Human Destiny

Some ideas discussed in this book may have proved distasteful, in some cases because a favorite activity has been shown up as essentially subhuman, in others because it may seem that the theory I unfold takes a cold, mechanistic approach to human aspirations. But by examining the long-term implications of this neurophysiological view of man's behavior, I can also show the enormous optimism it holds for the future, and can sketch out a system of beliefs and thought processes which, curiously enough, remove the machinelike characteristics of people and grant them infinite powers of individuality, freedom, and humanness. If my theory is true, this may be the only way to fulfill human destiny.

The very beginning of animal life is lost to us, but we can be sure that one-celled animals came near that beginning and we know from studies of present-day protozoa that they all seek some stimuli and avoid others. Without becoming lost in the philosophical question of whether amoeba "feels" pleasure when it finds a sweet solution, we can now see that only muddled semantics would prevent us from describing amoeba as a pleasure-seeker

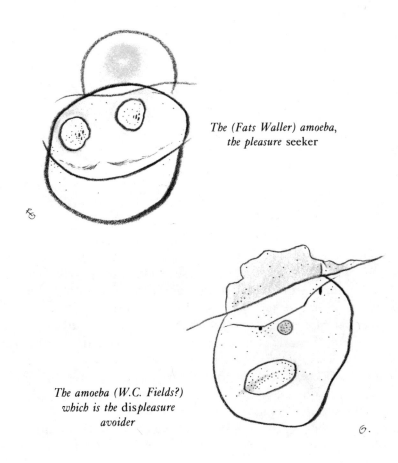

The (Fats Waller) amoeba,
the pleasure seeker

The amoeba (W.C. Fields?)
which is the dis*pleasure*
avoider

and displeasure-avoider. It should be clear, too, that both common observation and rigid scientific studies show that *all* animals have these same two characteristics. This is the only way in which we can sensibly distinguish between plants and animals; if an organism does not seek pleasure it is not an animal. The only way, also, in which we can sensibly account for what has been happening in evolution is to believe that the pleasure-displeasure mechanism has been the one universal, overriding force behind the increasing complexity of animals.

Once we accept the mass of evidence which totally predicates a succession of life from protozoa to man, disposing once and for all of the romantic and arrogant notion that there is something creationally special about the human species, we can see beyond the facile explanation that there has been survival of the fittest. What is or is not fit and fitter is largely a matter of opinion, and opinion has leaned very much toward physical prowess in combat as the acme of fitness. This idea rather neglects the fact that there are many more beetles and kinds of beetles than there are monkeys and kinds of monkeys; it neglects, too, the obvious fact that the largest and strongest animals—whales, elephants, rhinoceroses—have considerable problems in avoiding extinction; and it neglects the debacle of the dinosaurs. Surveying the animal kingdom as a whole, it is unarguable that weak, little creatures such as butterflies have done just as well over the eons as tough, big animals such as gorillas. Clearly, the driving force behind the succession of life has not been merely a tendency to become bigger and stronger. In fact, these two features were simply coincidental changes in groups which were relatively unfit.

When we interpret evolutionary advances in terms of the pleasure-seeking theory, we can see that the bodily changes produced by random mutations and crossing-over of chromosomes were "naturally selected," that is, endured when in some way they increased the animal's chances of obtaining pleasurable and avoiding displeasurable sensation. In some groups, the bodily mechanisms for doing this, coupled with their living conditions, became almost perfectly efficient at an early stage. The driving force diminished and so such groups have shown very little evolution since, and they have remained small and relatively weak but numerous and successful. In other groups each new feature produced only a small step toward perfection so the driving force of pleasure-seeking continued. More and more features were added, each one taking up some space, so the ani-

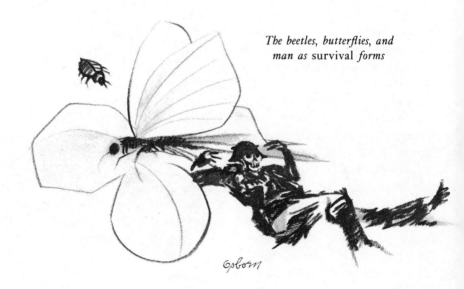

The beetles, butterflies, and man as survival *forms*

mals became larger and therefore stronger in the muscular sense of the word. But they were still less successful than the smaller creatures who had reached full development of pleasure-giving mechanisms. Obviously, larger size and greater strength would have advantages within any species, or among competing species of similar size; but size and strength do not confer biological superiority on an animal group. If these features happen to arise, they will be used in pleasure-seeking, but they have no special significance—they are not what is meant by evolution. If this had been clearly recognized long ago, then the shibboleth of survival of the fittest in terms of muscular power may not have arisen and we may have been spared at least some of the evil consequences of believing in the long-term power of Might. The lesson for man is to recognize that extending muscle power by the technological means of guns, bombs and rockets does not take us forward as a species, it does not make us any fitter than the gorilla. The same applies to daggers and football.

Since new features, to be useful in pleasure-seeking, had to mesh with the particular environment experienced by the animals possessing them, the groups diverged in form to produce a great variety of species, each exhibiting what has come to be called "adaptation to the environment." This standard biological term can be re-expressed as "built to derive the greatest pleasure from what happens to be around." It is not so elegant, perhaps, but carries a deeper meaning. All animals are adapted to their environment, some of them ideally so, and these remain in small areas with little change of form; others are only partially adapted, so they range over much space and change their physical makeup. They will do so until evolutionary changes enable them to extract maximum pleasure from their surroundings, for then no new features are of any use and when that happens evolution stops. From this point of view alone, we can see that man has a very long way to go yet. Man's special and unique equipment for pleasure-seeking has hardly been used. Most people are still using the predominantly sensory mode of activating their pleasure areas, even though evolution has given them a much more powerful tool for extracting pleasure from the surroundings. Despite possession of the necessary neural equipment, most people are *not* adapted to the human environment. One psychoneurologist has written that ". . . humanity behaves in general no more intelligently than animals would under the same circumstances," and an ethologist has said that this is due to ". . . that spiritual pride which prevents men from regarding themselves and their behavior as parts of nature and so subject to its universal laws." How has this come about?

We must first determine what kind of an organism is a newborn baby and what causes him to be a different creature later on. I shall draw attention to facts that many may find distasteful. But one of the ways to be a *human* being is to derive pleasure from knowing the truth rather than from believing nice but false ideas. Dispose of prejudice, whether romantic or religious, for our own good, for the good of our children and the people around us.

The plain *fact*, supported by a tremendous weight of evidence, is that the newborn is utterly mindless, soulless, totally lacking in personality and completely bereft of any human mental feature. Before going on to say what he *has* got, let me give a little evidence to support these negative claims. Much more detail can be found in the very readable and highly significant book *Physical Control of the Mind* by Professor José Delgado. Only a few years ago at the Massachusetts Institute of Technology,

J. Altmann, utilizing the elegant method of radioactive tracer compounds, showed that only about 10 to 20 percent of the normal complement of nerve cells are present in the cerebral cortex at birth, the other 80 to 90 percent appear during infancy *under some conditions*. Others have shown that the few nerve cells present in the newborn thinking regions have no connections with each other; only later, again under certain circumstances, do these cells come into contact, so that they can give and receive information. The fact that the great convoluted areas of recent brain are "empty" in the newborn is also shown by the observation that babies in which the cerebral cortex is entirely missing are virtually indistinguishable from the normal child for up to two months. Apart from these and many similar anatomical findings, there is also a wealth of neurochemical and behavioral evidence, such as the demonstration that neurones in the newborn cortex are very deficient in vital proteins and RNA, and that careful testing of behavioral responses reveals so little correlation that the researchers had to state that "there is no mental integration in the newborn child." Whatever loving parents or people of religious persuasion may wish to believe, men who spend their lives in the study of newborns, and neurologists as a whole, are forced to agree with Professor Delgado when he says ". . . we must conclude that there are no detectable signs of mental activity at birth and *that human beings are born without minds*" (his italics). Thus man at birth and shortly afterward has little more "works" inside his head than a fish. I hope to show that, far from deploring this fact, intelligent, rational people should seize upon it as the very foundation upon which a rich and varied human destiny can be built, for the individual and for mankind at large.

From the positive point of view the baby has a well-functioning sensory system in good connection with nicely developed pleasure areas. In the first few days or weeks of extrauterine life just about all the baby can do with his brain is receive sensory impulses that activate his pleasure and displeasure areas. The newborn is so poorly developed that he cannot even seek pleasure, but needs to have it brought to him. The way in which this is done is of paramount importance and is also fully controllable.

The baby's brain grows more cells but these become properly interconnected only under certain circumstances. These circumstances are quite simple and usual. First of all there are some basic general physiological requirements. If the newborn brain is to develop into that of a human being, the individual must have the set of genes which carry that potential; but the genetic endowment in itself is not enough. Indeed, it can be seen to be relatively insignificant for even with the enormous range of human genes only relatively few kinds of brains develop. Failure of the genetic basis, on the other hand, is quite different, and can have overriding influence on brain development. Secondly, the newborn brain must be supplied with oxygen, nutrients in the blood and thyroid hormone. Thyroid hormone is essential for providing the chemical "incentive" for the protein synthesis which must occur if cell connections are to grow, as has been elegantly demonstrated by Professor J. T. Eayrs of Birmingham University. Its absence results in cretinism. However, even if all these conditions are perfect, the newborn brain will still not develop properly. The brain must have a sensory input. Up to this point there may have been those who have decided that although the human baby may not have brain cells, brain connections, brain proteins and brain functions at birth, all these would turn up eventually as a matter of automatic development. This "nice" idea is also untrue. All the evidence shows that the development of a mind in the child is not a routine, inevitable part of development like the ability to move about. Minds have to be made.

Luckily this is no great problem. The number of cortical cells and their connections can be altered by exposing the newborn to high or low levels of sensory input. Brain cells in the seeing and hearing regions do not acquire their proper chemistry if the infant is deprived of light or sound. Artificial rotation of the body in newborn babies caused a 40 percent increase of RNA in the neurones concerned with balance and only eight days of high sensory input produced easily-measured increase in the weight of the cerebral cortex, its thickness and blood supply and in its content of enzymes essential for the transmission of information from one nerve cell to another. This and much more evidence like it proves conclusively that whatever potential there may be in the newborn brain, it will not become apparent unless it receives information from the world outside. Only then can its anatomy and chemistry move up the evolutionary scale, away from the fish toward the human.

But even this is not enough to produce a mind. The development so far could be brought about by flashing a lamp in the baby's eyes, shouting in its ears or joggling it up and down. The result would be a nice brain structure but precious little brain function. As Delgado puts it succinctly: "The brain is not sufficient to produce mental phenomena." Expressing it another way, and anticipating what comes later, we can say that different mental phenomena do not imply different brain structures. We demolish immediately the cry of self-absolution—"I haven't got the brain to do that." The evidence all points to us starting off with practically the same brains. What kind of mental phenomena occur later depends almost entirely upon what happens to us, assuming, of course, that we are normal.

The newborn must have a suitable level of sensory input if the brain is to develop properly. For the mind to develop at all, let alone properly, the sensory input must have meaning. From the point of view of the present theory, a sensory input has meaning if and only if it activates the pleasure or displeasure areas. When information is processed by the brain, preferred pathways are established, and there comes a time when certain stimuli give rise to nerve impulses that travel in certain directions to certain objectives, even though it is possible for them to travel by different routes to different places. A simple and crude analogy is the switching method on railways; a mass of lines and trains running about all over them with nothing to control direction does not constitute a "mindful" rail system. Only when the passage of a train from station A to station B is insured by switching out the irrelevant lines, can we profitably use the equipment. Strychnine takes all the "switches" out of the human brain and allows nerve impulses to pass along any pathways, and the observable effect of this compound is to produce a jerking, convulsive, mindless individual, quite incapable of thinking or even moving sensibly. Only brains that contain preferred pathways can exhibit the characteristics of a mind. And the kind of mind exhibited depends entirely upon the pattern of preferred pathways, which in turn depends upon what has happened to the individual. The setting-up of preferred pathways continues all through life, and if the conditions are right then some such pathways can be obliterated in favor of new ones. We then say that the person has "changed his mind"; in fact, there has been a change in a part of the experientially "lubricated" routing of nerve impulses in his brain. He may have brought this about himself (and will almost certainly insist that he has) but it is far more likely to have been induced by something in the environment. Thus the mind is: "the thought processes and behavior brought about by a pattern of preferred pathways in the brain." How are these pathways established?

In the newborn it is by sensory manipulation of the pleasure areas—the primitive neural system—that the mind begins to be formed. In normal circumstances the early period is straightforward. The mother brings gustatory, olfactory, thermal and tactile stimulation to her baby's peripheral receptors. All of these activate the pleasure areas; they are therefore meaningful stimuli because all we imply when we say that a stimulus is not meaningful is that it does not activate our pleasure or displeasure areas. With simple, crude stimuli such as are normally supplied to a baby, very little is meaningless, just as a plain white lamp is not meaningless to monkeys. For quite a while the baby responds to its mother in a way analogous to fish with their electrodes. She is a source of primitive sensory pleasure, nothing more. In fact, as Professor Harlow has shown with baby monkeys, she can be dispensed with entirely and replaced by a surrogate model made from a tailor's dummy, provided it is warm and of tactile interest. Brought up for a while with such a model, the babies prefer it to the real mother, running to it and clinging to it when the real mother is allowed into the room, even when the dummy has never supplied milk. Much the same happens from time to time with human babies, whose mothers die in childbirth or abandon them; and most mothers employ partial surrogates such as comforters, rattles and mechanical rocking. If we are to be realistic we must recognize that there is absolutely no more bond of "affection" between the newborn and its mother than between my crocodile and its electrodes. Happily, the situation does not remain like that.

The crude sensations supplied by the mother in the early days of the baby's life activate the pleasure areas and also travel along the classical sensory pathways to the cerebral cortex. Sensory input also promotes the growth and development of the higher regions. Thus there is a continuous impetus to the setting-up of preferred pathways between the pleasure areas and the thinking regions that involves the processes of attention, memory and association. Time and again as the image of the mother falls on the infant's retina, or the sound of her voice vibrates its eardrums, warmth, food and caressings activate its limbic pleasure areas. Nerve impulses speed along particular nerve pathways, oiling them, so to speak. Nerve fiber branches grow out to touch each other and so communication in higher regions begins; memories of sound and sight are laid down by the new protein stores; associations occur, so that when impulses arrive in one brain region, other impulses are immediately sent to another. Sensory input now does not just activate the pleasure areas, as in a fish; it sets up a highly complex dispersement of nerve impulses along many routes, and causes waves of electrical activity to sweep through various parts of the brain. The baby now *recognizes* sources of pleasure and displeasure, and its developing motor system enables it to try to get at them. All this is the beginning of mind.

But it is still subhuman. There is a common piece of wishful thinking, which is that lower animals do not have minds. As with the soul, this idea is clearly a mixture of arrogance and self-justification. As Konrad Lorenz has frequently pointed out, many people have a tremendously strong wish to feel that they are fundamentally different from lower animals; probably millions use the word "animal" to exclude the human species and conjure up biologically absurd phrases such as "I cannot treat her like an animal." They want to believe that their behavior is the result of special thought processes (even though often what they actually *do*, as we have seen, is subhuman) and that "animals" behave as a result of some other, inferior, unspecified mechanism. Knowledge of the essential distinction between human and subhuman behavior can no longer deny thought processes to lower creatures. The whole wide and fertile field of animal psychology could hardly exist if no thinking processes occurred in the animals studied. How else could we have circuses, horse races, and man's best friend by the fireplace?

The baby, with the beginnings of a mind, is thus rather like a pet dog. It is still entirely sensorially oriented, still id-controlled in psychoanalytic terms, or as Professor J. Z. Young states, ". . . the child is completely selfish and egocentric. The only features of the world that concern it are those that minister to its wants and *these are mostly the features and responses of men and women*" (his italics). The brain of the baby very soon comes to contain the information that rewarding stimuli are associated more with people than with objects. So it responds more to the presence of people, especially those who are most closely connected with pleasurable stimuli, like its mother or whoever reared him. This tendency to move toward a major source of subhuman sensory pleasure has come to be called love. It is not, one might hope, the only kind of love there is, but frank appraisal of bonds of affection among people will only rarely reveal one in which sensory pleasure is totally lacking. It will, of course, *never* reveal one in which activation of the pleasure areas is lacking; even when the righteous are "loving their enemies," they are getting some joy from doing so. The beginnings of emotional development arise only in the presence of a source of sensory pleasure and are *directed* at that source. Monkeys brought up with no more sensory pleasure than vital food supply have little emotional content and do not direct it at anything or anyone; something very similar used to happen in orphanages.

There comes a time in the baby's development when something fundamentally different from anything that has yet happened to it can occur in its brain. No one would be so bold as to say exactly when this is possible and most research workers would insist that there is nothing exact about it. More research is urgently required so that we can *know* at least within limits when our babies can start to be human beings, that is when sufficient brain maturation has occurred for nerve impulses to pass from the thinking regions to the pleasure areas.

At that time, the baby begins to respond with pleasure to stimuli which are not rewarding in themselves as sensory inputs but which evoke concepts and ideas, very simple ones, of course, such as approval and most importantly, pleasure in others. Now begins the long, slow development of a human mind, the establishment of preferred pathways for thinking pleasure. Just as with the "sensory mind" (preferred pathways totally involved with sensory pleasure) so the "human mind" is utterly and completely dependent upon environmental happenings for the degree to which it develops and the direction in which it develops. The child *learns* to think and behave in certain ways as a result of the preferred brain pathways brought into being by the rewards (activation of the pleasure areas) and punishments (activation of the displeasure areas) that occur in the environment. The environmental happenings *control* the development of the baby's mind. There are certainly genetic potentials, many that we do not yet know about, but the precise form that genetic tendencies take depends upon the interaction of the brain with the environment. Studies with identical twins have shown that the influence of genes on mental development can either be allowed to become apparent or can be partially or entirely obliterated by suitable environmental conditions. The point to fix firmly in our system of beliefs is that we can do nothing about the genes a baby possesses, but we are totally responsible for how its mind develops.

I have already mentioned brainwashing and mind control, and have drawn special attention to the way in which religious "truths" are embedded into the child's brain and political "truths" into the adolescent's brain. We must recognize that mind control cannot be avoided and has existed throughout the history of mankind. It happens in every church, school, kindergarten and home. It is inherent in the process of education. Without mind control there can be no mind because mind control *is the setting up of preferred pathways.* Any idea that children's minds should be allowed to develop without control, for whatever stated purpose, is based upon the false belief that an absence of systematic indoctrination results in no indoctrination. The similar suggestion that children should be allowed to develop "according to their own needs" is also biologically ridiculous, for the child has no "own needs" except the one to keep the pleasure areas active. Any other "needs" have been built into it one way or another as extensions of this primal one and can only be believed to be intrinsic if we reject the material evidence in favor of "I think so" philosophies. This makes life easy for the proponents of the idea, but it exposes the child's brain to random brainwashing stimuli which *must,* by inexorable biological law, encode with his brain sufficient preferred pathways to constitute a mind. We cannot expect such a randomly brainwashed individual to have a mind whose workings accord with any systematic social organization.

The rational approach is to accept the fact that children do not have souls, do not have personalities, do not have minds, as intrinsic items of equipment like their kidneys, and that parents and others are totally responsible for the kind of mind, the kind of personality that develops in the child. Rather than cavil at the concept of mind control, we should grasp it like a life belt for the savior of our children, relishing the fact that the newborn comes to us with an empty head and all the potential to become an honored accomplished citizen. Our task is not to avoid control of the mind, for that is impossible, but to pay great attention to how it should be carried out. In doing this effectively, deep-seated prejudices must be rooted out and rejected. Important matters such as how to bring up children, how to indoctrinate adolescents, how to eradicate antisocial behavior cannot be left to the uniformed whims of parents, magical tenets of priests, vested interests of commerce, or the power-seeking of politicians. They require the same kind of rational, factual, systematic study as has been applied to bodily disease or heating systems or bridge building.

The majority of people will not argue about what an aldehyde is, for that belongs to the realm of chemistry; or what an allelomorph is, for that is the concern of biology; or what a newton is, for that lies in the field of physics. By and large, people recognize that to argue sensibly about these matters requires a protracted, specialized process of indoctrination with evidence and knowledge. Yet most people, whose formal education finished in adolescence and whose contact with intellectual disciplines has been minimal, feel quite competent to decide with absolute certainty what is true, what is false, what is good, what is evil. It does not occur to them that these matters are just as much the proper subject for systematized, factual training as the phenomena of chemistry, biology and physics. We can now see the neurophysiology behind such intellectual arrogance. People at large label as true and good those things which activate their pleasure areas; things which activate the displeasure areas are labeled as false and evil. I cannot give examples of these categories because there is no universal agreement, for a very real reason. This misfortune arises from the demonstrable fact that what activates any given, average, untrained individual's pleasure areas depends upon the environmental influences that have affected his brain. His notions of the "eternal verities" are derived from the pure chance of what notions are held by the people with whom he comes in contact. Unless he seeks the difficult and purely intellectual pleasure of systematic, analytic, impersonal appraisal of observed reality, he will inevitably select his beliefs on the basis of which ones have been associated with pleasure and displeasure in the past. He deludes himself that they are thereby true, when in fact a large number of them are false and even larger numbers are logically doubtful, that is, there is not enough evidence to know whether they are true or false.

If good and evil are defined, not in terms of the effect that some things have on this or that person's or group's feeling of pleasure, but in terms of their actual demonstrable effects upon human life in the long-term view, then no one *knows* whether easy divorce, contraception, Communism, abortion on demand, drug-taking, fascism, sexual segregation, organ-transplantation, test-tube babies and many other such topics are good or evil. Claim to certainty in such matters is merely a demonstration of bigotry, arrogance and irrationality in the pretender.

Certainty, of course, is a very different approach from the viewpoint which says that because of such and such *evidential* rational arguments, we recommend that such and such a technique be tried. Experiments in the abolition of capital punishment are an example of this sensible approach to the control of human conduct. One of the features that has attracted many intelligent minds to Marxism is that, among an unfortunate welter of propagandist ideologies, there is a thoroughly scientific, factual, experimental approach to the structure of society which is very different from the totally ideological, that is, emotional concepts of democracy. But even though democracy is based upon undemonstrated magical ideas such as the edict that "all men have the right to X" when in fact the concept of human rights is scientifically meaningless, and the selection of X is arbitrary, it will come to be seen that democracy has features which will eventually be part of the ideal system. Everyone alive today must clearly recognize the *fact* that they are guinea pigs in the great experiments of human society, and that at the same time they are manipulators within those experiments.

Acknowledgment of this truth, together with the realization that *Homo sapiens* has not yet appeared in great numbers but that man's evolution is still progressing, might reduce our intellectual arrogance and produce intellectual humility. No one can yet state without personal prejudice what is the best way to live, but by observing facts it is possible to do two useful things. It is possible to state that some ways are better than others in terms of producing long-term pleasure and reducing long-term displeasure. And it is possible to state the most likely methods of finding out better ways of living and contrast them with present methods. I hope I have already made clear the rational, factual arguments that show that continuing to establish "truths" by any religious faith can only lead to disaster, in the same way that clinging to emotionally-based political beliefs, irrespective of the particular system, is likely to be holocaustic. The vast majority of people's beliefs, in big and small matters, are equally derived from primitive emotional involvement and such emotional development is founded upon sensory activation of the pleasure areas, upon subhuman behavior. This then is the biology behind Delgado's anguished cry that the majority of people behave like lower animals and behind Lorenz's sorrowful statement that ". . . some of the basic emotional responses of our species remain very similar and directly comparable to those of higher animals." Certain scientifically derived truths follow from this.

Progress toward a fully human destiny will be retarded while we place high value upon activities based on stimulation of peripheral receptors. Until such behavior is reduced to its true perspective as trivial, relaxational subhuman pursuits, all else that we may do will be of little avail.

Even then, and even if the majority of people obtain the majority of their pleasure from use of their higher brain regions, there is still the problem of finding the most suitable kind of thinking pleasure. There are some lessons from the past to help us and we should now know that the only way to find out more is to throw a great weight of scientific effort into the study of the individual and of society. This will be a long and expensive matter. A splendid example could be shown by the churches selling their enormous assets and devoting the money to the factual study of human happiness. Perhaps the top baseball players, who are paid more than the President of the United States, could lead lesser mortals in contributing to the mental welfare of the society to whose animal pleasures they pander. The cost of the Olympic Games would keep half a dozen research teams going for many years. More importantly, perhaps, those who are growing up with an eye to becoming sportsmen, priests or pop singers, might consider that a life spent in the factual study of man would give them a dignity and usefulness otherwise denied them. Most fertile and realistic of all, if everyone decided to embark on a systematic course of logic, leading to a real rather than imagined ability to think rationally, there would be a sound foundation of intellectual pleasure-seeking upon which to build the framework indicated by new-found facts. Universal logical positivism would take us a long way from the jungle.

But most people grow up with the preferred pathways built into their brains by parents, priests or teachers. These indoctrinated pathways represent the mental phenomena to which terms like "preconceived ideas" and "prejudices" have been given. Such pathways were established so early in life and so subtly that most individuals are no more aware that they "learned" them than that they learned to walk. The brainwashed character of these pathways becomes readily apparent under hypnosis or during psychoanalysis, but most people find it difficult to believe that these pathways which constitute their mind, their personality, are not really theirs at all in any self-generated sense. They do not like to believe that they are functioning like machines. Nevertheless a person whose behavior is based upon indoctrinated preferred pathways is no less a machine than the computer that behaves according to a preset program. Identical computers behave differently with different programs; identical brains have different minds if they have different preferred pathways. There is thus overwhelming evidence that the world is mainly populated by robots. It should be clear, then, that the most important form of mind control required for the proper fulfillment of each individual's biological birthright is self-control. We can only attain individuality, personal freedom and nonmechanical life if we determine our own preferred pathways.

Let there be no mistake. We can be mind-controlled into altruism or cruelty, whoever we are and whatever our level of education, unless we have been trained to think for ourselves. With regard to altruism, experiments by Dr. David Rosenhan of Swarthmore College, Pennsylvania, have shown how simple it is to indoctrinate children into giving to charity by acting out an example for only a few minutes, without propaganda or moralizing. Children one by one played a table-top bowling game with the experimenter. Every winning move was awarded two "gift certificates" that were redeemable at a neighboring store. With half of the children, every time the experimenter won he casually and without comment placed one of his two certificates in a box labeled "orphans' fund." With the other half no such contribution was made. The fund was never mentioned and the experimenter made no reaction to whether the child contributed certificates or not. After a short while the experimenter went away, leaving the child to play the game on his own. One-way observation during this period showed that no child who had not seen donations made contributed to the fund, whereas nearly half of the children whose partners had contributed handed over a large portion of the prized certificates. As Dr. Rosenhan says ". . . altruistic models, even in a narrow laboratory situation, serve to facilitate altruism in children."

Most of us take heart in such findings, but brain processes do not in themselves select only the good. In work done by S. Milgram and reported in 1968 in the *Journal of Abnormal and Social Psychology*, it was shown that anyone in a random sample of people would carry out apparently cruel acts if merely told that there was a fairly good purpose involved. Milgram used helpers to pretend to be subjects in an experiment. They were locked in an electric chair and the real subjects were told to press a lever if the man in the chair made errors in verbal tests, raising the voltage each time to produce a greater shock. Even though the real subjects had been given a sample shock of 45 volts they were prepared to shock the man in the chair right up to 450 volts, despite the well-acted pain and misery of the strapped-in victim. Some subjects protested from time to time but nevertheless continued to administer what they thought were shocks simply because the experimenter told them to, yet the experimenter was not in a position of any authority over them. This type of mind control to the length of cruelty has been confirmed many times in the laboratory. It explains, perhaps, the ease with which men can be induced to run concentration camps along Nazi lines, or set off bombs in political demonstrations, or torture for the sake of religion. Self-control of the mind could prevent that.

Only the human species is able to control its mind as far as we know, because only humans can introspect. Only humans can deliberately channel nerve impulses from one thinking region to another, which is what happens when we think about a particular topic, and when we engender in ourselves a particular attitude to that topic. The fact that most people do not do it is partly because they do not know how and partly because it is difficult and time consuming. There is more and more evidence that more and more people are born in each generation who can and do "make up their own minds" in this neurophysiological, nonarrogant sense of that phrase. But we do not have to wait for chance mutations to produce people who have high facility for doing it. Every sane, normal person can acquire the expertise that will enable him to establish self-selected preferred pathways in his brain, many of which may well coincide with ones already put into him. It is a matter of undergoing training in logic, refusing to accept without question the edicts of authority, examining impersonally the relation between present beliefs and facts, which means becoming acquainted with the facts, and rejecting everything that does not accord with fact.

This means that many activities and ideas about which we now hold firm beliefs will have to be relegated to the areas of "don't know." This in itself might prevent emphatic, riotous and militant attempts to replace one emotionally-based system with another equally subhuman belief. It should also enable parents to cease inculcating convenient, cut-and-dried wishful thinking into their children. It should persuade them to teach the modicum of good manners, decency and respect for others that is required for day-to-day living, while at the same time stressing the need for rational thinking and critical analysis, appealing always in the end to knowledge, not faith.

This approach to understanding and manipulating our own brains, this control of our minds, deriving the maximum activation of our pleasure areas from thinking activity, is very much a pervasive undercurrent in neurological, psychiatric and sociological circles today. Experimental work firmly based in all of these disciplines points clearly to the fact that once "thinking" takes on a systematic, rational character, it can serve as an "environmental influence." It can cause the rearrangement, establishment and re-establishment of preferred pathways in the brain, in a material manner, thereby conferring on each individual the power to make up his own mind with precision and control. If "freedom" is to have a real and not imaginary meaning, surely this is it.

The last chapters in Professor Delgado's book examine these new ideas at length and I strongly advise everyone to read them. He has kindly given me permission to quote in full his "postulates of psychogenesis," which now follow:

> 1. The mind does not exist at the moment of birth. 2. The mind cannot appear in the absence of sensory inputs. 3. Individual identity and personal behavior are not properties of the brain which will unfold automatically through neural maturation, but are acquired functions which must be learned and therefore depend essentially on the reception of sensory inputs. 4. The purpose of education is not the unveiling of individual mental functions but *the creation, the genesis of them*. 5. Symbols from the environment will be physically integrated within the brain as molecular changes in the neuronal structure. 6. Man is not born free but subservient to genes and education. 7. Personal freedom is not inherited nor is it a gift of nature, but one of the highest attainments of civilization which requires awareness and intellectual and emotional training in order to process and choose consciously and intelligently among environmental alternatives. 8. Education should not be authoritarian because then mental flexibility is reduced, handicapping creativity and forcing behavioral conformity or producing hyperreactive rejection and rebellion. Education should not be permissive either, because other kinds of automatisms are then being developed, determined by the blind chance of environmental circumstances.

Those postulates of beliefs that would lead to a psychocivilized society warrant deep thought. In essence, the tasks which face every caring individual are firstly to recognize the subhuman nature and social valuelessness of the sensory pleasure-seeking behaviors and therefore cease to be involved with them to any significant degree, cease to support commercial exploitation of them and cease to teach children that prowess in them has any human worth. Secondly, we must understand clearly the human methods of activating the pleasure areas as I have described, then we must recognize that all normal people possess the brain equipment to become involved in valuable human behavior. Thirdly, we must reject entirely any magical explanations of human conduct, human responsibility and earthly phenomena. Fourthly, we must undergo instruction and training in the human use of the mind, acquiring the facilities of rational thought and intelligent assessment of facts. Fifthly, we must develop in ourselves and others the quality of self-control of the mind, so that intellectual activation of our pleasure areas will occur at the level of human dignity rather than as the output of a robot. Sixthly, we must support to our utmost every endeavor made to initiate and foster research into brain function, mind control, behavior, education, sociology, and kindred subjects, so that men may have the relevant facts to tread as surely in mental matters as in moon walks.

I am aware that it is facile to write this and simple to read it, and that much time and effort are required to put these recommendations into effect. But after all, time and effort are available to everyone. Nor can there be any excuse about lack of brain power, paucity of intellectual ability. When war comes there is no great problem in taking men from shops or factories or similar unintellectual environments and turning them quickly into navigators, radar operators and other kinds of brain workers. The psychologist L. Hudson showed that men who had achieved great eminence in politics, law and science had no better degree than many less successful people. Twenty-three percent of Fellows of the Royal Society had obtained only second or third class degrees; this was only 2 percent higher than those with similar degrees who had not attained this highest scientific distinction in Britain. Further, 43 percent of the holders of doctorates had second or third class degrees. It was found that 66 percent of British cabinet ministers and 54 percent of High Court judges had poor degrees. There can therefore be no doubt whatever that whether or not a person engages in intellectual activities as a means of activating his pleasure areas is not dependent upon what is ordinarily meant by "brain power." For the majority of people, certainly all of those now leading "ordinary" lives, we may assume that they all started out at birth with the same potentially human brain. Their present status is due to their past environment and to the degree of mental inertia in them. But everyone is capable of altering his brain and therefore of changing his mind— his opinions, beliefs and attitudes—all of which are simply representations of preferred neural pathways. Let us, for our own salvation, dispense with the easy and comforting, but totally false, belief that "people cannot be changed." For centuries the world has been controlled by an intellectual elite, even in those regions where the lower classes seem to have power. In fact such lower classes often simply have power to listen and cheer the ideological indoctrinations of the thinkers who rule them, whether these are politicians or shop stewards. If attempts to correct this situation are made by brains driven by emotion there can be no enduring improvement, only an apparent change for the better which in a little while is again found displeasurable. Every individual must make the effort to insure that his thinking-pleasure is based upon fact and reason, and must make the effort to instill just such prepared pathways into his children or pupils.

An overwhelming force in retarding man's social progress is the great ease with which the pleasure areas can be activated. It is a sure and certain mark of subhumanness, and therefore should be a minor, relaxational part of our lives, not the driving force of our motives. The amount of effort put into the task of acquiring the facility to activate the pleasure areas predominantly by use of the higher brain regions determines in large measure the level of accomplishment reached in any field of endeavor. It also serves as a means of human evaluation. When we derive activation of our pleasure areas from the effort of intellectual activity as the major preoccupation of our lives, we can truthfully, factually and scientifically tell ourselves that at last we are human beings.

There is plenty of evidence that an increasing number of people have been doing this, even though they were perhaps not quite sure why. They now know why. And they also know that the laws of biology are on their side. Even though millions will continue to live in sensorially-oriented isolation from the human community that nurtures them, every generation will produce more *human* beings, not by accident but by the design of those who have recognized the truth of the psychocivilized society. It is for that, after all, that our pleasure areas evolved. Indisputably man has proved his mechanical superiority over lower animals in controlling his environment. Now, if never before, is the time to prove his biological superiority by determining the preferred pathways in his brain, thereby controlling his mind.

Glossary
Select Bibliography
Index

Glossary

ACTIVITY WHEEL. Chamber in which animals can "run" any distance yet remain in same place. Counting revolutions gives measure of activity.

ADAPTATION. A receptor is adapted when it no longer discharges nerve impulses, even though the stimulus continues.

ADRENALIN. A substance, for the purposes of this book, identical with noradrenaline (which see).

AMYGDALA OR AMYGDALOID NUCLEUS. A collection of nerve cell bodies in the temporal lobe of the brain, containing pleasure and displeasure areas.

ANOREXIA NERVOSA. Psychogenic illness in which, among other things, patient has no appetite, no appreciation of flavor, and refuses to eat.

ANTERIOR PITUITARY GLAND. Situated at base of brain, this gland manufactures and releases hormones that control the ovary, testes, thyroid, and adrenal glands.

ANTIANDROGEN. A chemical that prevents the male sex hormone from exerting its effects upon tissues. *E.g.*, cyproterone acetate.

ARCHICORTEX. First higher brain region to evolve and to supervise functions of archaic limbic system. Earliest cerebral cortex.

AUTONOMIC. The neural system concerned with normally automatic and unconscious matters such as heart rate, movement of intestines. Physical and emotional events cause extra activity in the system and awareness of this has been labeled fear, anxiety, excitement, etc.

BUCCAL CAVITY. Rather loosely, the mouth.

CAPACITANCE PROBE. A metal rod that generates an imperceptible electric field and detects changes caused in the field by the approach of an object.

CEREBRAL CORTEX. Latest, highest, and most complex part of the brain, overlying and controlling the archaic limbic system.

CINGULATE GYRUS. Old part of cerebral cortex lying in midline immediately above corpus callosum.

COGNITION. Sums up the manifold complex neural and psychological processes involved in *understanding* sensory input.

CONURBATION. The large urban masses caused by coalescence of neighboring townships or by very extensive expansion of single towns.

CORPUS CALLOSUM. Thick sheet of nerve fibers crossing the brain from one side of cerebral cortex to the other and distributed from front to back of brain.

DUALISM. *See* Monism.

EMPIRICAL. Based upon facts of observation and experiment, not theory.

ETHOLOGICAL. Based on ethology, *i.e.*, from considerations of behavioral observations only.

EXTEROCEPTORS. Peripheral receptors on the "surface" of the body in the skin, mouth, eyes, ears, nose.

HABITUATION. A region of the brain is habituated to incoming stimuli when it ceases to pass the information on to other parts of the brain.

HIPPOCAMPAL GYRUS. Very old part of cerebral cortex lying tucked into inner side of temporal lobe. Part of palaeocortex.

HOMEOSTATIC. All advantageous bodily processes and behaviors serve to maintain an equilibrium, for example of heart rate, blood sugar level, body temperature. Such processes and behaviors are homeostatic.

HYPOTHALAMUS. Very old brain region, part of limbic system, containing pleasure and displeasure areas, and regions for control of heart rate, respiration, blood pressure, temperature, hormone secretion, and similar "unconscious" functions.

INPUT. General term for the pattern of nerve impulses entering the brain or some region of it.

INTEROCEPTORS. Peripheral receptors inside the body, in the joints, mesenteries, blood vessels, intestines and other viscera.

INTRACRANIAL. Means inside the skull. In this book means inside the pleasure areas.

LIMBIC SYSTEM. Very old system of neural regions lying below the cerebral cortex, concerned with vital matters such as eating, mating, fighting. Contains the pleasure and displeasure areas.

MACROSMIC. *See* Microsmic.

MEISSNER'S CORPUSCLES. Complicated sense organs in the skin, sensitive to tactile stimuli and having the ability to discriminate between types of touch.

MESENTERY. Flat sheets of tissue lying between folds of intestines and between other viscera. Abundantly supplied with stretch sensitive receptors that signal "stomachache" and anxiety.

MICROSMIC. Animal groups in which the "smell brain" is poorly developed and the animals relatively unable to detect weak odors (*e.g.*, humans). The reverse are macrosmic groups, with highly developed olfactory system and acute sense of smell (*e.g.*, dog).

MONISM. Those who subscribe to the view that mind is solely a product of matter are monists. Those who postulate two kinds of universal "stuff"—material and nonmaterial—are dualists.

MULTIMODAL. Synonym for plurimodal.

NEOCORTEX. Most recent parts of the cerebral cortex, developing only in mammals and reaching its maximum in man. The thinking regions.

NEURONE, NEURON. Synonym for nerve cell.

NORADRENALINE. Substance manufactured and released by the outer layer of the suprarenal gland and also released at many nerve endings, transmitting information from one neurone to another.

OESTRADIOL. Female sex hormone manufactured in and secreted by the ovary.

PALAEOCORTEX. Embracive term for regions of cerebral cortex intermediate in age between archicortex and neocortex. Contains primary areas for sensation and movement.

PERINATAL. The period from just before to just after birth—a few days either way.

PHEROMONE. Substance secreted on the surface of the body which acts as an olfactory signal to other members of the species.

PHONEME. Smallest articulable sound units of languages. Very roughly correspond to letters.

PHYLOGENY. The main groups of animals are called phyla, *e.g.*, phylum amphibia. The evolutionary succession of phyla is called phylogeny.

PLURIMODAL. Sensory input derived from several sense modalities simultaneously.

PROGESTERONE. Hormone manufactured in and secreted by the ovary after ovulation. If pregnancy occurs progesterone is secreted throughout gestation.

PROPRIOCEPTORS. Peripheral receptors situated in the joints, which signal movement and position of limbs to brain.

REFLEXIVE. One's actions having an effect upon oneself.

RETICULAR ACTIVATING SYSTEM. A mass of short chains of neurones lying across the midline from the midbrain to the hypothalamus. All senses connect with it, and it connects with all parts of limbic system and cerebral cortex.

SACCIDIC EYE MOVEMENTS. Minute, unconscious, side-to-side movements of the eyes characteristic of mammals.

SENSORY MODALITY. Each sense is called a mode, *e.g.*, the modality of vision.

SEPTUM PELLUCIDUM. Most frontward part of limbic system, of pleasure areas and, in primitive vertebrates, of the brain itself.

SEROTONIN. Substance which occurs in some neurones and which can prevent information passing from one neurone to another. Inhibitory neurotransmitter.

SPHYGMOMANOMETER. Device with inflatable arm band for measuring blood pressure.

SUBSTRATE. That which underlies the topic of discussion. *E.g.*, the neural substrate of pleasure is that collection of nerve cells and fibers that compose the pleasure areas.

SYNAPSE. Junction between two nerve cells across which information passes from one neurone to another.

TELEOLOGICAL. Based upon concepts of purpose or function.

TERTIARY ASSOCIATION AREA. Parts of cerebral cortex concerned with highest functions such as speech, reasoning.

TESTOSTERONE. Male sex hormone manufactured in and secreted by testis.

THALAMUS. Large collection of nerve cell bodies lying above hypothalamus. All senses connect with it and information is relayed by it to specific parts of cerebral cortex.

TRANSDUCER. Device for converting one form of energy into another, *e.g.*, microphone transduces sound to electricity.

UNIMODAL. Sensory input derived at any one time from a single sense modality.

VESTIBULAR SENSE. Sensory mode by which we are aware of balance, twisting, etc., as a result of nerve impulses from semicircular canals associated with the ear.

Select Bibliography

About the Brain

H. J. CAMPBELL, *Correlative Physiology of the Nervous System* (Academic Press, 1965).

E. C. CROSBY, T. HUMPHREY AND E. W. LAUER, *Correlative Anatomy of the Nervous System* (Macmillan, 1962).

DEAN E. WOODRIDGE, *The Machinery of the Brain* (McGraw-Hill, 1963).

About the Mind

B. P. BECKWITH, *Religion, Philosophy and Science* (Philosophical Library, 1957).

josé m. r. delgado, *Physical Control of the Mind* (Harper and Row, 1970).

j. napier, *The Roots of Mankind* (Allen and Unwin, 1971).

e. slater and m. roth, *Clinical Psychiatry*, 3rd. ed. (Ballière, Tindall and Cassell, 1969).

j. z. young, *Introduction to the Study of Man* (Oxford University Press, 1971).

About Behavior

a. r. beisser, *The Madness in Sports* (Appleton-Century-Crofts, 1967).

i. eibl-eibesfeldt, *Ethology: The Biology of Behavior* (Holt, Rinehart and Winston, 1970).

c. e. m. hansel, *ESP: A Scientific Evaluation* (MacGibbon and Kee, 1966).

j. a. harrington, ed., *Soccer Hooliganism* (John Wright, 1968).

joachim kahl, *The Misery of Christianity* (Penguin, 1972).

j. h. leuba, *The Reformation of the Churches* (Beacon Press, 1950).

r. w. moncrieff, *Odour Preferences* (Leonard Hill, 1966).

ashley montague, *Touching* (Columbia University Press, 1971).

d. morris, *The Naked Ape* (Jonathan Cape, 1967).

———, *Intimate Behaviour* (Jonathan Cape, 1971).

Index

THIS BOOK WAS SET IN
PISTILLI ROMAN, L & C HAIRLINE
AND JANSON TYPES.
IT WAS PRINTED AND BOUND BY
THE HADDON CRAFTSMEN.
DESIGNED BY ANN SPINELLI